UNASHAMED

an autobiography

UNASHAMED

an autobiography

Christine Tailor

© Christine Tailor 2022, All rights reserved

First (eBook/paperback) edition: September 2022
ISBN: 978-0-6454624-9-4 (print)
ISBN: 978-0-6455762-6-9 (epub)

The right of Christine Tailor to be identified as the author of this work has been asserted by her in accordance with *Copyright Amendment (Moral Rights) Act 2000*.
All rights reserved. The author retains moral and legal rights. Apart from any use as permitted under *Copyright Act 1968*, no part of this publication may be reproduced, scanned, stored in a retrieval system, recorded or transmitted in any form of by any means, electronic, mechanical, photocopying, recording or otherwise, without prior permission of the author. This is a work of fiction. Any likeness to persons either living or dead is purely coincidental. Names, characters and places are used fictitiously.

Design: Luke Harris, WorkingType Studio
Cataloguing-in-Publication details are available from the National Library of Australia
www.trove.nla.gov.au

A catalogue record for this work is available from the National Library of Australia

AUTHOR'S NOTE

After living such a long, interesting and instructive life, which cannot go on much longer, it seems a shame to let the lessons learnt die with me. Those who are awake may learn from my experiences.

I am writing under my maiden name to honour my magnificent parents.

There have been name changes to protect the innocent, and not so innocent, because I feel that the story is more important than naming names.

*Dedicated to
my sister Jackie*

CONTENTS

Author's Note v

PART ONE   A naïve schoolgirl grows up 1
Chapter 1   Louisa and Bertram 3
Chapter 2   Sue and Ted 6
Chapter 3   Me 11
Chapter 4   WWII 13
Chapter 5   Mum's visit 16
Chapter 6   Tolworth 20
Chapter 7   Surbiton 23
Chapter 8   Farewell England 30
Chapter 9   The journey to Australia 33
Chapter 10 New to Australia 38
Chapter 11 Pooraka 44
Chapter 12 Final year at good old Thebie High 48
Chapter 13 Matriculation at Adelaide Girls High 52
Chapter 14 University students, so in love 56
Chapter 15 The Escape 60
Chapter 16 Teaching 66
Chapter 17 Married at last 70
Chapter 18 Married life, making decisions 73
Chapter 19 Curramulka 75
Chapter 20 Young couples 77
Chapter 21 My biological bull through a gate 79
Chapter 22 Army life, Puckapunyal 83
Chapter 23 Army life at Holsworthy 89
Chapter 24 Real life in Para Hills 94
Chapter 25 More real life at Para hills 101
Chapter 26 Erica 108
Chapter 27 Salisbury 110

PART TWO: Between husbands 119
Chapter 28 Able Street 121
Chapter 29 Back to University 129
Chapter 30 David 133
Chapter 31 One more year 141
Chapter 32 Murray Bridge 145
Chapter 33 May Holidays 150
Chapter 34 McLaren Flat Section 761 156
Chapter 35 Hillbillies 160
Chapter 36 How to settle into a country property 162
Chapter 37 How to settle into a country property part two 168
Chapter 38 Friends and Lovers 174
Chapter 39 My Man Paul 184
Chapter 40 Kathy the country girl 189
Chapter 41 Erica and Hiromi 195
Chapter 42 Am I still searching for Mr Right? 201
Chapter 43 It's raining men 207
Chapter 44 Neil visits 212
Chapter 45 The Letter 216
Chapter 46 Fun times with Neil 219
Chapter 47 A weekend in Melbourne 222
Chapter 48 Dad gives fate a push 227

PART THREE: Maturity ....
Chapter 49 Neil moves into 'Attention' 233
Chapter 50 The Garden Contest 239
Chapter 51 The Obligatory Trip Home, and what followed 241
Chapter 52 Golden Wedding 244
Chapter 53 The 50th birthday 247
Chapter 54 Lobethal and the tapestry 251
Chapter 55 Spinoffs from the Lobethal tapestry 256
Chapter 56 Goodbye Ted 259
Chapter 57 The depression we had to have 263

Chapter 58	Neil retires	268
Chapter 59	Both mums decline	272
Chapter 60	Wedding in Darwin	275
Chapter 61	The highs and lows as the century ends	277
Chapter 62	Paul and family in Adelaide	280
Chapter 63	Madang, Brighton and Woodend	283
Chapter 64	Zender and Max are born	288
Chapter 65	Black Crowe	292
Chapter 66	Events in FNQ	296
Chapter 67	We are going on a journey	299
Chapter 68	Last Christmas	303
Chapter 69	Pick yourself up, and move on	306
Chapter 70	The memorial	309
Chapter 71	The solo journey	311
Chapter 72	Settled in our home	314
Addendum		319
Acknowledgments		321

PART ONE

A naïve schoolgirl grows up

CHAPTER 1

LOUISA AND BERTRAM

Have you heard about the tummy line?

Well, it goes like this ... Kathy came from my tummy and I came from Suzie's tummy, so did Jackie. Suzie came from Louisa's tummy, but I don't know where Louisa came from.

You see, I have pieced together this story of my origin from my memories and those of other people, and the further back we go the sketchier the information becomes. The earliest anecdote Suzie told me was that Louisa would go to her father's tailor shop after school. For fun, she liked to help the men with the hand-sewn button-holes.

One day her father came in, found her sewing and said, 'Why am I sending you to school when you could be working here and saving me money?'

So, Louisa became a tailor. I sometimes think of her story as I would a fairytale.

In London, in 1890, there lived a lovely young woman called Louisa who worked in her father's tailor shop. In this shop, suits for gentlemen were made to measure. After a client was measured, a pattern was made for him. Most of the sewing was done on a sewing machine, but the finishing touches were sewn by hand.

One day, a gentleman named Bertram Bennett, who was from a wealthy family, came into the shop to be measured for a suit. When he saw Louisa, he thought that she was lovely. Sadly, he realised that she was working class while he was upper class. The dictates of the day said he should not even think about befriending her. However, he found himself looking forward to his first fitting with great anticipation, hoping that she would be helping the tailor to fit his suit.

The day arrived and there she was, passing the pins to the tailor. He smiled at her and she smiled back. That was the magic moment that sealed their fate.

Louisa was pressing his suit when he arrived early for his second fitting, so he watched her graceful, careful movement as she pressed. He realised that he was falling in love with this enchanting, industrious young woman. He dared not tell his parents, or even his brother, about this wonderful girl because they would look down on her as a most unsuitable companion for him.

Whenever he wore that suit, the one that she had pressed and finished, he found himself thinking of her. Eventually, he felt that he must tell his parents about Louisa because he wanted to court her and ask her to be his wife. They were furious that he should even think about such a girl. They could not, would not, accept such a person into their family! He said no more on the subject, but he continued to think of her.

One day he said to himself, 'If I was to court Louisa and she did agree to marry me, what would happen?' The answer was obvious. 'My parents would never speak to me again and I would not inherit any money when they die.'

Swept away with thoughts of the lovely Louisa, Bertram thought with his heart more than with his head. The internal conversation continued. 'Well, I earn enough money to support a wife and family without any help from them, and I would rather live with Louisa than with them. Why am I waiting?'

Bertram went to her father's shop that very day to order another suit and asked Louisa to 'walk out' with him. Well of course she said 'yes' because he was like a prince to her. They grew fonder with each meeting. They strolled the streets of London and into the parks. They probably visited the Crystal Palace that had been relocated from Hyde Park to Penge Place, Buckingham Palace, Westminster Abbey, The Tower of London, Trafalgar Square, and, of course, Kew Gardens. Yes, they would have been well acquainted with the sights of London.

Soon, Bertram asked Louisa's father if he could marry her. And her father, after giving it some thought, was happy to agree. He would be losing an excellent unpaid worker, but he could see that his daughter would be well cared for by such a rich young man.

Chapter 1 *Louisa and Bertram*

When they were married, Bertram's parents indicated their disapproval by not attending the wedding and not attempting to even meet Louisa.

A few years of wedded bliss followed and they had many babies. There was Donald, young Louisa, young Bertram, Winifred and Ruth. They loved their children and each other dearly.

In 1914, King George was on the throne, and another baby was due. But a catastrophe happened. World War I broke out. It was a terrible war. Lots of young men were killed in the trenches. No one was spared from the war effort.

Bertram became an intelligence officer on a warship. He sent coded messages to other ships to try to avoid German warships.

Louisa sent Bertram a photograph of his family when baby Suzanne was born. It is in the photograph collection nestled within the pages of this book.

Sadly, Bertram's ship was sunk in battle. He never returned to hold his baby, and little Suzanne never knew the love of a father.

CHAPTER 2

SUE AND TED

When Bertram was killed in World War I, his parents were saddened. However, it didn't inspire them to check on his family. They refused to help Louisa raise her children. She had to bring home tailor finishing work to do at home while she cared for her children.

The older children, Don and Lou, were soon sent out to work to support themselves, but Bert, Win, Ruth and Sue were very young children. Sue was four years old when WWI finished.

In time, Louisa grew tired, run down and unhappy, and she took to drink and neglected her children. The four youngsters were taken from her by child welfare. Bert was put into an orphanage for boys and Win, Ruth and Sue were placed in an orphanage for girls. The cold charity of an orphanage had to be endured. Here, life was strictly regimented and corporal punishment was rife. It was crude but effective. No wonder Sue carried a fear of authority figures all through her life! If anyone in the orphanage was sick no inmates were allowed to go to school. Consequently, their education was very limited.

They were kept clean, dressed and fed, but they only had each other for affection. I have been told that Sue often said to her sister, 'Colour me, Ruthy, please colour me,' when she needed a cuddle.

The girls would cuddle together and Win would tell them that soon their mother would come and rescue them. She would take them to a lovely little cottage in the country where they would play in the sunshine and be loved by her. They never gave up hope.

Eventually, their mother was deemed good enough to reclaim her children. Their home was in London, not the country cottage dreamed up by Win. They had to walk to school. Sue was terrified of the rough London kids that she encountered during the walk and in the playground.

Because of her limited education she could not read or understand what was going on around her. She quickly learned to cheat in tests and to mouth the words that other children were reading when they 'read' all together aloud in class. Somehow, she learned to read and add up by the time she left school.

In those days, if you were fortunate, you went into a trade. Your parents paid a master craftsman a lump sum and he agreed to train you on the job to be a proficient worker in his trade. Bertram had been considered a wealthy man, so there was money in his will for each child to be apprenticed. Win became a florist and Ruth a milliner. Sue wanted to be a hairdresser, but when her mother took her to a hairdresser to seek an apprenticeship the hairdresser said that Sue was too short for the job. So that was that. Her mother sent her to be a clerk at Somerset House. This was a government office where births, deaths and marriages were recorded and filed. Somerset House is now dedicated to the arts.

Sue fumbled and cheated her way through work, and worked out as many ways as she could to get sick leave. All she did was filing because she had learnt her alphabet. She could arrange papers alphabetically or by date. Despite all her shortcomings, she had a lot of fun with her workmates and loved to go ballroom dancing.

Since her mother was a dressmaker, there were boxes of fabric in the house which Sue and her sisters would use whenever they needed a dress. Sue could make a dance dress in a day. It was not very neat nor well finished off, but it was a new dress that she could wear dancing that night.

In the 1930s, when Sue was in her late teens and early twenties, the two chief forms of entertainment were the movies and ballroom dancing. Ballroom dancing was much more graceful, formal, and intimate than it is today. The gentleman 'lead' the woman around the dance floor. Sue was light and moved easily and had a good sense of rhythm and timing, so she was good at 'following', which is what women were supposed to do when ballroom dancing. Finally, here was something that she could do well. Sue loved it! And that is where she met Ted.

Ted's father was a poorly paid butcher. He brought home bacon or sausages tucked under his coat so that his family could eat well. Ted did quite well at school and joined the Boy Scouts, which was a huge adventure for working class boys. Here, they learned how to look after themselves and to do all the jobs necessary to live in a simple tent. As a result, the boys would go on cheap holidays like cycling tours around Britain, and even a camping holiday in France.

Ted's two brothers, Fredrick and Alfred, were apprenticed; one as a toolmaker and one as a baker. Ted liked to work with wood and hoped that he would be apprenticed to a carpenter, but when he turned twelve his father said to him, 'Alf tells me that they are taking apprentices as toolmakers at Glacier Works. You better get on down there and get an apprenticeship tomorrow.'

Without discussion, Ted became a toolmaker.

This meant that he could pay his mother for board, buy his own clothes, pay his bus fare, and buy any other luxury that he fancied, like a book or a pair of running shoes, by saving up the few pennies left. Each year he would get a raise in pay, and he managed his money well enough to buy those books and sporting gear. He attended athletics meetings, amateur at first, but later when he found he could win cash prizes he became professional. Anything extra was welcome. He wanted lots of things, like new clothes to impress the ladies. So, he found extra work when he was not at the factory. He started by selling ice creams at the dog races and graduated to a bookie's clerk. He understood pretty soon how gambling worked and won a few bets on the side. It became a lifelong hobby of his. He also learnt how to play card games. By the time he met Sue at the *Palais De Dance*, he was a sharp dresser and always had a few quid in his pocket. Ted, always a man to live by his wits, learnt to dance by watching others. Fred Astaire was a great dancer who featured in musical movies of the day. Ted copied Fred Astaire's moves and incorporated them into his dances.

Sue was pretty, petite and could 'follow' well. He dressed well, loved a joke, and would not hold back when it came to buying a round of drinks for a group of friends. He was a popular chap. Sue and Ted danced well together and soon Ted was teaching Sue his Fred Astaire moves. They moved to the music of Victor Sylvester and George Gershwin and danced all the modern dances of their time. They could Charleston and jive with the best. They entered dance competitions, and even won a few.

And as they say, one thing led to another and they wanted to get married.

However, there were complications. They could not afford for Sue to give up working, which she would have been obliged to do if she married, and 'living in sin' was frowned upon in those days. Attitudes have relaxed these days, but the prevailing view was that married women should be supported by their husbands.

The answer was obvious. They needed to cheat the system.

No one had enough money to make it a grand affair. Sue was only nineteen, so she needed her mother's permission. Her mother agreed on the condition that Sue wore a long white dress and they were married in a church.

With a little thought and planning, the complications were overcome.

They planned the wedding for Christmas Day because Boxing Day was a public holiday. That was their honeymoon.

Sue had borrowed her sister-in-law's wedding dress for the big day. Ruth, the milliner, made her veil. Win, the florist, made the bouquet. Fred, the baker, made a lovely wedding cake, and Ted organised the church. After the ceremony, everyone returned to Sue's mother's home for a 'knees up'. They ate and drank. They sang and danced to all the old cockney ditties.

After the party, Sue and Ted travelled by underground train to their flat in Lewisham with the remains of the cake on Ted's lap. Boxing Day was their honeymoon. The day after that, Sue took off her wedding ring and dressed for work, not forgetting her high-heeled shoes.

This using of his wits to get around difficult situations was one of Ted's endearing, though not always legal, traits. One example of this was he was part of a crew that sold raffle tickets around the pubs for a Christmas dinner during December. They pocketed the takings and one of them was always nominally the winner. Then, during World War II, whenever there was an air raid warning he would enter an air raid shelter from a different direction to one of his mates and they would pretend to be strangers. During the course of the evening one of them would suggest a card game. A few men would join in to alleviate the boredom. Ted and his mate had secret signals about the strength of the hand they had been dealt, enabling one of them to win the hand. They met later to divide the spoils and select a different shelter for the next night's game. They probably told each other that 'all's fair in love and war', or 'a fool and his money are easily parted' or 'there is one born every minute'. Thus, their basic wages were supplemented, and Sue and Ted were a happy couple, snug in their secret for four years.

Then I wanted to be born.

CHAPTER 3—

ME

Mum often spoke of how happy she was to stay home to care for me. Naturally, a Silver Cross, the Rolls Royce of perambulators, was purchased. After bathing and feeding me, Sue would put me to sleep in the perambulator and place it outside in the sunshine where she could peep out at me as she did her housework. She was a young woman of 23 and she thought it was great not to have to go to work. One day, she took me to the shops and left me sleeping in the pram outside, as you did back in those days. Sue wandered the shops for a while and then bought herself an ice-cream and wandered home. When she arrived at the flat she realised that something was missing ... the baby!

She ran as fast as her legs would carry her back to the shops to find me sleeping peacefully and being admired by passers-by.

My appearance did not curtail Ted and Sue's dancing, and I was never excluded from the fun, even though I was a baby. Sue would often dance until she was too tired to walk home. Silver Cross perambulators were sturdy, and Sue was a petite woman, so she would get into the pram and cuddle me while Ted pushed us home. The Silver Cross was also used to carry the camping gear when we went on holiday by train.

My parents adored me. I was called Christine, after Mum's best friend.

When I was three, I had a cuddly stuffed toy called Peter Penguin who had a strong, reinforced beak. He was my protector. If it came to a fight in the sand pit he would defend me. On quite a few occasions another child's mother would report to Sue that I had hit her child. Sue would then ask me, 'Did you hit Freddy or Alice?' to which I would honestly reply, 'No, Mummy. Peter Penguin did.'

We could say that I was assertive, imaginative and willing to defend myself, even as a little girl.

Mum wanted me to be a ballerina, so off to dancing class I was taken. Picture a class of four-year-olds, all decked out in their tunics and ballet slippers. The teacher claps her hand and says, 'Now, children, I want you all to stand in a line across the studio facing me.'

A line begins to form, but this studio with its huge mirrors and adoring mummies, was bewildering to most of the potential ballerinas. Annoyed with the delay, one girl stepped out of the line and took matters into her own hands. Taking each bewildered student by the shoulders, she placed them all firmly into the line, returned to her place and smiled at the teacher. Job done.

Yes, that was me—impatient—but also an organiser and problem-solver.

What a monster I could have grown into, aided and encouraged by my doting mother!

I remember my cousin's wedding. I was seated on the piano, singing along with all the other guests in Auntie Lou's front room. The room smells of beer and cigarette smoke, but that does not bother me as we all sing 'Roll out the Barrel', 'Knees up Mother Brown', and other similar ditties while Aunt Doris tickles the ivories. I know all these songs and sing out loud and clear.

Quite the entertainer, wasn't I? And what a good memory!

CHAPTER 4

WWII

When war broke out in 1939, Ted volunteered to work in the submarines. He'd found out that sailors in the submarines were paid danger money. He figured everybody was in danger during a war, so being paid for it appealed to him. However, when it was discovered that he was a toolmaker currently working at the Woolwich Arsenal, he was sent right back to work.

Because the arsenal was a target for German bombs, it was split into several arsenals around the country. Ted was posted to one, so Mum and I moved to live with Aunt Lou and her grown up daughters, Madeleine, Dotsie and Joan. The girls were like sisters to Sue. They went to dances together, shared clothes and even drew the line down the back of each other's legs to represent stocking seams. Silk or nylon stockings were such luxury items, they just could not afford them.

Mum was terrified of the bombing and was always the first into the air raid shelter when the alarm sounded.

My sister Jackie was born during the war. One of my earliest recollections is of being five years old and in an isolation bed in hospital with cold tight sheets and I wanted my mummy. I had missed being evacuated with most London children because my mother did not want to part with me and then I developed dysentery. By the time I was released from hospital, Mum was afraid for me and Jackie. She had missed the government evacuation scheme, so she had to find accommodation for both of us girls. She found a nursery for Jackie and foster parents for me in Yorkshire.

My foster parents were Johnny and Lilly Barker. He was a coal miner, and she was a stay-at-home mum. She always wore her hair in a hairnet. They had a daughter about a year younger than me who was called Our Doreen. Most children were called Our something, but I was not because I did not belong to anyone. I was useful to take smaller children to the park, where we made daisy chains. I suppose they were paid to keep me. Mother often sent me dresses that she had bought on the black market, though I never saw them. They were carefully kept until they fitted Our Doreen.

I remember Guy Fawkes Night and the build-up. Weeks beforehand, the local children made a scarecrow figure out of someone's father's old clothes stuffed with rags and straw. Boys would push Guy around in a wheelbarrow, begging for money to buy fireworks.

'Penny for the Guy, mister?'

As November 5 approached, flammable materials were heaped up on the land behind the toilets in readiness for the communal bonfire. Then on the big night, Guy was placed atop the bonfire and it was lit. We gathered around it to keep warm, and potatoes were pushed into the ashes around the base. When they were cooked we ate them greedily, never mind the burnt bits or the charcoal. And then finally, fireworks! Wow, the noise and the beauty of them! The boys threw squibs and bangers into the fire, their staccato explosions making the girls squeal with delight. Then a rocket would rush skyward, carrying its magic. When our necks ached from gazing upwards, the rocket would burst into glittering fairy dust in the shape of a ball or a waterfall. Our collective 'aaahh' was its applause.

I remember washing day. The copper in the corner of the kitchen was lit and Aunty Lilly spent the whole day washing. We came home from school to a kitchen full of steam and a meal based around cold meat, the leftovers from the Sunday roast.

I remember picking the scabs off my knees. I must have fallen over a lot to always have had scabby knees. School was good. I was a normal citizen there.

I also remember head lice, caught from the other children. I remember how they were dealt with. I can still see Aunty Lilly sitting by the stove in the kitchen with a newspaper on her lap. She would call me to kneel in front of her and rest my head on the newspaper. She took a very fine comb called a tooth comb and gently combed through my hair from my neck to the top of my head. As she did this the lice would drop onto the paper, making a little plop as they landed. She would trap them between her fingernails and squeeze them to death with a click. It was a very slow process, but Aunty Lilly carried it out fastidiously.

Just thinking about it makes my head itch!

CHAPTER 5

MUM'S VISIT

This is a letter I wrote to Jackie in August 2007. It was to celebrate her 65th birthday and tell her that 65 was no big deal, I had survived it and was now 69.

Dear Jackie,

I do not remember your birth, although I was four years old. The first memory that I have with you is visiting you with Mum in the nursery that you lived in as an evacuee during the war. You must have been about two and a half, or maybe as old as three. Do you have any memories of the place? The 'orphanage', for want of a better word, was out in the remote countryside of Yorkshire. It was winter and the country was covered in snow. Mum, city slicker to the last, was fashionably dressed down to the inevitable very high heels.

We picked you up in the entrance hall, a large, light space with many doors and an ostentatious staircase. It was probably a stately home pressed into service, as they were during the war. There was a huge window on the eastern wall and the morning sun was streaming through. The light was fortified by reflection from the snowy landscape outside to absolute glare. The children were lined up in preparation for their morning walk and the runny noses were being dealt with by an attendant with a roll of toilet paper. Watching the process made me wince. War-time toilet paper was not the soft, downy creature it is today. You were a sturdy, chubby child and seemed quite at home in the somewhat rough and rowdy world you inhabited. But I pitied you because of the nose wipe procedure.

Mum took us for a walk, out into the fairyland of glistening snow.

Chapter 5   *Mum's visit*

With one daughter in each hand, we can only guess at her joy. At least a year of separation made us strangers to each other, yet it was warming to know that we had a mother who cared enough to visit us in our respective hideouts. Of the walk, I only remember standing on the top of a hill and looking over the pristine sparkling snow covered countryside and marvelling at the beauty of it in the clear cold sunlight. Mum's shoes were silly strappy creations and soon became saturated and her feet frozen, so you can imagine her response when I suggested that she should carry my poor little sister.

¶

When the war was over, Dad brought me home by train and taught me to tell time during the journey. I thought that he was so clever and he thought that I was pretty smart too. I have a strong memory of the first blissful evening together. We were in the middle room of our house in Tolworth. After tea, we sat around a fire just drinking in the togetherness. Mum was mending and I tidied her sewing box—it was such a mess. I wound up all the loose ends of cotton onto their reels, stuck all the pins and needles into the pin cushion and rolled up the tape measure. It took me all evening. I was so happy to be with my own Mummy and Daddy again, warm and together. The contented feeling comes back whenever I think of that night. We were indeed a lucky family to have all come through the war unharmed. We had been sent to different parts of Yorkshire while Dad had been working in the Woolwich Arsenal, Mum had worked in the Hounslow bus garage as a chassis cleaner. That's where she met the Stanfords, George and Else. Remember their children, Terry and Valerie? Yes, Valerie of our Star Girls Concerts.

Do you remember the banana incident? Bananas were not available during the war. So, when they first came on the market, Mum and Dad wanted us to experience the 'treat' and bought some. You did not like them. Can you remember why? Mum made a custard for dessert and put chopped banana into it without saying what it was. We were all happily digging in and saying how lovely pudding was when she said, 'It's banana custard.'

Immediately you spat it out with an, 'Uuugg, it's horrid!' but we all laughed because you had been tricked into enjoying it just a minute before.

I know you remember Sunday lunch in that house. Mum and Dad made such a big deal of it. I suppose because we had roast meat and potatoes with vegetables and gravy. These were things that had been in very short supply during the war years and they thought we should feel as pleased as they were and scoff the lot, but we were picky and didn't want this or that, we just wanted to 'get down' and play. So, the hard word was put on us, by Mum, of course. She was the disciplinarian, poor thing. 'You are not leaving the table till your plate is clean.'

And we stayed there, even until there were islands of fat floating in the gravy. During the war the British had been exhorted WASTE NOT WANT NOT and to them not eating such a good meal was a terrible waste.

We were often left alone because our parents were working. We would have to enter by the side gate, find the key and let ourselves in by the back door after school. I remember once peeing my pants because I couldn't get the gate open quick enough to get round to the toilet.

Do you remember the concoctions we used to make ourselves to eat? Things like cocoa mixed with sugar and butter. Yummy!

They also left us home alone occasionally to go dancing. We would go to bed early because Mum would promise to come into our bedroom to show us how she looked when dressed for the dance and kiss us good night.

'Oh, Mummy, you look like a princess' or 'You look like Cinderella dressed for the ball' we would say in deep, heartfelt admiration. They would kiss us goodnight and go and we just went to sleep. No babysitters or phone numbers to call in an emergency. We were okay, fast asleep with visions of our beautiful mother dancing at a ball.

Chapter 5   *Mum's visit*

A final memory of the Tolworth house was how they redecorated and smartened up the garden in readiness for selling. I remembered planting pansies in the front garden with Mum and when a couple were viewing the house you were so proud of your father's efforts in making the house look good that you bragged to the viewers, 'There was a big crack over that window. My Daddy fixed it all up before he painted this room so now you can't see where it was!' You were whisked quickly away before you could give away any other secrets.

Have a wonderful 65th birthday.

Lots of love, Chris

CHAPTER 6

TOLWORTH

Looking at our semi-detached home from the front gate, you saw a very small scruffy garden with a path on the right leading straight to the front porch. A cement path ran along the left side of the house all the way down the garden to a timber tool shed. Mum and Dad were not gardeners, and I cannot recall the grass ever being cut, although there were a couple of apple trees. I have many memories from my time in that house.

Because Dad was a toolmaker, he knew how to make moulds and so decided to make lead soldiers as children's toys. Mum was his first employee and they worked in that tiny garden shed at the bottom of our garden.

The soldiers sold well and Dad needed to increase production, so he rented a garage at the end of the road and had about four girls working there with Mum. Later, it was discovered that lead was very bad for children and he had to quickly find a new medium and new subjects for his factory. He turned to bride and groom statues for the top of wedding cakes, using plaster of Paris.

I would frequently call in to the factory after school and entertain the girls with songs and poems that I had learnt at school.

There was a housing shortage after the war, and Mum and Dad bought the house cheaply because it had squatters. We hardly ever saw or heard them, even though they had use of one of the upstairs bedrooms and the front downstairs room. The next room back was our living room. It held the dining room furniture and a couple of lounge chairs each side of the fireplace. Jackie and I looked out of that window one Christmas Eve wishing for a White Christmas. As we stood and watched and wished, gentle snowflakes fell, drifting softly over the path until it was completely hidden.

That whole Christmas was another very happy childhood memory. For

Chapter 6   *Tolworth*

the past few weeks, when we had been in bed, not quite asleep, we could hear activity downstairs. There was sawing and hammering going on, but each morning the house looked just the same when we got up. On Christmas Day all was explained. Dad had made us each a small, upholstered chair with a seat that lifted revealing a box to keep our toys in. We were delighted!

The larder occupied a space in a cupboard under the stairs, which we used to raid after school before Mum got home from work.

If we were sick enough to be put to bed, Mum made a special treat for us, bread and sugar soaked in warm milk. She always served it in an old-fashioned designed bowl with crazed cracks that she had inherited from her mother. We considered it very special and called it the 100-year-old bowl.

Pig bins were a left over from the war. Pig farmers would leave garbage bins at the roadside, which they would empty a couple of times a week. People would put organic rubbish into these bins. The contents were a welcome food for pigs.

I don't think that we were naughty children, but I do recall being sent to my bedroom as punishment and staying there crying. Jackie was more obstinate and refused to cry, even when she was spanked, which just infuriated Mum. Anyway, after what felt like hours, alone weeping and freezing, Dad would come in and say it would be alright if I apologised to Mum. So, I would come downstairs and say, 'Sorry, Mummy.'

She would retort, 'I should think so too!'

My rebellious inner voice would say, *'Then I'm not sorry at all.'*

Even so, we were well loved and disciplined as most children were in the 40s.

On Saturday mornings, we loaded dirty washing into my doll's pram to take it to the laundry. We returned with the previous week's load washed and pressed and packed neatly into the pram while we walked home eating ice-cream cones. Sometimes, I took Jackie to a nearby town so that we could go to the Saturday matinee at the picture palace. It was great fun! There were cartoons and even a serial like *Lassie* or *Hop-along Cassidy*.

While we lived in Tolworth, I attended a church school called St Matthews. We were promoted on ability, but I caused a dilemma for my teachers because I was very bright, but my book work was untidy. We wrote with pens that were dipped into ink wells which always smudged, and my fingers were always covered in ink. However, I was promoted and was usually the youngest in my class. At school fetes, we danced country dancing and maypole dancing to entertain our parents. It was all great fun.

Tim and Josette, his Belgium war bride, lived next door with Tim's sisters. Josette and the sisters didn't get along, not only because she was foreign and used quite a lot of makeup, but she already had a child of her own.

One Easter, Dad asked Tim and Josette if they would take me to Belgium when they visited Josette's family. I was only a kid and was bamboozled by the foreign language, but I loved the village street parade, people in their colourful national dress, and the silly kissing games they delighted in. Then there was their septic tank in the back garden that had its annual clean out while I was there. It was huge and I did not need French to work out what it was and what was happening. Poooo!

CHAPTER 7

SURBITON

Dad was good at running his factory and keeping his workers happy, but he was terrible at managing cash flow. When things were going well he was very generous, but he did not think of putting capital away for a rainy day. The rainy day inevitably came and his business was crumbling. He took sleeping partners to finance him, so 'Cake and General Novelties' was born. They moved the factory to bigger premises, allowing Mum and Dad to buy a bungalow near Surbiton.

Dad was delighted with our new home, as 'The Haven' stood on its own piece of land. He called it an 'estate' because we could walk right around the house. There were apple trees and he showed us how we could pick and store them in the attic, spread out so that they did not touch each other. That way a bad apple would just rot away all by itself and not spread the rot to the other apples.

On school days, Mum would plait our hair very tightly to keep it tidy. Brenda would call for Jackie and me to walk to school, jumping ditches. Not that they were in our way, there were drains down the side of the road. It was just a fun thing to do.

A small bottle of milk and a cooked lunch was supplied at school to ensure that all children were well fed. The whole school sat at trestle tables in the hall while the monitors served the lunch. Teachers sat at the end of the table to make sure we ate it.

For me, the big event of our time at 'The Haven' was sitting for the 10 plus exam. If you passed, you went to grammar school, with the hope you could progress to university. Dad had his sights set on that as my future. If you failed, you were sent to a secondary modern. The exam had three papers—Arithmetic, English and General Intelligence. I was okay at arithmetic, terrible at essay writing and spelling, but I enjoyed the weekly intelligence test.

Dad was not an educated man, but he coached me. I'd repeat times tables 'parrot fashion' every evening and then he'd bombard me with rapid-fire jumbled multiplication questions.

What to do about English? We were both phonetic spellers and since he was a Cockney, his pronunciation was often incorrect. Still, he persisted. Each weekend I would have to write an essay on a topic he'd dreamed up. One weekend it was 'going swimming with the school'. I did my best, then he went through it with me, correcting some of the spelling, and on this occasion he inserted a phrase 'when we reached our destination, the swimming pool', then I had to re-write the whole essay. It was quite the ordeal, but he loved me and I him, so I put up with it, even though I would rather have been out playing rounders in the street with Jackie and our friends.

As an added incentive, I was promised a brand new bicycle if I passed.

I still remember some of those stray thoughts that passed through me on occasion.

Gosh, why did Dad want me to pass so much? It would cost him a packet if I passed, and then he was offering a bike as well. Oh well, Dad, if you want it so much I'll give it my best try.

On the day of the exam, Dad drove me and my friends to the hall in the work delivery van and we felt like royalty. The arithmetic was a breeze and the intelligence test was fun, but English was a worry. I would probably fail the English.

Sorry to disappoint you, Dad.

However, I could not believe my eyes when I saw the essay topic—'An excursion with the school.' Well, this was an intelligence test in real life! I had no moral dilemma. I remembered my practice essay with Dad, and trotted it out right down to the destination. So, I passed and Dad bought us both brand new two wheeler bikes; Jackie's was red and mine was black.

Sir William Perkins was a British chemist who lived and worked at the end of the 19th century. He founded Sir William Perkins School for 25 boys. It had since grown and become a grammar school for girls. The uniform was very special. It was sax blue with a magnificent blazer with an embroidered pocket, a matching hat, which was shaped like a sailor's hat, and everything was so special, but when Mum got the list of extras she began to complain ...

'Indoor shoes, a complete change of clothes for gymnastics and sports, hockey and netball in winter, and tennis and cricket in summer ... this really is too much!'

Dad came to my rescue. 'It's a very special school, hun. She passed the exam. We will find the cash somewhere.'

Another thing they found the cash for was my continued ballet dancing, while Jackie took up horse riding. Big mistake! If only Mum had wanted me to be an actress. That is where my talent lay. I just did not have the physique for ballet.

Since Christmas was Sue and Ted's wedding anniversary, it was always a special day for us all. The lounge was out of bounds for at least a week before the big day. Mum and Dad would secretly convert the room into a Christmas fairyland. On Christmas morning, we would each find a gift-packed stocking at the end of our bed. In its toe was always an orange, which we knew must be kept for the next day because oranges were imported, a special treat that had disappeared during the war. We'd play with the small gifts, anxious for the main event, eventually waking Mum and Dad. In the kitchen, a full English breakfast had to be consumed with patient decorum. We knew we would not be permitted the big treat until the breakfast dishes were washed and Dad had lit the fire. Then we ceremoniously walked down the passage together and entered ... magnificent Christmas-land! There were so many marvellous presents that it took all morning to unwrap and examine them. A sumptuous lunch followed, then with overfull bellies we all slept until 3 pm for the King's speech.

On Boxing Day, we were taken to a pantomime. An orange from the stocking's toe must have been a tradition in many families, and the smell of them being simultaneously peeled in the interval was a heady experience.

Our summer holidays were usually camping holidays. We all slept in a big tent and Dad would cook on a primus stove. He'd cook a full English breakfast followed by fried bread and treacle. It was scrumptious.

One August we had just returned from camping and Mum and Dad did not have to go back to work until the Tuesday, and they felt like squeezing in an extra day off, so they shoved all the unopened mail into the cupboard next to the radio. Had they read that mail we might never have gone. Being full of carefree holiday happiness, it was decided that we would go in the work van, which was full of pink petrol. Pink petrol was for commercial use only and illegal to use for private purposes.

'After all, there won't be any inspectors out on a public holiday, will there?' Dad said.

We arrived mid-morning, selecting a lovely spot on the riverbank, with a good view of the water's edge. The picnic blanket was spread, just to the side of a tiny bay. We changed into our bathing costumes, just wanting to get into the water for splashing fun, even though it was muddy. There was a gradual slope into the gentle flow of the river, overhung with shady willows. Ted was instructed to be in there with us for safety's sake.

After a bit of fun, I decided to show off my newly acquired swimming ability, even though it was pretty shaky, and took off into the river. I swam a small loop, estimating that I would stop just short of Dad.

Oh no! I can't touch the bottom!

I just went further down and down. Struggling upwards, I reached the surface for a gulp of air only to sink again. Each time I rose to gulp air I could see Jackie and Daddy talking. Then as a foothold was denied to me, I sunk into the murky waters of panic and fear of drowning. Dad's strong hands eventually grabbed my flaying arms and hauled me coughing and spluttering back to the slippery edge. I climbed the bank and lay down to gain my breath while Dad explored our 'safe' area.

'Don't go any further out than that fallen willow.'

Frankly, I didn't feel like going in at all. However, Dad knew not to let a little scare like that become a phobia, so I was encouraged back into the water. Holding onto the fallen willow, I practiced my kicks in the deep water.

We played and lazed and ate lunch while other families arrived, with each respecting each other's space and continuing to be happy with in their own area.

Chapter 7 *Surbiton*

Mum liked to watch other families, and then she said, 'Oh, Ted, one of those boys is in trouble!'

'Where?'

'Where Chris was this morning.'

Ted was gone. This was a time for action, not words. He dived over the willow behind the boy and pushed him onto the ledge. As he climbed out, people were silent for they could see blood in the water. Dad struggled onto the bank clutching his right thigh and fainted.

From another blanket arose a man saying he was a nurse. He took charge of Dad's condition and had someone call the ambulance, while we just looked on agog.

Mum was especially concerned. 'If he goes to hospital, how will we get home? I can't drive and the van is full of pink petrol.'

The male nurse, having dispatched the hero off to hospital, turned his attention to us and Mummy confided our woes to him.

'That's alright, Mrs Tailor. I will drive you home and then catch a bus home. Your husband did a very brave thing this afternoon, it's the least I can do.'

Not only did he see us safely home, but he also wrote an account of the event to the Royal Humane Society, leaving out the pink petrol bit. Dad received the vellum scroll by mail as he declined attending a presentation ceremony. Once he recovered he had a lot of missed work to catch up on because he was self-employed.

The male nurse just disappeared from our lives. Mum forgot to ask his name in all her anxiety.

But you ask, 'Why would we not have gone if they had read their mail?'

In that pile of mail, shoved so hastily away, was a letter telling Dad to come into hospital to have an operation on his varicose veins that very day, so they would have spent the day preparing for that instead of going out for the picnic.

Sue and Ted were a happy, loving couple and were content with their little family, but like most couples they did not want their children under their feet all weekend. When they discovered a Sunday school a short distance from home, and they knew that I was responsible enough to take Jackie, Sunday became the day to enjoy *quality time* together.

I loved Sunday school. I loved the Old Testament stories about characters who lived a long time ago and were good or bad, calm or subject to outrageous passion. And all were on a direct phone line to God, as you were in the olden days. I was secure in my parents' love, but it was good to know there was an ever-loving, all-powerful father-in-the-sky watching and caring for me too. On some Sundays, my parents might decide to plan a family outing to which I would object. Dad would then come down strong with, 'I am your father.'

My response was, 'You are my earthly father. My Heavenly Father wants me to go to Sunday school!'

An earthly reward for Sunday school was the annual Sunday school outing. Everyone from the Sunday school boarded a bus with a bag of swimming togs and towel. *Whoopee!* No parents to regulate us and control our screams and laughter. The 'teachers' supplied a lunch of sandwiches and cake, then it was back to the fun. We sang 'Yes, Jesus loves me!' and 'All thing bright and beautiful' all the way home, then we would collapse exhaustedly happy into our parents' arms.

Jackie was my junior by four years which made her a bit of a nuisance because I had to take her with me everywhere. I didn't mind taking her to Sunday school because she was in a younger class. Mum and Dad never fussed if we were home late, so we used to have adventures on our way home. Once we became lost in the woods, as my sense of direction was never very good. And once, we followed a river for what seemed like miles, but I knew we could just follow it back again. We didn't get lost that time.

Whenever we knew that the Stanfords were coming to visit I organised a concert. Our dining room became the stage and the audience, comprised of proud parents and neighbours, like the Gristocks from over the road, sat in the lounge with the adjoining doors flung wide open. On one occasion, my friend Elaine and I wrote a very short play. It was called 'The Spinsters of Lush'. But Jackie made a big mistake! She said, 'She was with a female!' when she should have said 'male'. When the audience laughed, she stamped her foot in anger and said, 'It's not funny!'

Mum told me afterwards how funny the adults had found the incident. Mr Gristock had to stuff his handkerchief into his mouth to control the noise of his laughter.

CHAPTER 8

FAREWELL ENGLAND

Here is a letter that I wrote to Jackie in August 1982 ...

Dear Jackie,

In my last letter I raved on about passing the 10 plus and going to Sir William Perkin's School for Girls or SWPSG. Well, it wasn't easy when I got there. There were so many clever girls there who had not cheated on their English essay. I was in awe of all the brains.

I fell in love with the Maths teacher, Miss Bishop, because Maths now contained algebra and geometry, both endlessly fascinating. One special technique that she taught us was a method for solving mathematical problems. I have been able to adapt her method to real life problems. It goes like this:

1. Read the question carefully. Be sure that you understand what the problem is.
2. Look at what you are given, what you have to help you solve the problem.
3. Where are you going? What is the answer you are looking for? What you wish to achieve?
4. What vehicle will I use to get me from the beginning to the end?

Science was very limited. After all, we were girls and expected to excel at languages.

Mrs Cooksey, English, must have wondered how I ever arrived in her class, and the sewing teacher, Miss Derry, told us outright that we were not ladies. We were mere scholarship girls! Somehow, we were persuaded to become ladies, to speak properly, to deport ourselves elegantly, to always wear our hat and gloves when travelling to and from school and never, absolutely never, eat an ice-cream in the street!

It became harder for Dad to help me with my homework, as he had no idea about algebra and it took longer to explain the problem to him than it did to just work it out for myself. Inevitably, I came to realise that my education was outstripping his. Then, when he offered to play in the cricket team of fathers v girls, I shrank with embarrassment to hear his cockney vowels conversing with the other posh parents. I wanted to disown him. I am ashamed now to think of how I could want to disown that lovely man who had done all that was in his power to get me to that position of privilege. He continued to bat for me against the deadly Miss Duncan, the headmistress, when he was called up to hear that I had wandered into a toilet cubicle with a classmate on sports day so that we could continue our conversation, uninterrupted by the fact that we both needed a pee. Disgusting behaviour! Then again, she was displeased when I stood up to her in an English class. She asked us to raise our hand if we thought we would not read three books between now and Christmas. I was not a reader as the other brains were and explained that eating tea and doing my homework occupied the entire evening.

'What do you have for tea?' she stridently asked.

'Bread and jam with tea!'

'How many loaves?' brought a titter from the class.

'About half a loaf.' I would not let her face me down, but she was too affronted to ameliorate the situation with some kindly advice. Instead, the conversation stopped there.

Mum and Dad listened to what this superior being had to say and reported back to me. They thought the toilet situation a bit of a laugh and it was thereafter called 'A Sweet Pea'.

In general, I really loved my time at SWPSG, even if I was out of my depth with French, English and Gymnastics. History and Geography were interestingly taught and Maths, Science and Art were delightful. Then Dad decided to move us to Australia. Remember how he could always see the adventure in the unknown and taught us not to be afraid of something new?

Do you remember listening to the radio in the kitchen at 'The Haven'? Dick Barton, special agent, and Pollyanna were our favourites. Pollyanna was the daughter of a poorly paid missionary, but she played a game called the Glad Game where she always looked for the bright side of any situation. I remember in one episode they received a parcel from the mission and Pollyanna was hoping for a doll to play with. When they opened the parcel there was no doll but a pair of crutches. After some thought Pollyanna said, 'Well, we can be glad that we do not need the crutches!'

Mum and Dad wanted us to be Pollyannas. They also taught to have faith in other people.

'If ever you are lost don't be afraid to ask someone for help. If you are stuck on a bus and do not have the fare, you can give your name and address to the conductor and he will claim it while you stay on the bus to get home.'

He frequently dropped these pearls of wisdom within our hearing. I remember another one, 'Try to see the other fella's point of view.'

So why did Dad decide to move us to Australia? I'm glad he did, aren't you? I would never have got to uni in England, and we have both had great lives here!

I've been looking for Mr Right for years and have come to a realisation. The men I've been dating are looking for Miss Right. She is young and impressionable, earning a good wage, has no children and is willing to live with him in a neat suburban home near to where he works. I am not her. I will still go on dating, just as men do, for the sheer pleasure of it, but with no expectations. I will live happily ever after, just me, the kids and the animals at 'Attention'.

Well, Sis, have a happy 40th birthday on your fruit block and please let me know how Denis's experiment of keeping all the fruit trees goes.

Love, Chrissie

CHAPTER 9

THE JOURNEY TO AUSTRALIA

'Let's migrate to Australia! If another war comes it would be better to live in the larder than on the table!' Dad proclaimed.

Dad always saw change as a great adventure. Mum was more pessimistic, but she had been promised that she could return to England if she was not happy after two years. I was inclined to be swept along by Dad's delight in the new, as an impressionable 13-year-old. Jackie was nine when we left. We were off on a voyage and a New Life in a New Country.

In order to qualify as 'Ten Pound Poms' we had to be healthy, interested in taking on something new and be useful citizens to Australia. We were examined and questioned at Australia House. I remember only that we were all dressed cleanly and neatly. Mum would always see to that when we went out as a family. We were told to speak up when we were questioned. A very basic medical was followed by a conversation to check our intelligence and enthusiasm. We passed with flying colours.

There was a limit to the household goods that we could take and Mum had to leave her prized lounge rug behind. This was her first disappointment. Then there was leaving her extended family behind. We children were easily convinced by Dad that this was a big adventure, bigger and brighter than a holiday, but Mum had many reservations. We did a tour de family and friends to say goodbye.

Ted must have convinced her at some point that the sea voyage would be like a cruise with parties and dancing every night because we went shopping for two new dance dresses.

The very day that we set sail, King George VI died and Queen Elizabeth II came to throne, and the ship was in mourning for a whole week. This meant absolutely no fun for the first week of our voyage, but I was seasick for the entirety of that week, so the King dying didn't spoil my fun.

Because we were a family of four and the cabins accommodated six, Mum, Jackie and I were put in a cabin with another woman with two children, while Dad was in with other men. On the first morning, I fainted because the cabin was so stuffy. How was Sue going to cope with all this stress without her Teddy to lean on?

By the second week, I had achieved my sea legs and the fun began too. There really were parties and dances every night and no shortage of dance partners because Dad had befriended the other men in his cabin and they were mostly single men. I fell in love with three of them and danced all night. Dad must have had a quiet but firm word with the guys ... 'Absolutely no hanky-panky!' So, I sailed on with my own sweet romantic ideas of love.

Although, I do recall that I had felt the embarrassment of realisation one evening when everyone was singing 'Roll me over in the clover' and I was happily and guilelessly singing along. The words ... 'Now, this is number one and the fun has just begun. Roll me over, lay me down and do it again. Roll me over in the clover. Roll me over lay me down and do it again!' All the happy smiling adult faces beamed as they sang.

Then in my head something went, *'Click!' This is a rude song. This is about sex. All these people know that this is a rude song and they merrily sing along like part of a conspiracy. I am singing it too. Do they think that I know it what it is all about? Do they think that I am part of this big conspiracy when I am not? Oh dear! How am I to get out of this terrible situation?*

The verses rolled on and on and got ruder and ruder. I looked questioningly at my dad and he just gave me a wink and a grin.

No help there. All I could do was sit quietly and wait for it to finish. I felt sick, but I did nothing and said nothing. I was frightened and ashamed by what I had realised. Then I grew angry.

It is not my shame! It is a shame on you! You adults! You trapped me into singing this song. Why don't you just tell me what this is all about? I will not sing that song again! Ever.

Another couple joined our group of evening revellers, Pam and Jimmy Taylor.

Chapter 9   *The journey to Australia*

Pam was very young herself and I suppose they were what we now call DINKs (double income no kids), which is a great way to become rich. They became firm friends with Mum and Dad. I was jealous of them. They always had money to splash around on expensive gifts for each other, but it did not bother Mum and Dad that all their money went on raising Jackie and me. The friendship with Pam and Jimmy was long lasting. They were later always introduced as good friends who came out on the boat with us whenever they came to parties.

At Port Said, on the Suez Canal, our boat had to wait for access and we were beset by a swarm of hawker boats. Commerce was carried out by yelling, pointing, bargaining and ultimately goods sent up in a bag on a rope. The cacophony and Dad's bargaining skills of 'How much? Too much!' eventually brought forth large grass woven sun hats for all four of us and a large raffia woven hamper for Mum. She took it as a dirty clothes basket, but its oriental shape and the novel way of shopping in a tropical setting made me imagine that there was a genie inside.

One evening the entertainment on board was 'housey-housey'. It's called 'Bingo' today and I won the princely sum of twenty pounds.

'When we get to Algiers I'll take you ashore to the kasbah and you can buy yourself a piece of jewellery to remember the occasion,' promised Dad. This would be a great event. I would take my wealth (I had never had money of my own before) and go shopping in a foreign jewellers like a grown up. What a wonderful adventure this was becoming!

Dad was as good as his word and we went ashore in Algiers. My first shock was when an Arab sidled up to my father with a furtive, 'Psst. Dirty post cards, sir?' He produced an envelope full of picture cards of nude women.

'Disgusting! Oh, Dad!' I burst out.

They were quickly pocketed as we went on our quest of jewellery for me. I purchased a lovely ring with my twenty pounds, a sapphire set in diamonds. It was magnificent in a very conservative way. I was so proud of it that I wore it all the time.

Another big event in my eyes was the children's fancy dress competition. All of Mum and Dad's friends were happy to help produce the fancy dress. The boys were pressed into making crepe paper flowers for a lei while

Pam and Jimmy produced a raffia 'grass' skirt that Hawaiians would have envied. I was smeared with a cocoa solution and borrowed a pretty two piece swimming costume from Mum to make it modest. They all wanted to teach me appropriate arm movements and hip swings to carry off my role as a Hawaiian maiden.

Jackie was very shy till Dad came up with the idea of housey-housey. A large cardboard box had a roof added so it was the shape of a standard house big enough for her to be inside with just her legs free for walking, and some slits for vision. It was covered with 'bricks' of housey-housey blanks. We both won prizes. (All the children won prizes!) It was all part of the entertainment to keep the passengers from going stir crazy on such a long voyage. Just as 'crossing the line' was. That involved a faux King Neptune and the squirting of much water. All first-timers were issued a certificate.

We also went ashore at Colombo, Sri Lanka, where Dad asked a taxi driver to show us the important sights. We were driven out of town to a huge water tank.

'Water supply for Colombo, very important.'

And that was Colombo.

In time, we arrived at the Promised Land. Perth was our first experience. We had a day ashore. It was so hot that the Botanical Gardens, Kings Park, was the coolest place to be. We also visited a milk bar (our first) and partook of local delicacies; milkshakes and chocolate frogs.

Australia was going to be fine!

Upon reaching Port Adelaide, South Australia, we were carted by train to Bonegilla in Victoria. The railway compartments were normal sit up compartments with a passage running along one side with one toilet per carriage. It was a three day, two night journey with no provision for sleeping. Small children were put to sleep in the overhead luggage nets. I cannot remember how we were fed and watered. I just recall that it was very hot and seemed to go on forever.

In Bonegilla, we were housed in Nissen huts. It resembled a military camp. The accommodation was spartan and we were called to meals by means of a German announcer over a loudspeaker. It was soon dubbed 'Stalag 52'.

Chapter 9   *The journey to Australia*

The showers were in cement floored tin sheds, and there were drop toilets that were moved each month. You could see where the toilets had been two months previous because extremely healthy tomato plants had sprung forth.

Each bed had sheets and two army blankets and on each fresh pillow was a packet of aspirin. Mosquito repellent would have been more useful. Jackie's face was so badly bitten that it resembled a large red fruit with lumps on.

'Maybe that's why we are called Pommies. We resemble pomegranates!' Dad joked, but Sue was not amused.

She soon began to ask, 'When can we go home? This is so primitive.'

We were told that our stay in Bonegilla Migrant Camp was necessary while they sorted us to find the best destination for each family. We were guests of the Commonwealth Government while we were there and Dad, as usual, helped us to make the best of it and regard it as a free holiday.

One day, we went for a picnic by Lake Eucumbene and I swam out to the middle. I really did swim too far and as I tried to swim back I became very frightened and called out 'Help! Help!' to the rest of the party sitting on the shore.

Jimmy Taylor swam out to me. He didn't let me touch him. He kept just out of my reach and said, 'Come on, Chris! You can do it. Just keep swimming, I won't let you drown.' He continued to swim near me until we eventually made it back to shore. I was very grateful to him for showing me that I could do it on my own. I realised that had he not been there I could have drawn back the fear and swum back, proud of my own ability.

After a couple of months at the Bonegilla Migrant Camp, we were herded aboard a train for Adelaide. We undertook a two day and one night slow train journey under the same dreadful conditions.

Clearly, this Department of Immigration did not know how to organise anything, and we emigrants had to suffer. I took my lead from Dad. This was one of those instances when one just had to grin and bear it, having faith that we were heading to a brighter goal.

CHAPTER 10

NEW TO AUSTRALIA

In Adelaide, we were housed in a hostel in Finsbury, a western suburb of Adelaide. From here, men were expected to find employment, a home and schooling for their children. Jackie was soon enrolled at the local primary school while I went to Thebarton High School. We would take our allocated lunch sandwiches back to the canteen and replace the nutritious fillings with jam or sugar.

To reach our schools we walked through a few blocks of factories then went our separate ways. We met up again for the return journey. I was always asked to look after her.

Upon entering Thebarton High, I was placed in 2F (the top girls class for my age because I had been in grammar school in England) and given a choice of which science subjects I would take—Botany or Physics, Physiology or Chemistry. I selected Physics and Physiology because they appealed to me and I had enjoyed both. This choice turned out to be a bad one.

I found the whole school experience novel and soon made friends with three girls in my class. They were Janet, an English migrant with normal family, one younger brother, working parents and a grandmother who did the housework; Constance Joy Sturt, the only child of an older Australian couple, her father was the self-employed manufacturer of Sturdy Strollers. Her name was chosen because she would be a constant joy to her parents. That speaks volumes. She insisted on being called Joy. Well, who wouldn't? And then there was Olga, a white Russian refugee. Her family comprised a mother, grandmother and a stepfather, who her mother had picked up in a refugee camp in Yugoslavia. We became firm friends from 1952 to 1954, and we spent our lunch hours walking round the school oval deep in conversation.

Janet had dancing lessons, Joy did elocution, while Olga was sent to work in factories whenever it was possible. I took up ballroom dancing as soon as a suitable school could be found.

Joy lived in a proper established house with her father's factory/shed in the back garden. Janet's father had joined a self-builders club upon their arrival in Australia. He helped other members to build their own homes and in return they helped him to build his. Olga's stepfather was going it alone. He had built the back half of a house which included a bathroom and kitchen. They lived in a caravan and these rooms while they saved for the materials for him to continue. There were quite a few of these half-houses scattered through the Adelaide suburbs at the time.

Another very clever girl in the class, Marilyn Potter, was always top in Physics and Maths, probably in Chemistry too, but I didn't mind. I never defeated her, but once I scored second to her first in Physics and considered that a victory. I knew then that I was good at Physics and it became my favourite subject. Miss Chattery, a rather informal and chatty teacher, taught us physics and after one exam she could not help herself, she had to tell the story of a student in 2A (the male equivalent of 2F) who scored 99%. The amazing thing about the story was that he was not happy with this and asked her most politely, 'Where did I lose that 1%?'

We all giggled with amazement at the tale and asked who this genius was? He had a very funny Czechoslovakian name starting with an X, so none of us bothered to remember it. Boys classes were on the other side of the school and we would probably never meet him anyway.

We remained in the hostel until our home in England sold, then Dad went into partnership with an Irishman, Mr McCourt. They bought a large piece of land in Pooraka, north of Adelaide. The aim was to build a dwelling to house both families then teach the McCourts the plaster ornament business which would increase our joint fortune until they could build sheds, buy chickens, and run a chicken farm. Then we would share income from both plaster ornaments and chicken sales.

The house was built and we all moved in. Mum did not like living in 'the bush', which abounded with creepy-crawlies and there were a lot of chickens to feed.

I had to cycle to the Northfield railway station. The flies swarmed onto the back of my navy blazer as I took off each morning. Even though the chicken farm was not in the vicinity of Thebarton High School I continued to attend it because of the trouble I had had settling in.

You see, the curriculum in my school in England was not exactly in phase with the Australian school. Some subjects were ahead of England and others were behind it. I was a cheeky rascal and enjoyed making my classmates laugh, especially in the subjects where I was bored. The teachers soon worked out who was disrupting the class and it was mentioned in my school report. Dad went to the headmaster and complained.

'This is not my daughter; she is an excellent student. She was in grammar school in England.'

'If this is what the teachers report then this is true,' replied Mr Flaherty, the headmaster. I have never come across a headmaster who supported his teachers so emphatically in all my years of teaching. My father conveyed this message to me and I realised that I had let him down. My behaviour improved forthwith.

The Adelaide railway system was a series of lines radiating out from Adelaide city. The school and home were on different train lines, so I had to change trains in Adelaide. I could save time, however, by getting off one train at the stop before Adelaide and racing across the parklands to catch the second train at its first stop. It was quite a strenuous run for me, loaded with my school bag, but it saved a long wait at the Adelaide railway station.

We lived at that first home for about a year, Dad optimistically working away at the chickens and the plaster ornaments kept us fed and housed. Neither he nor Mr Mc Court had looked deeply into how to run a business in Australia.

My clearest memory of life on the chicken farm is of being woken at night by Mum's smoker's cough. Her way of stopping it was to get up and smoke a cigarette. She said that it relaxed her. Also, Jackie's horse trod on my foot! Yes, as soon as it was possible Jackie had a horse and I was dancing.

Dad was still no businessman. The business was wound up in due course and sold along with the land and we were back in a migrant hostel, Gepps Cross Hostel, this time.

What did me and my girlfriends talk about as we walked round and round the school oval at lunchtime? What were love and sex and how do they relate to one another? Why is it that boys are told to 'sow their wild oats' while girls were expected to be virgins until they marry? And then there were the bigger questions. Was it the truth in mathematics? Was it the ingenuity of Archimedes, Galileo or Newton from our physics lessons? Was it the neat and beautiful human body? How the systems complement and cooperate to make this marvellous living thing? Or was it the beautiful poetry that we were introduced to in English? Our favourite was Wordsworth and his love of nature. He seemed to see how the economic world was overtaking the natural world when he wrote, 'The world is too much with us; late and soon, getting and spending, we lay waste our powers: Little we see in nature that is ours; We have given our hearts away ...'

I think we all saw the hand of God in the magnificence of nature. Besides this, I thought that if we did believe we should be compliant and obedient to His laws, that is, the Ten Commandments.

Despite my desire to be compliant with God's will, I was beginning to question the Bible. We had religious instruction teachers who permitted questions and so one day I questioned the 'begats', you know, the piece in the Bible where it says Adam begat Cain and Cain begat this bloke and he begat another bloke, and so on and so on, ending up with Joseph, proving that Jesus was descended from Adam and Abraham.

'Well,' I said to the instructor, 'what's the point of all this begetting going down the male line when Joseph had nothing to do with Jesus's conception? He was born of Mary, The Virgin!'

Obviously, our teacher had had this question before, as he pointed out that Mary and Joseph were from the same line. It's just that they don't mention that in the Bible.

Why, I thought, should such an important fact be left out of this Bible?

Obviously, women had no part in writing the Bible and were considered too insignificant to be mentioned!

During this period, I had switched from ballet to ballroom dancing because of my wonky knees and, I must admit, I enjoyed it more until a couple of unsavoury episodes occurred.

I frequently travelled by train. There were lots of funny old trains on the rails in the fifties. There was a carriage system called 'dog boxes'. With dog boxes, a compartment had two rows of seats running from one side to the other facing each other. The aisle between them joined the doors so that access could be gained from either side, but there was no passage joining the compartments. One evening I entered such a compartment, sat in a corner and took out a homework book, totally ignoring the *gentleman* who was already seated on the other side. No sooner had the train started to move when he came and sat right next to me, uncomfortably close to me. I tried to ignore him, but he started talking.

'You are a very pretty girl. Do you have a boyfriend? I would like you to be my girlfriend.'

He insinuated one arm around me to grope my breast, while the other hand crept across my thigh. I was amazed, horrified, stunned, cornered and immobile for a few seconds that felt like hours. I wriggled free, but there was nowhere to go.

All I could do was say, 'No! No! No!'

I stood, retrieved my books and bag, and walked up and down the aisle until we reached the next station when I could leap out. Fortunately, he was not aggressive and my actions were enough to put him off. I was still shaken when I reached home, late, to tell Mum and Dad the story.

You may ask, what has that to do with ballroom dancing?

Well, at this time, I was having private tuition for ballroom dancing at the White Academy. *'Learn to dance the White way'.* My teacher was Mr White. The lesson took place in a remote temporary hut with a good floor, a few chairs and a record player. On the Wednesday following the train incident, Mum and Dad were to pick me up after work. The lesson was spin-turns. To achieve a smooth spin-turn, the couple face each other in a firm ballroom hold. Right legs are forward and left legs are back so that as the man steps forward right, the lady steps back left with a simultaneous movement. They spin and rock and so the spin progresses.

Mr White was saying, 'Relax, Christine! Your thighs are much too tight!'

This did not relax me. 'I cannot relax and rock and spin all at the same time.'

'You do not have to relax all your leg muscles, just your inner thighs.'

To indicate which muscles he meant, his hand was between my legs and slapping from side to side on my inner thighs. This definitely did not relax me. A man's hand did not belong *down there*. I pulled away.

'Okay, let's try again.'

There was absolutely no escape from this situation. Mum and Dad would not arrive for another ten minutes. I was red with embarrassment and tears were beginning to well. He ignored my reaction and continued with the lesson. I will never know if his actions were a crude attempt at seduction or a genuine attempt to improve my spin-turns because when my parents arrived I leapt into the car and burst into tears.

'I'm not going back to him again!'

When the whole episode was explained my father wanted to return and give Mr White 'what for', but Mum and I restrained him. We just decided to find a different dance school.

What had these experiences taught me?

Previously, I had been taught people are trustworthy. If you are lost, do not be afraid to ask an adult. They will help you.

Now we have a slight change to that philosophy.

These instances were not my fault. There was nothing for me to be ashamed of. Not all people are to be trusted. Some are nasty, but most people are good and can be trusted, in general, most of the time.

CHAPTER 11

POORAKA

Glenda's dancing school had rooms on North Terrace Adelaide, right opposite the Adelaide railway station. Private students were put through the medals system of exams and competitions for which one needed a partner, at about the same level of competence, so you could take your private lessons jointly and practice together in your own free time.

Enter Dino Pastro. I did not like his appearance. He was at least four years older than me, a grown man of Italian descent. His face was large, with large lips, a large nose, large bushy eyebrows, and one redeeming feature, large brown eyes. He had a permanent five o'clock shadow, which was far from fashionable in the 50s. However, he was a very polite, strictly Catholic Italian boy living under his parents' control. His family lived in the city near the parklands where they kept a cow. His job every morning was to rise early and milk the cow.

I found this amazing! Medieval even!

He was working as a chartered accountant, so he was not dumb, but he was totally controlled by his parents and boss. The ballroom dancing must have been his only personal outlet. However, it came about, we were brought together to dance and dance we did. We were awkward at first, but with practice and private lessons our style improved greatly and we passed our medals and even won some competitions.

The proximity of the studio to the Adelaide railway station proved a boon. At the railway station was a magnificent ladies room where, for a small fee, one could take a shower, change clothes and apply makeup. So, on dance nights, this caterpillar of a schoolgirl could transform herself into a lovely butterfly.

Although Dino was four years my senior he had no friends. I was a chatty,

Chapter 11   *Pooraka*

friendly girl, so we became firm friends because we shared the dancing experience and found we could talk to one another. He was oppressed at home and at work, so he enjoyed having someone to talk to who did not control his every move and thought. We would go to the Palais on Saturday nights and dance for practice and fun, then he would walk me back to the railway station and I would catch a train home.

We had moved from Gepps Cross Hostel to a rented house in Pooraka, and that was a new experience for us. Washing was done in an outside laundry in a copper that had to have a fire lit under it on washdays. Mum found this very primitive, she was used to sending her washing to a laundry where someone else did the washing and the ironing. The house had a large backyard and some sheds. Dad soon set up his plaster ornament business again. He employed three or four girls working in the shed. One girl called Irene caused us much mirth. She once tried to describe a new Australian that she knew and the thing that he ate.

'He takes eggs and mixes them up and puts other things in with them as he cooks the eggs.'

'Perhaps it's an omelette?' said Mum.

'Oh! I don't know what nationality he is! I'm just telling you how he cooked eggs.'

One morning she told Mum that she had dreamed that Ted had asked her to go to Melbourne with him. He would drive and they would have some fun! (Nudge, nudge, wink, wink). Mum listened attentively to Irene's dream and laughed it off. Later, she had the opportunity to tell Dad the story without Irene knowing. Then, later in the day, Dad approached Irene and asked her to come to Melbourne with him, just as he had in the dream. Irene was so embarrassed, thinking that her dream had come true. Then all the girls began to laugh and she realised that the joke was on her.

In the 50s, one only had to pass a written test to get a driver's license. Learning to drive was up to you and your family, you didn't necessarily need official lessons from a registered provider. So, Dad taught me around the back roads of Pooraka. However, Dad was taking a trip to Melbourne to deliver orders from his factory and suggested that I go with him to practice my driving skills. I jumped at the offer and I drove the deserted dust road that connected Adelaide to Melbourne at the time.

In the middle nowhere there was a fork in the road and I took the left fork. Dad exclaimed, 'You should have turned right there!'

There was a little track joining the two branches of the fork. When I saw it, I decided to take it to get me back on track, but I didn't slow down. Instead, I put the car into a swerve and before we knew it the car was lying on its side

'Oh, Dad, I'm so sorry, I'm so sorry, Dad!'

'It's all right, Chrissie, calm down. We just have to get the car back on the road.'

Instantly, someone opened the upper door and said, 'You folks all right? Let us give you a hand.'

They helped us out and helped us to push the car back on its four wheels. Oil was leaking out, but the motor started and our helpers simply suggested that we stop at the next service station to top up the oil, then they waved us goodbye. We did not know these rescuing angels or where they came from. We just thought, 'We must have encountered Aussie mateship.'

My father insisted that I take the wheel when we hit the road again. I was not allowed to develop a fear of driving, but I had to learn from my mistakes, not dissimilar to my swimming incident while we were at the river Thames.

A slightly more mature Christine ended 1953. I remember Dad confiding in me about a few of his money worries. Not that he expected me to do anything about it, just to let me know that life wasn't all beer and skittles and he still ardently wished a better life for Jackie and me.

'Because,' he said, 'you didn't ask to be born. It was my action that created you, so it's my duty to give you the best life that I can.'

His overriding message was that whatever LIFE threw at you, you did not sit and feel sorry for yourself. You got up and got on with it! He was preparing me for what life could have in store.

My favourite poem from this year was *Ulysses* by Tennyson. My favourite quotation from it was, 'For I am a part of all that I have met; yet all experience is an arch where through gleams that untravelled world whose margin fades forever and forever when I move.'

Chapter 11   *Pooraka*

At the end of this school year, we sat for our Intermediate Certificate. We went to the Wayville showgrounds and sat at individual desks in a huge hall for a three hour written exam for each subject that we had studied. It was nerve wracking, but we survived and most of us passed.

CHAPTER 12

FINAL YEAR AT GOOD OLD THEBIE HIGH

In the 50s, many people still thought that education was wasted on a girl. What was she going to do with it? All a girl did was marry and have children. If it was necessary for her to earn some money there were plenty of menial jobs she could work at. This was not Dad's attitude, especially since I had passed the 10 plus in England. I was going to be someone. If I could get to university he would support me.

Thebarton High had a girls section and a boys section. At the end of each year, the number of girls in my class diminished, as the girls were deemed old enough to be sent to work Joy, Janet, Olga and I were all survivors. At the beginning of 1954, there were about twenty girls left at our year level. This was too few to make up a class. Twenty-five boys, the best academically, were selected to be put into a class with us. We had the only mixed class in the school! The competition and standard within that class were the highest I have ever encountered. Homework was always done, discipline and attention to teachers was keen. It soon became clear that we were all expected to pass all our subjects and the teachers seemed to enjoy teaching us. Many of the students went on to professional careers and many are still my friends more than 65 years later. Becoming a self-proclaimed Education Snob probably started here … no, it probably started with Sir William Perkin's School for Girls. Remember, we were told to act like ladies and no eating of ice-creams in the street. That was common!

Max Hocking was our brilliant Physics and Maths teacher. His explanations were so clear, his appreciation of the topics so evident, his demonstrations in the laboratory so enthralling, at least, that is how it seemed to me. In Maths, I was swept away by the dizzy heights of Euclidean geometry and algebra that ran on to trigonometry. One night, a particularly tricky proof was set for homework. I spent a good hour on it before I cracked it. I was so proud to be the only student who had managed to complete the proof.

But, oh, how devastated I was when told that we had now finished with Euclid! We had learnt all his theorems and all the techniques for solving his geometric problems. Moving right along, we spent a few weeks on logarithms. That is now a superseded method for working out big sums accurately. It was displaced first by the slide rule and now the calculator.

Physiology was my second science and I enjoyed that too. Halfway through the year, Max Hocking took me aside and said that if I wanted to go on to study science at university, and I did have the ability to do that, I should be studying Chemistry as my second science. He was willing to help me with it, but I enjoyed Physiology and found Chemistry really foreign as I had no previous grounding in it. So, I abandoned it, not realising how true his words were until too late.

English was not so hot. I enjoyed the poets, the novels and the plays, but our teacher, The Dragon, did not aim to help us to improve our style or grammar or spelling. She just set the work and we had to do whatever we could. It is a miracle that I passed.

French, well, I had no aptitude, but I had to try to come to terms with it because it was a prerequisite for entry to university for a science degree. I failed to see the logic in this, and failed to pass it too.

I did not play sport, but I had my ballroom dancing and my run across the northern parklands to keep me fit. Then Jerry Phillips and Peter Narraway decided that we could put on a school production. Gilbert and Sullivan's *Trial by Jury* was too short as a standalone production, so a short play called *Happy Death Limited* was also produced. Janet, Joy and I had parts in this and so did Peter Whitford. I was awarded actress of the year for my part in *Happy Death Limited*. The prize was a year's free membership in the Adelaide Repertory Company.

Sue and Ted argued that 'Acting is not a real job! It would be better if you concentrate your time on real study and become a maths teacher like Miss Bishop or Mr Hocking.' So, I did not take up the offer. Instead, I took up the offer to become a preliminary probationary student with the South Australian Education Department. They offered a small 'wage' in exchange for signing on the dotted line and promising to teach for four years after graduating.

This was a formative time for another reason.

I was amazed by Xavier Jancarik, a Czech boy in our class who studied Drawing for most of the year. When he discovered that French was a prerequisite for Medicine, he switched to French in the last term and passed. He was the clever boy with a funny Czech name starting with X who had asked Miss Chattery where he had lost that 1%! He had drive and initiative, that boy! He intended to go straight on to university next year, as it was possible to do that then. He had been held back at school by two years so that his English could be brought up to par, and he said that his parents could not afford for him to spend a year in matriculation. Both parents worked full-time and they took in boarders. Because he was the oldest child, he was child-minder and interpreter for the family. In the holidays prior to Christmas, he worked as a postman.

I was very impressed. He was what I call a biological bull: tall, strong, athletic, good-looking, very good at schoolwork, ambitious. He will be a doctor!

Wow, I admired him greatly.

The big questions of life still puzzled me.

What is love? What is sex? Are they one and the same? I have my periods and am told by Mum that it's all okay. It's a sign of maturity. I must keep myself clean and change the pad daily. Carry a pad when you are expecting it to come. Although I am now mature at this age, I still do not know what sex or grown-up love is. Why are parents so coy or embarrassed to talk about this? I listen to Shakespeare and theorise on the love poetry by Burns that we read in English, for instance, 'My love is like a red, red rose that's newly sprung in June'.

So, love is everything sweet and beautiful and pure, and at the same time it is heroic, strong and everlasting. What has that to do with sex? My friends

Chapter 12   *Final year at good old Thebie High*

and I talk amongst ourselves as we walk around the school oval at lunchtime, but none of us ever reaches a satisfactory conclusion.

One afternoon, towards the end of the year, Xavier offered to teach me to play chess if I would stay back after school. We stayed in our classroom after the others had left. We set up the pieces on one of the middle desks and started a game. It was so complicated! I wanted to impress him as he had impressed me, so I concentrated. After a few minutes Mr Hocking passed the window and called into us.

'Xavier is teaching me to play chess, Mr Hocking,' I chirped up.

'Ah! Xavier go and open the door would you, son? You shouldn't be in there with the door closed.'

'Yes, sir, right away.' Xavier was up and opened the door immediately.

I did not see the innuendo of a girl and boy being shut in the classroom alone after school, but clearly Mr Hocking and Xavier did.

Some of the boys took an interest in the girls. I remember Janet and John Fine were keen on each other, but after a brief romance they went their separate ways. Sue Anderson and Graham Alexander paired up; later they married and spent a long and happy life together.

And I was impressed by Xavier. At the end of the year, we had a class party, played silly games, brought a plate to share and dressed in clothes other than school uniform. I had nothing suitable because I was either in school uniform or ballroom gowns, so Mum found a dress of hers that fitted me, and in my first high heels I tottered along to the party. Fortunately, Xavier met me at the railway station so I could take his arm and teeter more confidently to school. During the party, Mr Hocking made a little speech about what a wonderful year it had been for him, thanking us for being such dedicated students. He usually taught boys and commented what a great bunch of girls we were and said that he couldn't blame the boys for liking us so much.

The years at Thebarton high taught me the self-discipline necessary to be a good student, but I was young and invincible I kept the reigns of my own future in my own hands. I stuck to Physiology. What a silly, headstrong girl.

CHAPTER 13

MATRICULATION AT ADELAIDE GIRLS HIGH

I did my matriculation at Adelaide Girls High School because Thebarton did not have a matric class. I would catch an early train and Dino would meet me. We used to walk the streets of Adelaide for about an hour before school started, then I went to school and he went to work. We seemed to have so much to talk about it filled that hour every weekday. His main contention was that although he was 21 his life was not his own. He was ruled by his parents at home, by his boss at work, and the Catholic Church everywhere else.

I thought he needed to talk to my father about his life and how he could improve it because my dad was a wise man. So, one day I invited him home and he told Dad about his predicament. After consideration, Dad gave him some advice.

'Why don't you go to Melbourne? Break free from your boss and parents, and start life anew.'

Eventually, in 1956, that's what he did. We were still such buddies that I would phone him a couple of times a week from the public phone on the corner of our street. On school holidays I visited him. I stayed at the Hotel Cecil in Melbourne city and we went about together and danced and talked and had a great time. We never became lovers, his faith constrained him. We cuddled and kissed, but both of us remained virgins.

Matriculation at Adelaide Girls High was very intense. My close Thebarton school friends went their separate ways into the big wide world. Janet and Joy disappeared into the world of commerce, while Olga took the shortest path to becoming a teacher which was a two-year course at Teachers College. They were all capable, intelligent girls, and I would have been the

Chapter 13 *Matriculation at Adelaide Girls High*

richer emotionally if we could have continued along the academic road together. However, there were still five girls from Thebarton in my class.

I studied Year 12 Maths one and two, Physics, English, and Year 11 French, which I had failed the year before. Marilyn Potter, remember her? The unreachable one, she became my buddy for Maths and Physics. Physics was studied at Adelaide Boys High. A group of us walked to ABHS during our lunch hour to be there for our daily lecture while a small group of boys walked in the opposite direction to study Botany.

I had always been poor at English, but at Adelaide Girls High was a marvellous teacher, her name was Elsie Morrison. She was so enthusiastic that she carried us along. She reasoned that if we could write a critical essay then an imaginative essay would come easily. So, every weekend she set a critical essay about books, plays, poems that we were studying. She collected the essays on Monday morning and by end of that school day they were returned to us, marked. She soon discovered that I needed help with my spelling. So, as she marked my work she listed my spelling mistakes and asked me to learn these words by Wednesday morning when she would give me a test in her study. I strove to improve.

It took the whole weekend for me to write my English essay with a dictionary in constant use. When I got to school on Monday morning a friend, Alison Friar, would read it through and correct any spelling errors that she found. Still the errors got through, but Elsie was delighted with my essays and encouraged me greatly.

She could read Shakespeare and Chaucer in such a way that we understood and enjoyed it. She is responsible for a turnaround in my attitude towards English and reading. French was a drag, but I just had to do it and did manage to pass. Maths and Physics were fun to me and filled a lot of my time. I passed them easily. Every evening I settled to my homework and worked for at least two hours. This was the year I learned to persevere at unpopular subjects.

Our English studies on *Hamlet, Anthony and Cleopatra*, and Chaucer's *Canterbury Tales* introduced us to very human characters; human, in that no one was perfect. They all had feet of clay. Last year I was of the opinion that love was sweet and strong and all good, but now I see there is no longer black and white, wrong and right. This helped to prepare me for things to come.

My life at this time consisted of travelling to school, working at school, travelling home, eating evening meal, doing homework, then sleeping. It was my 'year of the nerd'.

There was to be an end of year school social for all the matric students from Adelaide Girls High and Adelaide Boys High, and it was to be held in the big hall at Adelaide boys high. By this time, I was a beautiful and graceful ballroom dancer. I had reached the silver medal level. I thought that it was time for me to show off to the teachers and students of these schools, so I invited Dino. Dressed in one of my lovely ball gowns, made by Suzie, of course, with layers of tulle, I went to the school social. I was unique and stood out like a sore thumb, but I wanted to say that they may excel at tennis, netball, football and other sports, but I was a dancer. I don't remember anyone talking to us between dances. After a handful of dances, we left the children to their social and he walked me to the railway station. So much for Adelaide Girls High, I thought. Looking back at it now, I feel it was a very hollow victory. What thoughtless, unnecessary showing off!

While I'm embarrassing myself thinking about the 17-year-old me, I am reminded of another incident that took place that summer. One Saturday evening, Dino and I were dancing at Glenelg. This means, of course, that I was fully rigged out in a tulle ball gown with flowers on the dress matching the flowers in my hair, make up immaculate. It was announced that Chips Rafferty was visiting the dance hall.

'He is searching for new talent, so gentleman, if you think that the girl in your arms is beautiful and talented, take her over to meet Chips and his producer at the table at the back of the hall.'

Dino was immediately inspired to such an act. 'Chris, you are beautiful and talented. I'm taking you over.'

I, however, immediately panicked. 'I—no, no, no, Dino, I can't! it's too sudden.'

'This is a now or never opportunity.'

Chapter 13   *Matriculation at Adelaide Girls High*

'Please, no, I can't!'

My pleas were overridden and before I knew it, I was standing before Mr Chips Rafferty himself.

'Mr Rafferty, I would like you to meet my partner, Christine Tailor,' said Dino respectfully.

'Please sit down. Hello, Christine and …?'

'Dino.'

'Dino and Christine, how are you both?'

I blushed, I was flustered, I tried to answer and the words would not come out.

This was Chips Rafferty! I had seen him in films. Smiley *was a lovely movie.*

I thought all this, but nothing would come out of my mouth I was absolutely struck speechless. My usual self-confidence had flown now that I was face-to-face with greatness. After a few attempts to strike up a conversation he said, 'We seem to have struck a very shy one here.'

There was nothing for it but a hasty retreat by an embarrassed Dino and a scarlet, flustered Christine. I was so cross with Dino that he had rushed me into the situation. I was in complete shock, and also devastated as it could have been the start of my acting career. I had revelled in the stage work we did at Thebie High the previous year, but this year there had been nothing, so when faced with a wonderful opportunity I was just a wimp.

So that's the 17-year-old Christine Tailor. She had worked very hard to gain her matriculation and had passed Leaving French so she was all prepared for university. But, as a person, no development had occurred at all. She needed some education in LIFE.

Well, it was all about to happen.

CHAPTER 14

UNIVERSITY STUDENTS, SO IN LOVE

I spent two years at Adelaide University where I studied Pure Maths, Physics and Chemistry one and two. Rock and roll was *the* dance and Elvis was *the* heartthrob.

I loved everything about Adelaide University—the spacious, well-kept lawns where our gang met for lunch, the individual buildings for each department set apart and each one a world apart from the others, the quadrangle abutting the canteen with its sandstone arches and walkways. I only needed to visit the Maths department, the Physics department and the Chemistry department in the real university. Some of us who were preliminary probationary teachers were employees of the Education Department—remember we signed up in 1954—so we also had to attend Teachers College for our teaching subjects such as Hygiene, Teaching Methods and the like, all pretty ho-hum.

Xavier had studied first-year medicine in 1955 and therefore did second and third year medicine during these two years.

Dino was in Melbourne and at the beginning of that time I considered him my boyfriend, but I was very busy with my studies and confused about boyfriends because Xavier kept inviting me to university events like the Commencement Ball. I felt I had to sort it out with Dino, so I planned a trip over a long weekend, wrote to him and arranged that he should meet the Melbourne Express on the Saturday morning, as he always had done, so that we could talk and I could feel secure that we were a couple.

He did not meet the Melbourne Express, so I booked myself into the Hotel Cecil and went to where he was living. He had a small flat in the back garden of that address. When I arrived, I asked the owner of the house if Dino was home and they told me he was not.

Chapter 14   *University students, so in love*

'He had gone out on Friday and not returned. It was commonplace for him to do that,' they said.

I was most confused. I sat around his flat for most of the day, then left him a note to bring him up to date with my situation, asking him to call me at the hotel when he returned home. I returned to the hotel and looked at my financial situation. I had the money to pay for the hotel and a very little bit over. I calculated how I could survive on this money until it was time to catch the Melbourne Express home on Sunday evening. I phoned Xavier and my parents to bring them up-to-date. Then, because I had nothing to do, I remembered an essay that I was supposed to write. I sat on the bed, put pen to paper and wrote the essay, stopping only to go out for the cheapest meal I could find.

I thought all this was very strange, but perhaps it was the best way that Dino could think of to break off our relationship. Clearly, there was someone else in his life and he was spending the weekend with her. I never did find out, despite more calls and letters.

Xavier was at the Adelaide railway station to greet me, as I knew he would. Prior to this, after the Commencement Ball when I was being coy about his advances, he said, 'I can see that you are a one man woman, Chris. I just want to be that one man.'

Xavier became my boyfriend by default and was quick to seduce me. The mechanics of starting the sex act seemed rather awkward to me, but it meant that he cared for me and I was trembling with anticipation. When it came to a climax I was blown away!

This is why they do it!

I remember my thoughts at the time.

So now not only do I admire and respect Xavier, I adore him. I do not know why, I just do. He is marvellous and I just want to be with him, near him. I want him to adore me the same way. I want him to think that I am beautiful–intelligent–desirable above all other girls.

I was smitten. I would do the sex thing whenever he wanted it because it pleased him. But despite the pleasure, it was tinged with fear. I was terrified of being caught, falling pregnant, or losing him. 'If you love me you will have sex with me' was a hidden message at all times. I was not really psychologically mature enough to really enjoy the ride.

So, now I had a boyfriend. It was back to university, studying and enjoying lunch on the Barr Smith lawns with our usual crew of friends from 'Leaving' at Thebarton High School.

These were great years for science! Sputnik circled the Earth on 4 Oct 1957. Marilyn Potter was my buddy in Maths and Physics. We worked together in our Physics practical and we had a secret weapon, Xavier's practical book from the previous year. Science for first-year medicine was the same as for the first year of Bachelor of Science. The practical experiments had not changed and if we could not get a good result for our experiment we could always fall back on his meticulous book.

Xavier did think that I was a clever girl. At one time he told me about a girl in his class who was so introverted that she did not want to deal with patients. She had decided to become a pathologist.

'You could be a doctor. You are brighter than her. Why not?'

I loved that I had impressed him. 'Yes, why not? I would love that!'

But then he backtracked. 'On second thoughts, it's better you stay a teacher. Two doctors in one family would be awkward!'

Xavier's friends were all doing well too. Hamish was doing medicine. Karl was studying dentistry and Rolf was doing science. These friends all succeeded in their degrees and Rolf became an Industrial Chemist.

Xavier played rugby for the university team and so I went along to cheer him and the rest of the team every Saturday. After the match, we went to the Botanic Hotel to drown our sorrows or cheer our win. Rolf joined the rugby team, although he was most unlikely candidate for rugby. He was more of your studious academic but we, New Australians all, tended to stick together and enjoy each other's company and friendship.

There was one particularly romantic occasion that I will never forget. Xav had been away at National Service so we had not seen each other for a few weeks. On his return we took a motorbike ride up into the Adelaide hills and found a lovely spot overlooking the city. He brought our lunch with him. It was a rockmelon, the first I had ever encountered. I was delighted by its succulent perfumed flavour. We were so happy to be together again on this lovely summer's day with a warm gentle breeze blowing ... Yes, I thought to myself at the time, 'Love is a many splendoured thing.'

And while I moved on to university, Jackie moved on to high school and we moved onto Henley Beach to a rented house. There must have been another shift in our family fortunes. I must admit that I was more wrapped up in passing my exams and Xavier at that point. Over the summer holidays, I was able to work as an instructor in the Learn to Swim campaign. It didn't feel like work, just splashing around in the shallow water with the beginners, but I developed a lovely tan and had cash in my pocket.

Ah yes, I remember now. Dad's business collapsed because small Japanese trinkets flooded the shops, so he moved on to making plaster sheets for ceilings. This must have been a big upheaval for Mum and Dad, but Jackie and I just proceeded with life as normal. She decided that she would like to win the sports cup at high school. She rose early and ran every morning without disturbing the household and practiced her events at school. Then one day she came home with the cup. She had said nothing to any of us, just made her own plans and got on with it.

We were all amazed!

She decided that she did not want to try to follow in my footsteps and make her way to university, instead she took an apprenticeship with an Adelaide hairdresser, Arturo Taverno. He was a hard taskmaster as I learnt one morning when I had to call him to let him know that she was sick and could not get to work. She entered the real adult world ahead of me, meeting Denis Parsons at a New Year's Eve dance and forming a serious relationship with him.

CHAPTER 15

THE ESCAPE

During this period, Xavier told me something about the background of the Jancarik family and the fate of Czechoslovakia during the Second World War and afterwards. I present here as near as I can their history from pre-WWII until it merged with mine.

Prior to outbreak of war, the Czechs were informing London that German troops were building up on their borders and they needed help to repel the Hun. Britain was too busy building up arms for her own defence to pay any heed to the little European nations. Hence, the Germans marched easily through Poland and Czechoslovakia and these were occupied territories throughout World War II. We British thought that we had a hard time during the war, but it must have been harder for the occupied countries because the Germans would have taken resources for their own troops first, leaving the residents to scrounge for leftovers. Although they were disappointed by the Allies lack of help, the Czechs did what they could to sabotage the German war machine. Xavier told me how the boys, Xavier, aged 12, Jan, aged 10, and Pavel, aged 6, discovered that a coin placed on a railway track could derail a train and so they did this as often as they could. They trusted no one in uniform, but superficially they befriended their invader in the hopes of favours and information. At one stage their father, Jan senior, was sent to a concentration camp. He was released as a walking skeleton and had to be gently nursed back to health by his loving wife, Maria.

They were delighted when war ended, but freedom was not to be theirs. Communist Russia 'liberated' the eastern countries and their Iron Fist was worse than the Germans. Jan Jancarik senior was too outspoken for his own good. He refused to join the Communist party and so found himself unemployed. Some of their relatives lived in a rural area, so Maria and the boys

Chapter 15   *The Escape*

went to live in the country where at least they could eat. Meanwhile, Jan travelled the country, officially looking for work and a place for his family to live when in fact he was searching for a means to escape Czechoslovakia.

Eventually, in 1949, he found a house on a hill overlooking a railway station, so close to the German/Czech border that it was deemed a no-go area. He asked his relatives if any of them wanted to join his nuclear family in an escape. Maria's sister Fran and her husband, Vlastick Cerney, with their two small boys joined the group. Jan and Vlastick watched the railway station for days to observe the movements of the armed guards. They observed that whenever a train came into the station from Germany, the guards moved onto the platform to check passengers who might be smuggling food or weapons. This left the road which ran parallel to the railway unguarded, with just one large roll of barbed wire marking the border.

Jan took his sons into the woods and whenever he came upon a large bramble he would throw a rug over it and ask the boys to clamber over as a challenge. They did not know why their father invented this activity but enjoyed the game. Meanwhile, the women were planning what each person could carry and packing survival packs in knapsacks and packages small enough for each person to carry.

The authorities had discovered that a family was living in no man's land and they were ordered to move. Jan informed the police that they would move on a specific day by catching a certain train travelling from Germany to Pilsen, so the soldiers were not surprised to see a hand cart and a group of people walking down the hill towards the station to catch the incoming train. As the train pulled into the station the guards moved onto the platform to check alighting passengers, which meant the train was blocking their view of the Jancariks and Cerneys. Timing was of the essence. At a signal from Jan senior, the blankets were thrown over the barbed wire and some adults and the bigger boys clambered over and packages were thrown to them. Once loaded, they ran full pelt down the road. Almost all was done when Maria realised that young Pavel was still standing in bewilderment next to the abandoned hand cart wondering, 'Why is my family running away in what I have been told is forbidden territory?'

Maria yelled out in desperation, '*Utikej Pavlicku, utikej*!', meaning 'Run, little Pavel, run!' He ran to her and found himself tossed over the wire and into welcoming arms. On the German side were German citizens and guards, watching the escape, so when the Russian guards realised what was going on they could not fire at the escapees for fear of hitting a German civilian and causing an international incident.

The family survived in the refugee camps on the German side because they stuck together as a family and obeyed their father in his every word. I'm sure he felt that his family's survival depended on their unity and obedience.

Xavier told me about life in the camps. One story stuck in my mind. The boys used to go onto the streets and pick up cigarette butts, bring them back to their hut, break them open to glean out the tobacco then roll new cigarettes for their father or to sell among other refugees. Their rations here were very meagre, but the family survived on the hope of migrating to Canada. One evening, Jan returned to his family with the sobering news that the next available passage to Canada was at least 12 months away. However, a boat bound for Australia was leaving in one week. This greatly influenced the decision to go to Australia and they duly set sail on the *S.S. Nelly*, a converted USA troop carrier. The crossing was slow, but finally they arrived in Sydney.

From Sydney they were trucked to Bonegilla where they lived for some weeks. From there they were trucked to Mildura where Jan and Marie took work as fruit pickers to partly offset their ever increasing debt to the 'Australian authorities'. Eventually, they found their way to Mallala, near Adelaide, which was a holding camp for immigrants. Maria and the children stayed in Mallala while Jan senior found lodgings for himself at Mile End and work as a labourer at Pope Products in Finsbury. He soon earned enough to buy himself a bicycle, and dutifully rode to Mallala every Friday afternoon to spend the weekend with his family, and then rode back on Sunday afternoons.

After a time, they were able to rent a small house in Leslie St, Kilkenny, so that the whole family could be together with the children in school and Maria was able to find work. She also found room to take in two young Czech men as boarders, anything to help pay their way.

Chapter 15 *The Escape*

They had escaped from post-war Communist-rule Czechoslovakia with only what they could carry. However, there was value in what they carried. Throughout their year-long transit there was virtually no assistance from any source and they had to pay every step of the way.

Their ability to live so modestly stood them in good stead. Maria worked her magic on the cheapest cuts of meat and used vegetables and fruit from their own garden. They put in a huge effort because their aim was to see all three boys with university degrees and professional jobs. They would show these Aussies, who called them Bolts and Dagoes, how much intellectual and physical strength Czechoslovakians have.

Had I known the full story when Xavier and I first met I might have had more sympathy for Jan and Maria.

I learnt how fugally they lived when I shared my first Christmas with them. The Christmas meal was a feast, of course, and I gave Xavier a gramophone record as a gift, 'My prayer' by The Platters. He took me aside afterwards and said that Christmas presents in his family were not of a frivolous kind. The boys were given three pairs of underpants and three pairs of socks which were to last them the year. A shirt or another pair of socks would have been more appreciated than a gramophone record. I felt hurt and crestfallen; but I realised what a small budget this family lived on.

Clearly, I did not understand the sacrifice and effort necessary to carry this family through its 15-year plan.

The fact that he had chosen me as his girlfriend came in for much criticism.

'Why pick that girl? English! Clearly spoiled and frivolous, look at all the pretty dresses she wears! There are many lovely Czech girls that we know. Why don't you select one of those?'

But he was smitten and I was the one he wanted. I was among the brightest in the class, pretty, vivacious, and very impressed with him. In truth, we both decided that our parents knew nothing about our tastes and we just wished that they would leave us alone.

Our romance continued and we would sneak away whenever possible to be alone together, and yes, we were sexually active. Of course, I was terrified of becoming pregnant and yes, once it happened. Xavier managed to procure some abortion pills. I took them under his instruction and when I stopped the course my menstrual cycle resumed.

Phew! What a relief! That little episode drew us closer together. We were fellow conspirators.

About this time, Dad must have realised that we were sexually active and sought a way to put a stop to it. He said to me in confidence one day, 'A man does not spoil the flower that he intends to wear.'

I was miffed at first and then worked out what this rather old-fashioned saying was supposed to imply. So, to answer him back I asked Xavier to declare his intentions to Dad and ask for my hand in marriage. He spoke very respectfully to Dad and explained that we wanted to be married as soon as possible. Naturally, we could not marry while we had no income, so he had applied for scholarships with New Guinea, the Navy and the Army in exchange for a bond of four years' service after graduation. He was successful with the Army application.

I think Dad was surprised by this formal approach and could only wish us well. I was listening in from the passage and thought to myself, *Put that in your pipe and smoke it, you old-fashioned, old prude!*

The only way to raise the income to provide for a home was for me to abandon my studies, start teaching and earning. This was possible only with the consent of my parents, so I pleaded with them to let this happen. Actually, I was finding university study heavy going and dreaded the thought of third year in any of my chosen subjects. My father eventually succumbed to my pleading and visited my 'guardian' in the education department. But Dad actually sought a way to separate me from Xavier and asked that I be placed in a one-teacher school way out in the country. However, since I was only 19 my 'guardian' thought it best that I remain in a suburban school. I was appointed to Brighton High School, but Dad basically succeeded in his aim. We hardly saw each other that summer. I taught swimming in the 'Learn to Swim' campaign while Xavier took work driving a bulldozer for a gang that was clearing bushland. This enabled him to buy the traditional engagement ring.

This was yet another step forward towards our marriage. I saw Dad's attempt to separate us as racial prejudice and dug my heels in. I was not ashamed of my association with this foreigner. His hard work bought my engagement ring. I was justifiably proud of the man and the ring!

CHAPTER 16

TEACHING

For two years, I taught at Brighton High. They are happily blurred together.

Now I felt that I had entered the adult world and became friendly with other female teachers, even though I was only 19. I heard their stories and learned that married life was not all beer and skittles. But then, I thought, they were not married to the perfect husband that I had selected.

I got on well with my pupils because I was a softie and enthusiastic about the maths and science that I taught. Here is a quotation from a book called *Growing up in Adelaide in the 50s*. The article is written by Claire Hayes:

> The most exciting class was science, where controlled experiments took place with such things as phosphorus, dissecting of frogs and mixing heating various liquids in beakers over Bunsen burners. All this was conducted by a very pretty young English woman called Miss Tailor, who was engaged to be married and had a very positive outlook on life. She was a favourite of the students.

In those days there were no drama teachers, so if the school was to do a production it was a matter of staff volunteering for extra duties. I reached an agreement with the music teacher, Mr Pruul, that if he would teach the music side of things, I would take care of the dance, speech and stage management so that we could produce a Gilbert and Sullivan opera. Once we had managed to persuade enough boys to join the crew we had a wonderful time with *The Pirates of Penzance*. The really lucky break was when I was approached by the granddad of one of the girls. He had been a member of the Doily Cart Company and knew a lot about producing a Gilbert and Sullivan.

Chapter 16 *Teaching*

I listened to all he had to say and put as much of it into practice as possible. He was encouraged by my enthusiasm and proceeded to help even more. He went to the John Martin Theatre shop and organised proper costumes for our leading roles. We still had to enlist the aid of students' mothers to dress the chorus, but the costumes that he acquired at no cost really gave a professional touch to the whole production. It was a huge success. However, I feel that it was mainly due to this granddad's much appreciated help.

We lived at Marino at this time and I travelled by train to the Hove railway station and walked the kilometre to school. How vividly I remember running from school to the railway station in my high-heeled shoes. What a silly thing I was. Also teaching at this school were Monica Depasquale and David Farmer. Monica and her other half Paul had been friends of mine at university and I first enquired about the Catholic faith from them. To me, they were a model of a Catholic couple and I frequently had deep conversations with them about the Catholic faith.

David Farmer was engaged to Marilyn Potter, my university buddy. He had been studying to become a priest in the Lutheran faith but had abandoned it because of his conscience. He and Marilyn were sexually active before marriage and he felt it would be hypocritical of him to preach against things he was doing himself. I was very impressed by his honesty. But he still needed to make a living and teaching seem to be the only thing open to him. I was proud to call them my friends. They would not live a hypocritical life. They had each other and battled on together.

My sister Jackie, working as a hairdresser, was in love too. Her boyfriend was Denis Parsons, an engineering student that she had met at a dance.

As my wedding date slowly approached, my parents were having a hard time financially and emotionally. They could see that they were going to have to accept Xavier as a son-in-law, even though they thought him a selfish, domineering man, and they were dragging together the money so that they could afford to give me the wedding that they thought I deserved. Dad took a job at Moomba, the gas field. That meant he spent three weeks away followed by three weeks at home.

Then Jackie and Dennis approached them one evening with the news that Jackie was pregnant and they wanted to get married. This was really too much for Mum and Dad. They tried to persuade the couple that an abortion was the best way out for them because they were so young and Dennis was in the middle of his studies. But Jackie and Denis stood firm. He would change from a degree course to a slightly shorter course, a Bachelor of Chemical Technology, so that he could get to work sooner. Jackie would work for as long as she could and they would live carefully. Dad could not dissuade them and eventually washed his hands of them. He went back to work and left it to them to sort out. I sympathised with Dad. Their timing was a distraction to the build up to my big day. We had battled our families' prejudices by waiting until I was 21. Now I see our hypocrisy and admire the fact that Jackie and Denis were not ashamed to declare their love, to face up to the decision to marry and start life on the bottom rung, while Xavier and I sought to have the false, pristine show wedding so as to launch ourselves into married life with a goodie-goodie conventional image which we thought our parents should applaud.

Our aunt Ruth came to the rescue, offering them a home-catered wedding. It was all organised. We even feared that Dad would not be in town for the wedding. In August, just before her 17th birthday, Jackie was a voluptuous and beautiful bride. And Dad? Dear man, his love won through. He took time off to come to the wedding.

Xavier and I knew that we had met the right person and we would be married and carve out a future for ourselves. Our parents, however, saw it very differently and both sides criticised the mate their child had chosen.

After an enjoyable date, we frequently sat in the car talking and his parents' criticisms were levelled at me. They increasingly eroded my self-confidence and I was losing confidence that I was entering into an equal partnership. However, I interpreted the situation that I should be honoured that such a man would stoop to marry a mere mortal like me. I would be elevated by the union.

I was proud of my catch. He was big and strong and intelligent, good at sport and in his studies. He was going to become a doctor, while I was a mere teacher. I was deemed too frivolous. I told jokes at parties. He was so impressive. It disturbed me to think that he was taking these criticisms of me seriously.

I did not pass on my parents' criticisms of him because I did not want to rock the boat. I wanted my husband and my parents to admire each other as I admired them. I frequently went indoors after a date and cried myself to sleep. My father kindly enquired why I was upset? Was I sure that I really wanted to marry this man? All he could see was the upset.

Xavier, modelling himself on his autocratic father, liked to be in control and liked to win. He had rules for many things in *his* life, which was to become *our* life. He noticed that when babies arrived into a family the husband was frequently pushed aside and all the woman's love and attention was devoted to the children. This was not to happen in our case.

Despite seeing the hard side of his nature, I was still very much in love and despite my shortcomings so was Xavier, hence we proceeded with plans to marry in early 1960.

However, religion was another problem. He was a Catholic and I was an Anglican. I'd had conversations with my friends at university, but I took instructions in the Faith from a delightful priest called Father McGehity and could see very little difference between our two faiths. I thought family life would be simpler if we all had to the one faith and so decided to convert to Catholicism, much to the dismay of my parents who had many false impressions of the Faith. I took the religion seriously, regularly confessed my sins, our sins, and wanted a nuptial mass when we married. This meant we both had to go to confession before receiving communion at an actual mass. Xavier found examining his conscience to this depth quite a chore and complained greatly. But I had God on my side and insisted. He eventually decided that he should comply.

So endeth my last years as a single woman. I was deliriously happy.

CHAPTER 17

MARRIED AT LAST

So, they were married and lived happily ever after.
A wedding is a beginning, not an end. Ours was full of conflict between parents and each of us. In fact, no one was completely happy. Neither set of parents was happy with their child's choice of mate. Perhaps nationalism—Czechoslovakia vs. England—was at the root of it. My parents were willing to pay for 50 guests, for a hotel celebration. The Jancariks were willing to have a self-catered bigger event at their home. My parents were unhappy that I had converted to Catholicism and had organised a full nuptial mass. Xavier was uncomfortable about the pre-nuptial confession. I disliked the fact that Mrs Jancarik had gone shopping at bargain basements until she found a pretty but 'not me' white organza gown that I was pressured into wearing. Helen, Xavier's young sister, was to be flower girl and the daughter of a friend of Mrs J, Mariana, had been asked to be a bridesmaid, without consulting me. Whose wedding was this? Mrs J's reasoning was that we would get good wedding presents.

My closest girlfriends were both in Robe, married to poverty stricken fishermen, and I finally found that Marilyn Potter, now Farmer, bless her heart, was willing to support me by being a bridesmaid and paying for her dress to match Mariana's. These dresses were one thing that I chose and adored—they were plum-coloured shot silk. I persuaded Xavier to accept my parents' kind offer to finance the hotel reception to compensate them for it being a Catholic wedding. This offended Mrs Jancarik. I wanted flowers in the church and a bouquet of frangipanis for which I had to pay myself.

With the advantage of hindsight and having attended weddings through my life, I realise what important events these are to all the people involved, not just the bride and groom, which was how we viewed it. My parents had made do with a makeshift wedding because neither they nor their parents had any spare cash for such an event. When they had children, they vowed they would give their children a better life than theirs and that included a hotel wedding reception.

The service took a whole hour, but the reception went off without a hitch. It was a relief, after all those squabbles and tension, for us to escape to a nearby hotel. We had drunk too much and just collapsed onto the bed. Consummation had to wait till morning. Then we headed to the small hotel at Nelson for the joy of waking up in the same bed, having steak and eggs for breakfast, spending the days in idleness in the sun and lying down together each night. The immediate consequence of such delight was inevitably a pregnancy. But that's another story.

A Czechoslovakian cautionary tale
Once there were two newlyweds riding the groom's horse back to his village after their wedding. The horse stumbled and the groom said, 'That's once!'

They continued along their way and a little later the horse stumbled again. The groom said, 'That's twice!'

They continued on their way and a little later the horse stumbled again. The groom told his wife that they were going to dismount and remove their belongings from the horse. When they had done that the groom shot the horse.

The bride was furious. 'You silly man! Now we have to walk, to carry our belongings and we have lost a very useful servant!'

The groom turned to his wife and said, 'That's once!'

I do not know why Xavier told me that cautionary tale during the course of our honeymoon, but it was a sour note and left me stunned. I would always strive to do everything he wanted, because I loved him, I adored him, I worshipped him. I did not need to be threatened. Perhaps it is an old Czechoslovakian custom to be sure that a wife knows her place. I never found out because I did not ask.

Perhaps it would have been better if I had.

That might have led to a more equal relationship. The relationship was not equal. Xavier liked to win. Even if we might have a play fight on the bed, he would rapidly overpower me and pinning my arms above my head would give a triumphant grin and wait for me to surrender before releasing me. I learnt it was no use getting into a physical fight with him. I glossed over the shock of the cautionary tale and we continued to delight in each other's company. I hid his dominance from others. I was so proud of my catch and so in love that I was willing to go to any length to appease him. My whims were also considered. We rounded off our honeymoon with a trip to Melbourne to see the theatre production of *My Fair Lady*.

CHAPTER 18

MARRIED LIFE, MAKING DECISIONS

Our first real home was a dear little furnished house courtesy of a friend of Marilyn's who was taking a year's holiday. It soon became evident that I was pregnant. Urine was promptly taken for a frog test and when the result came back ... positive! My heart momentarily jumped for joy.

'We cannot have this baby,' Xavier said, and my heart sank.

'Our parents all said we should have waited before we married. I am only in my final year of medicine. This baby would be born just when I am swotting for my finals. We cannot have a crying baby disturbing my sleep. We need your wages to stay afloat financially. We have to wait for children at least until I am through my Intern year.'

Of course, he was right. We had a dilemma. An abortion cost five hundred dollars and a trip to Melbourne. We could not afford that. We could not, would not, turn to our parents for help. This was our first trial and we would handle it ourselves. We thought that they would be all 'I told you so' about it. So, it was hot baths and plenty of gin for a week which had no effect.

You may ask, 'Didn't you take any precautions to prevent pregnancy?'

Oh yes! We had. I had been fitted with a Dutch cap. However, my medical student husband had examined the cap and decided that a better seal would occur if the cap was inserted inside out. Perhaps the manufacturers knew better.

Meanwhile, the brain of Xavier was working overtime for other options. With no regard for the church ruling, he thought that he could perform a D&C. He had seen it done in med school. It would not have to be a full curette, just enough to destabilise my uterus and cause it to go into spasm. Then my baby would abort of its own volition. He could borrow the necessary equipment and sterilise it thoroughly at home.

He was firm. 'Agreed?'

'Yes, I suppose so.' I indicated my ambivalence. After all Jackie and Denis had survived a pregnancy well enough.

He pressed his position of power. 'You do trust me, don't you?'

Of course I did, he was all powerful and capable. I had every faith in him so my 'yes' sealed the deal.

Then, with me sedated by good old gin, we spent three evenings in our makeshift operating theatre, the kitchen table. Yes, I was terrified, but I did trust and love him.

Saturday brought on some bleeding and a griping belly ache. We were scheduled to appear at the Jancarik's place for lunch. We decided that we should go so that if anything happened it would all appear normal. So dressed in our best we went. I had to leave the table with the gripes and when I sat on the toilet everything came away with a huge splosh. I knew the deed was done. Feeling very shaky, I returned to the party and asked if I could lie down. Some hours later, Xavier took me to the Queen Elizabeth Hospital where a blood transfusion revived me and we started the charade of, 'Oh dear, we have lost our baby!'

The gynaecologist could not decide whether I was still pregnant or not, so he ordered a urine test for the next morning. It showed that I was not pregnant and so was booked in for a full D&C to stop my bleeding. Parents visited with their questions, but we had set up our story and held steadfastly to the lie. If they had suspicions they did not air them, knowing that we had dealt with everything. I did not have time for regrets. I knew that in the fullness of time we would have children. All would be well. His graduation would be our ticket to success.

I had to return to work pronto and so did he, to his studies. We were now one. Secure in our secret, knowing that we had well-founded faith in each other.

We lived happily on our very restricted income. Xavier kept a very close watch on when bills were due. They were to be paid first. Whatever was left was for shopping. I mean food shopping. Some weeks there was not much. We would go together to the supermarket to get the most we could for the least, and we were surviving.

CHAPTER 19

CURRAMULKA

Xavier was anxious to earn real money now that he had graduated, but the terms of his agreement with the Army dictated that he was only to work for them for the next four years. We had December and January lying vacant in front of us so naturally we turned to the cash system. We came to know of a desperate doctor with a large practice in Curramulka who needed a holiday. Curramulka is a dot on the map of the Yorke Peninsular, South Australia.

We visited and were invited into the kitchen where Mrs Desperate Doctor was preserving apricots. The doctor showed us round while explaining the job. The house was large and cool but had a very primitive bathroom and toilet. The consulting room and waiting room were situated in a separate building at the front of the house adjacent to the footpath. The consulting room was joined to a small pharmacy. Patients were to be consulted and a prescription written. Then doctor and patient would walk into the pharmacy and the doctor became the pharmacist. There was a hospital next door with a very capable matron, but the doctor was expected to do a ward round every morning and he was on call 24/7. The Curramulka surgery was used most days, but on two mornings he went to Port Broughton to assist patients living there.

'Well, young man, do you think you can cope?'

'Certainly, sir.'

'Welcome aboard. When can you start?'

Within a week he was off on holiday and we were installed in his large house.

It was clear what the doctor had to do, but what does a doctor's wife do? Well, firstly there is the obvious—clean the house and cook the meals. Fortunately, we didn't have children or preserves to bottle. I soon discovered that a doctor's wife has some very special uses. I was his secretary and his support team. The telephone had to be answered and messages taken and passed on. When he came home for lunch or dinner, I listened to how exciting his morning had been, problems he had solved, patients he had cured and ultimately the one he could not save.

In the middle of the night, he was called to the hospital to a girl with cystic fibrosis. Her parents were with her, they knew she was near the end. He did all he could, but she died and he was extremely distressed. The girl's parents were consoling him. They knew her life would be short. When he got back into bed he was inconsolable. I've told you how he liked to win, but this was one that he had to lose and that night I became a security blanket, a cuddly teddy bear, an understanding companion. I felt that we were binding, that he needed me to hold him together through this rough episode. Then the next morning we got up bright and early and I saw him off in his freshly ironed shirt, with a confident, optimistic face, a good doctor going about life as normal.

Thursday, just before Christmas, he came home from Port Broughton with a large parcel. A fisherman had paid his bill in kind, as they do sometimes in the country. It was a huge snapper. Fortunately, my school studies in Physiology came to my rescue and I was not squeamish about dealing with this large fish. I put it into the bath to remove the scales. I gutted it and washed it and cut it in to single serve sized pieces. It took me the whole of the next morning to cook the pieces as crumbed cutlets.

How would we ever consume all that fish? I needn't have worried. The Jancarik family descended upon us. They were anxious to see Xavier in his new role. I only had to make a large potato salad and there was a meal for the whole family.

That Christmas he gave me a real pearl necklace and earrings.

We had arrived, Dr and Mrs Jancarik.

CHAPTER 20

YOUNG COUPLES

All my friends were having a hard start to married life. Neither Olga nor Janet made it to my wedding, both being married to hard-working fishermen and living in Robe. Robe felt like a long way off, but we visited them both once and saw their simple, hard lifestyle. They had both borne sons and the parallels did not stop there.

In 1960, they both lost their husbands at sea in separate accidents.

Olga really hated Robe and its introverted isolation. Her husband, Chuck, had no life insurance so his death left her destitute. However, the fishing community looks after its own. The hat was passed around and she was given a healthy sum. Because she was pregnant with her second child she sought refuge with her mother. Some other kind soul who had a truck moved her to her mother's home in Thebarton. After the birth, she returned to teaching and began life anew.

Janet was in parallel but different. Again, it was only with rare letters and even rarer visits that I learned her story. Because her husband, Bluey, was lost at sea the insurance company would not pay out immediately because there wasn't a body to prove death. She had to find work to pay for a home and keep for herself and son. She found work as a laboratory assistant at Cooper's Brewery, which lead to other events later in her life.

Jackie and Denis worked on together, keeping their heads above water but secure in their relationship. Sue and Ted eventually warmed to them and their children when they saw what a good provider Denis was and how they worked together as a team. However, they never warmed to Xav.

Another couple who were friends of ours early in our marriage were Monica and Paul. They were university contemporaries of ours and were practicing Catholics. Their family quickly grew to four while we were still holding back and trialling every contraception known to modern medicine. The thing that I found amazing about them was that they could discuss an issue without it becoming an argument. They each valued the other's point of view. Any difference of opinion in our household quickly descended into a row and the row would have to be settled today, or now, would be even better. I quickly learned to surrender early. It was the easy way out and so Xav ruled. But they would have ongoing discussions for weeks and months while they nutted out the best solution. Later, they discussed their Catholic faith in depth and eventually left the church. It appeared to me that all young couples had a tough period to work through at the start of their marriages. I envied Monica and Paul their mutual respect, but I accepted Xavier as the head of our household in all respects and never questioned his right to dominance. I was completely overawed and willing to dance to his demands. He really was a powerful man.

CHAPTER 21

MY BIOLOGICAL BULL THROUGH A GATE

Another challenge came our way. We had only been married for two years, but we had moved from the cute house and now we resided on the first floor of some austere but brand new flats at Henley Beach where our penury continued. Hope of a brighter future buoyed us up. Not long to wait now, only this one year of internship to get through then real money would come our way. All the floors were tiled. It was not very cosy, but it was easy to keep clean. We gradually bought bits of furniture. A laminex kitchen table and four vinyl covered chairs. Then we looked for something to lounge upon. We could afford a 3-piece suite or a lovely large recliner. Xav really liked the recliner.

I thought, *I do not have time to recline, but when he comes home from being worked to death at RAH he could flop into it.* So, we bought the recliner, and it looked very lonely. It was the only piece of furniture in our lounge. I was teaching at the Henley High School and Xavier was doing his residency year at the Royal Adelaide Hospital. I was delighted to get a posting so close to home so not much time was spent travelling.

On the other hand, a doctor's residency was constructed to be difficult. It was a roster planned to disrupt life. One day on duty was followed by one night off duty, then a long shift of 24 hrs. The long shift meant that the doctor slept in a back room whenever there was a lull in activity. This was followed by a day off, followed by a night duty. I'm sure it was designed to test a budding doctor's stamina. Perhaps some doctors slept through most of their days off, but not Xavier. 'If I have to work hard, I will also play hard' was his motto. So, whenever he was not at the hospital we went out for the evening to a party or a movie or visiting friends. Of course, I could not be running around with him when he had a day off unless it was a weekend. I had to fit the laundry, shopping and housework and school lesson preparation in the times that he was on duty. I also tried to catch up on sleep and visit my parents who lived nearby when he was away. The roster did not fit in with the normal seven day week, so it was all a matter of do what you can, when you can.

Despite the messy roster, Xav, as his university mates called him, continued to play rugby for the Adelaide University first fifteen. We thoroughly enjoyed our Saturday's out through the winter. We usually did the shopping in the morning and came home to soup and toast for lunch, then it was off to the game. His physique made him a forward, but he also had the speed of a back when the opportunity arose. I would run up and down the sideline yelling words of encouragement to the uni team with the rest of the supporters. No sitting in stands for us. It was a workout for one and all. After the game, the players took showers if they were available then rugged up and went to the nearest pub for a post-mortem. Mine was brandy and lemonade, his was beer. All the players sat around telling each other how well they had played, telling jokes or singing rugby songs like this one that is sung to the tune of Botany Bay.

Black jerseys from SA love rugby.
Black jerseys from SA love beer.
Black jerseys from SA love women,
And that is the reason we're here.

Then someone would volunteer their home for the night's party. We would buy some supplies and head home for a clean-up, put on some glad rags and grab a meal. The girls would knock up a few savouries in the kitchen while the boys continued the conversations from the pub. Later, we might dance and sing to the Beach Boys or the Beatles while we continued drinking and talking into the night.

'Those were the days my friend.'

I'm sure you know the song.

On one such Saturday afternoon, the game was progressing with the usual gay abandon on a wet ground. A wet ground was preferred because you could jump confidently into a tackle knowing that you and your opponent would

Chapter 21   *My biological bull through a gate*

slide along in the mud as he came down. The boys were heavy with mud but warm with their activity.

As the second half started there was a lot of slippery scrumming around and bodies were strewn on the ground. Xav saw an opportunity to scoop up the ball and make a dash for the try line. An opponent was determined to stop him and dived in to tackle his legs. He was anticipating another slide in the mud, but a fallen player was behind Xav making a solid anchor for his boots. While the inertia of Xav and the tackler kept going in opposite directions, *snap* went both the bones in his lower left leg. We heard the snap and the yell of pain from the sidelines followed by a deathly silence and then the referee's whistle stopping the game. Doctors ran onto the field and rapidly splinted his legs together and phoned for an ambulance. I was distressed, as you can imagine, and was bundled into the ambulance with him. Xavier took the situation very calmly while I was extremely upset, shaking and crying as though I was the injured party. He spent most of the trip to the RAH consoling me.

We were both attended to at the hospital. He was whisked into surgery where, to help the bones heal in the correct position, screws were used to anchor them together and a full leg plaster applied to immobilise his ankle and knee so that the injured area was immobilised for six weeks. I was gradually calmed, but I did not leave until he was out of surgery and tucked into a pristine warm bed with the full leg plaster cast suspended in the air.

Having recovered from the anaesthetic, Xavier realised what a predicament he was in. If he could not attend to patients and do ward rounds his year of residency would be cancelled and he would have to repeat it next year. He would not graduate with his year. What an utter waste of time! Then there was the army scholarship that we were living on. Next year he was due to be on active service to start repaying the bond. Lying in bed was not to be countenanced, despite the ministrations of beautiful nurses.

'When will I be mobile again? Teach me how to use crutches!' he cried.

They were soon mastered and he could swing along faster than most people could walk. After all, his walking action now had its fulcrum at his shoulder so he progressed with huge swinging strides. He mastered the stairs to our first floor flat and rested in our spartanly furnished lounge. 'What a good job we bought this big reclining chair instead of a three piece suite. Now I can at least rest with my feet up.'

Bathing was quite a circus because in those days a plaster was made of plaster of Paris, which must not be wetted and was very heavy. His arms and weight-bearing leg soon grew as muscular as a weight-lifter's while the encased leg withered greatly by comparison. For a few days he sat at home in the recliner while I was off at school, but I knew he could not stay captive for long. Getting to the hospital was impossible without a car. His right leg could operate the gas and brake pedals, but what about the clutch? Sitting there at home he drew on his inner resources. We all have them. He did not sit back and say 'poor me'. He did not let the setback hold him back. He worked out how to have our car modified so that the clutch could be operated by hand. We then drove to a friendly mechanic mate and got it fixed. This 'find a solution and get on with life' is just what Ted had taught me as a child.

Hence, within a week he was back to 'normal' work, parties, everything. He just sailed right through the experience like a bull through a gate. It's just the sort of man that he was. By his stubborn effort the year was not lost and he graduated with his class having sailed through with flying colours, as usual.

CHAPTER 22

ARMY LIFE, PUCKAPUNYAL

Xavier was called to work at Puckapunyal in Victoria, but there was no house available yet so his orders told him where and when he was to present himself, baggage to follow. That meant me and the furniture.

Sue and Ted were living in the same block of flats as we were, and since we did not know how long I would be waiting we decided that I should carry on teaching at Henley High and live in Mum and Dad's spare room. They thought it was lovely to have me home again, but I longed to be with my husband. Once while chatting to Suzie, I discovered that they had had sex before marriage and I was angry. I said nothing to Sue but inwardly boiled at my hypocritical father who had said, 'A man does not spoil the flower he intends to wear'.

So even you, my dear, wise father, have feet of clay. You are just a man like any other.

Before the baggage was invited, my husband found a Czech couple living in Melbourne who would give me full board so that we could be nearer. We could visit each other at weekends and I could drive up to Puckapunyal some days when he was free.

Yes, I had my own car. It was a little red Fiat coupe. I felt very glamorous driving it.

Dad was worried that I would be tired driving all the way to Melbourne by myself, so he decided that we should drive together up to Eagle on the Hill and park my car there for the night. Next morning, he drove me back up to my car so that I could proceed, refreshed on my journey to Melbourne. Xavier met me somewhere outside Melbourne and I followed him to my new residence. How they both cosseted me! No wonder I was not learning to think for myself.

The army viewed me as baggage which I found annoying. We were a couple repaying the army for the scholarship money that had enabled us to marry. By the time the baggage had a house and was settled in, Captain Jancarik was due a few weeks leave so we took a holiday on the Gold Coast and conceived our firstborn.

I see my children as the jewels of my life. They give reason to my being. For me, nearing the end of my life, the fact that I can point to three healthy, well-adjusted offspring who are living productive lives gives me a huge sense of satisfaction. From 1963, when I had my first child, the lives of my children have been entwined with mine.

When we knew that I was pregnant we were delighted. Finally, we were in a position to have a baby and to give it security. Xavier was a captain in the army and we were living at Puckapunyal. The quarters were simple timber three-bedroom boxes, but everyone furnished them according to their own personalities and so inside each one was different.

We finally had money, so we splurged. We bought a white shag pile carpet for the lounge, a good lounge suite and yards of curtaining that I made into full-length curtains to completely hide the utilitarian windows. Maternity clothes were hard to come by, so I had to make my own. I managed one beautiful dress for affairs at the mess and several smocks. I bought a maternity swimsuit because there was a pool at Puckapunyal and I love to swim for exercise. The lifeguard used to walk alongside me as I swam, as though I was a big worry.

I remember one particular day while we lived in Puckapunyal. I was watching over our Labrador bitch who was whelping while I was ironing and listening to the radio. I was listening to a live broadcast from America as President and Mrs Kennedy drove through the streets of Dallas in an open top limousine when suddenly he was shot. I was shocked and distressed! Here was a president that I admired and now, dead in an instant. How clear that memory remains.

I know Xavier wanted a son, but I felt sure that I would fail him. You see, I was already losing my self-confidence, as many women do when they are swallowed into domestication. Then the birth came late, which was much to Xavier's annoyance. But eventually, there I was in a Melbourne hospital

Chapter 22 *Army life, Puckapunyal*

delivering my first baby. I was delivered of a beautiful boy and couldn't believe my luck. Xavier was over the moon and was heard to run around saying, 'It's a daddy, it's a daddy, I'm a baby!'

In those days, a new mother spent a week in hospital resting and learning how to look after baby. I gave my lessons serious attention. I was going to get this right. In Xavier's eyes, I had already done one thing wrong by delivering late. Working on the scheduled date he had taken two weeks leave so that he could be with us as we settled in at home. However, since Paul was born one week late and I was to spend another week in hospital his precious leave would have to be spent taking daily trips to hospital. No fun at all. He convinced me that a better idea was for him to visit Adelaide, stay with his parents and catch up with old friends. It was his holiday after all. I did not like the idea but thought that I would be being a drag if I opposed the plan. So off he went with my blessings.

I loved my baby. How could you not love your baby? They are part of you, they shared your body for nine months, they rely on you. As they feed you notice the innocent greed and even when they are finished there are those eyes that look at you for every need and comfort that you alone can give. They are secure in your love and you in theirs and you know that this bond will go on forever.

I devoted myself to my lessons in baby care and my beautiful boy. I followed all instructions to the T. My swollen breasts delivered plenty of milk and my infant thrived. The first problem I faced was trying to cut out that 4 am feed. When the district nurse told me I could, I decided I would stop it.

Xavier insisted that because he was the breadwinner he was not to be disturbed during the night. It was my responsibility to attend a crying baby. However, the first morning after neglecting to give the baby his 4 am feed my breasts were as swollen as footballs and leaking milk in the bed. I could not move.

'Please go get the baby, I can't move!'

Reluctantly, he obeyed and the relief was immense. For the rest of the week Xavier had to fetch Baby for his first feed. Gradually, we settled into the new routine so that we did not have to disturb Father's sleep.

Under the watchful eye of the district nurse Paul thrived.

Naturally, we did a trip to Adelaide for his baptism. His uncle Jan/John was his godfather and so Paul took the name Paul John. We took loads of photographs of him eating, learning to walk, running around without clothes. We were typical doting parents with their first child.

Life in an army camp can be very boring. Xavier decided that he would like to study to be a surgeon and he was given a day off every week to go to town to study under a surgeon at the Prince Alfred Hospital. I thought about returning to teaching and enquired at Seymour High. The headmaster was very glad to have me start in the new year. I found a local girl who wanted nothing more of her life than to stay home and mind babies so we were all set for a more interesting life.

At the beginning of 1964 the school year had not commenced but Xavier was having his day in town and I was doing housework, ironing, in fact. When I finished the ironing I unplugged the iron and left it standing to cool on the ironing board. I started running Paul's bath. He was always fascinated by watching the water run into the bath, so I left him standing in the bathroom clutching the side of the bath and gazing at the cascading water while I went out to open the gates ready for Xavier's arrival. I noticed that the dustbin needed to be brought in. So, I returned it to its spot by the back door. As I approached the kitchen door I heard Paul screaming and rushed inside to find him entangled in the electric iron cord trying to push the iron away from him. It was still hot. He must have toddled from the bathroom to the lounge and pulled the iron down onto himself while I was outside. I could see he was badly burnt the inside of both legs and across his crotch. I screamed and wept then calmed myself to think of the sensible thing to do. I phoned the locums and begged him to come to see this catastrophe. He was horrified too and looked at me as if I were the worst mother on earth. Paul was rushed straight into the Seymour hospital. I was told to visit next day so I went home and was in bed with a book by the time Xavier arrived home

I told him what had happened. He was annoyed and disappointed in me. Or was he perhaps just a little guilty that he was so late home. I never asked.

Next morning, we went in to see our suffering child. He had been put into a 'no touch' sterile situation. This meant he laid naked on a sterile sheet with his arms tied to the side of his cot so that he could not touch his wounds. He was pleased to see us and looked pleadingly at us. His eyes asked us to release him from his bondage. It was pitiful to see him in this state. Xavier became angry with me which only added to my own self-abhorrence for allowing this to happen to my precious son, I was utterly ashamed of myself.

Paul lay like this for six weeks. During this time, I started teaching. There was no point moping around at home and Tricia, his babysitter, was employed in readiness for his return home. The burns left a lot of scarring but no deep damage. What a relief. There just remained a burden of guilt in my heart.

Sometimes, when I felt that things were very bad in my relationship with Xav, and I felt that he was not listening to me, I would write him a letter. I would pour out my feelings on paper. I wanted him to know how I felt. However, he never read any of those letters because once I had got it 'off my chest', as the saying goes, my passion was spent. I calmed down, tore up the letter and went on with my life. In hindsight, I realise that I should have given him the letter and defended my position. Things might have improved if I had managed to communicate my feelings to him. He was so self-assured that I could never make my opinion count.

Because of the isolation of an army camp, we had to make our own entertainment. I joined a drama group and acted in one little play. We mainly played cards with our neighbours of an evening for entertainment. Of course, drinking went with it and usually a flagon of sherry could be consumed during an evening of canasta or bridge. I preferred canasta because Xavier was very controlling and took bridge and winning very seriously. He ruled that after a few searching bids he would always have the last bid so that he could play our hand which sometimes worked well and when it didn't I always felt that it was my fault. We often played with the couple living opposite, Brenda and Bert, so we became good friends with them. One day Brenda, all tears, came over to see me. Xavier, on a visit, was in the act of kissing her when Bert had walked in and all hell broke loose. She was so sorry that this had happened and Bert was insisting that we broke off our social contact.

This was a big surprise to me and I was disappointed, but I thought that if I made a fuss an argument would follow and he would manage to turn the argument around until it was my fault so I decided against that. Maybe he interpreted this as condoning his actions. It was certainly another blow to my ego, and I continued my friendship with Brenda during the daytime to avoid the macho animosity.

During our time at Puckapunyal came the Preludin phase of our lives. Xavier had access to the drug cabinet of the regiment and we tried Preludin. It is a pill that is taken by truck drivers to keep them awake on long hauls. We found that it enabled us to work more efficiently, so by taking one in the morning I whizzed through my housework and had more time for fun in the afternoon. However, sleeping then became a problem so we took sleeping pills to put us to sleep.

Very silly children, weren't we?

When we were about to move to Holsworthy and another pregnancy was planned, we decided to stop pill popping. We both had the strength of character to control and stop the pills—it was a youthful experiment which did not go too far. The thought of a happy time together creating another beautiful baby was foremost in our minds and gave us strong motivation.

CHAPTER 23

ARMY LIFE AT HOLSWORTHY

The Holswothy married officer's quarters were more substantial than Puckapunyal. Even though they were identical houses they were red brick, which I liked, and once again our own furnishings stamped our personality onto the regimental abode.

Army life provokes alcoholism. For a few months, as we joined in the social life of the new Mess, we became alcoholics. We were only really happy after a couple of drinks, in the company of other drinkers. I could feel the slow, comfortable slip sliding away into dependency. The Officer's Mess had so many good functions and the alcohol was so cheap. We drank and joked and ate well, but it gradually soured for me.

'Do we have to be sloshed to enjoy each other's company?' I found myself asking. I cut back my intake substantially and felt a lot better for it. I was strong enough to overcome any addiction, except perhaps my love of Xavier and my children.

As it is with most young happily married people, sex was abundant in our marriage. However, conception was controlled by the book. Women should have two and a half years between each child. This was calculated to the month and I lived in dread of conceiving too early, which put a bit of a damper on my libido. Hence, when it was time to conceive the next child, sex was a joyous thing and conception soon occurred.

When Kathy was born, it was still deemed necessary for a woman to have bed rest for a week after giving birth, just as it had been after Paul's birth. In Prince Alfred Hospital, Sydney, the baby was kept mainly in a nursery so that the mother's sleep would be undisturbed. The baby was brought to her for feeding every four hours. This way help was at hand if there was any trouble inducing the newborn to suckle, to deal with sore nipples, bowels, waterworks, sore bum or any other troubles that the pregnancy and birth process had induced, and at about day four, the mother was taken to the nursery and taught how to bathe baby. After this week, the mother returned home relaxed and confident that she could care for her child with a little help from her husband or a good friend to maintain her other home duties. A new routine had to be established which included feeding and bathing baby and nappy washing.

Xavier had organised a week off to be my helper in that week at home from his job as a medical officer in Holsworthy Army camp. It was to be one week after the calculated due date. Unfortunately, Kathy's birth was a few days later than calculated. The magnificent bouquet of colourful gladioli duly arrived from loving husband, with cards and gifts from other friends and relatives. I lay back to wallow in the week of relaxation.

By day three, he was at my bedside with an idea. He had a week off starting from now. What was he to do with himself? Holidays were precious and he did not want to waste it. I was being well cared for. He needed a holiday. He would drive to Adelaide, with Paul. His mum, Babi, would love to care for Paul while he visited friends. He would return in time to take me home, spend a couple of days getting us settled into our new routine before he had to return to work. It would have been churlish of me to expect him to spend those few days pottering around our home, caring for Paul and visiting me daily to share the joy of our new daughter as most husbands did.

He was not most husbands; he lived his life fully and five days of holiday were there to be enjoyed. Naturally, I could not argue with that. It would have been mean-spirited of me to say how much I enjoyed his company and would be lonely without his visits. I was being well cared for and Paul would be adored by his grandmother. Xavier's arguments seemed reasonable. To buck against his desires for my own selfish pleasure was not in my nature. I cared deeply for this man and wanted him to continue to care for me, so it seemed fair to consider his happiness on a par with my own. We were strangers in Sydney, neither of us had friends at hand.

He went.

By day four I was miserable and told the nurse so. She told me in a

Chapter 23   *Army life at Holsworthy*

comforting way that day four was called Blues Day and that it would pass and today I was to walk to the nursery and bathe baby Kathy.

Four more days passed. I occupied myself with keeping the gladioli fresh, feeding my baby, reading magazines and cards from my friends and writing letters back to them. When I thought of my dear husband, it was to hope that he was having a good time, but not too good a time, without me.

On Sunday, the Salvation Army band was playing in the grounds of the hospital and I was slowly waking from an afternoon nap, still in a stupor, with the sun streaming across my bed. It was a mild, calm, bright day and the music wafted in through my open window. I was relaxed and if not really happy I could play the 'glad game'. What a lucky girl I was to have a private room in a good hospital, to be so well looked after, to have two such beautiful healthy children.

On our way home, Xavier stopped the car and told me that he had organised a helper for me, Jean. She was a nurse friend of his from his intern year at RAH and was coming to us on a week's holiday. She was already installed in the spare room and opened our front door to greet us on arrival. She was so good-looking that I instantly hated her. Jean made herself very useful, so I enjoyed easing myself back into my home. The day before she was due to leave was a Saturday, so Xavier was off duty. He suggested that as a thank you for giving me a week of help he should take her for a day out and drive to the Jenolan Caves. I felt obliged to agree. Why didn't I say, 'Well, the car has four seats. Why don't we all take a day out together?' What a wimp!

I suppose in my heart of hearts I knew it was to be a romantic day out for them just enjoying each other's company. I know in hindsight that I should have put my foot down here, but I was just putty in his hands and I knew that he loved me and the children in his own way and that she would be gone tomorrow and I would be queen of my castle again.

I had adjusted the feeds satisfactorily when I brought Paul home and he was soon sleeping through the night without a feed. Xavier suggested that I cut out a night feed and I acquiesced. After all, he was a doctor and knew about these things. We must have made the change too suddenly for Kathy, or she was a more demanding child. Whatever the cause, she was soon a crying baby and she cried when her father wanted quiet. The cry would change from a pitiful cry to an angry cry. Xavier would not put up with it.

When it turned to the angry cry, he would march into the nursery, remove the nappy and slap her bottom until the anger turned to pain. After a while the crying would abate. Now the sleep times and feed times were all messed up and I was pained myself by this spanking, and my breasts would swell in sympathy. After just two days I said, 'It's my fault that this has happened. I will return to the feeding routine that we had in hospital and when she has settled we will work out a better way of changing things.'

Immediately, the four hourly feeding had been re-established, we had a contented baby again. It was then that I started my habit of waking at 4 am. I would put my fed, clean baby down to sleep and make myself a coffee that I would sip while washing the nappies. When they were on the line I breakfasted, Paul would wake for his breakfast, then Xavier would wake for his. By the time father was off to work it was time to feed and bathe the baby and do whatever needed to be done for the day. The time between 4 am and 7 am was so quiet and all mine, and I loved it.

I also loved feeding my baby. I took up the routine that I'd had with Paul. For the first minute I would watch the innocent greed of the child at my breast and then I would read while she suckled. Ten minutes each side with a burping session after each ten minutes. At the end of 30 minutes, we were both comfortable and relaxed.

Paul was two and a half by then and was intrigued by his baby sister. He liked to watch the bathing and feeding and even asked to taste the milk. I complied. We have a lovely photograph of him sitting on our front doorsteps, holding Kathy wrapped in a tight bundle.

To go shopping for our weekly supplies was quite a performance when I had a toddler and a baby to take along. All had to be loaded into the car with the stroller, bags, list and cash, then all unloaded at the shops. But I did not regard it as a chore. It was an outing to be enjoyed. There was a pop song at the top of the charts at the time, *Pretty Woman*. It had a happy walking beat and would often be playing on my car radio as I reached the shops and it continued playing in my head as I walked around the shops. I identified with it. I was a pretty woman. I was not told so at home, but the song told me that I was and cheered me along.

Naturally, a trip to Adelaide was in order with the baptism ceremony and party. I asked Monica and Paul to be her godparents, but since I didn't like Monica's first name I asked her second which was Marie. So, Kathy became Kathy Marie. To me she would always be Kathy-o after another pop song of the day.

Now we were counting the days to our release. Xavier was bonded to the Army for four years after his graduation to repay them for the wages he had received while still a student. The war in Vietnam had started and Xavier did not want to go. Luckily, his bondage ended in time to avoid an overseas deployment and we were all set to return to Adelaide.

Xavier drove the car over, but I flew to Adelaide with my two infants. This was a luxury, even though I had to feed my baby mid-flight. Fortunately, I was never shy about such things.

So, what had I learned during these four army years? Alcoholism had been faced and conquered, never to bother me again. Same with pills.

With the birth of each child a new blossom of love opened in my heart. By the end of the four years, I had three loves. Since Xav was adamant that the children were my responsibility, I spent a lot of time caring for them while my caring for him was a routine. Sex was very enjoyable when the fear of pregnancy was absent.

But a new fear was arising. Xavier needed more excitement than I had the energy or imagination to give. In short, I was not enough for him and I had the sneaking suspicion that he enjoyed other conquests. I felt like Julie Jordan in *Carousel* who asks herself, 'What's the use of wondering if he's good or if he's bad?' but concludes that she loves him and is resigned to whether he is good or bad.

Yes, I was resigned to my situation. I had no intention of upsetting the applecart of our marriage. There was still more joy than pain.

CHAPTER 24

REAL LIFE IN PARA HILLS

Para Hills was our entree into real life, because in the Army so much of your life is organised for you. Since our house was provided we had spent our money on cars and furnishings, so when we arrived back in South Australia the first priorities were work for Xavier and a house.

Xavier went into practice with his brother Jan, who had finally graduated. I was sent to the bank to ask for the mortgage and strolled in well-dressed with my two children in the pushchair. I told the bank manager our situation expecting that he would easily agree to the loan required. Since Xavier had graduated, institutions seem to fall over themselves to lend us money, but the bank manager was different. He looked at my two beautiful children and asked, 'Do you have any other liabilities?'

I found that extremely rude and left the office without a loan. I was only the doctor's wife. The manager found it easy to dismiss me. Women were not taken seriously in the financial world. Xavier must have taken the matter in hand himself and we soon had two mortgages to buy 9 Rialto Avenue, Para Hills. It was a brand-new house so the grounds were just a building site. We had to have a cement driveway installed to accommodate our cars and I was commissioned to landscape the garden. The brass plate announcing that this was a doctor's residence was mounted on the front wall and we set about living in the same merry way as we had in the Army. This meant parties every Saturday and hangovers every Sunday. During the week, I was the housewife and he was the doctor. However, since keeping house and minding two small children was virtually nothing, in his eyes, he always left me with a few little phoning chores to be completed before he returned for lunch.

Once children had been fed, bathed and settled at some game, I felt free to sit beside the telephone in the passage and attempt to make contact with the people on my list. I never got through immediately to the person in question. There was always a secretary to tell me how busy they were and when they might call me back or I might call them back or that I should try a totally different number. All of which meant that these little jobs spread right through the day and were never completed by lunchtime.

I was happy though overworked in this little house. I found time to do some redecorating and laying out the garden. I remember Easters when we would sit Kathy in a highchair and give her an Easter egg in its shiny foil and watch for the havoc as she worked out how to remove the foil and consume the delicious interior. She did consume most of it, but a certain percentage always found its way around her face, her body, the chair, and the floor.

Xav's brother, Jan, and his fiancé Anne were married in January, I remember their wedding because it was a lovely, warm occasion and I wore a glamourous new silk suit which was twisted and creased by Kathy, as she was permanently attached to my hip. Pavel, his second brother, and Dorothy were married in May. They lived their first married years in the senior Jancarik's spare room. I cannot think of anything worse than having my mother-in-law so close.

I remember the Christmases in Para Hill with pleasure. How Xav and I set up the tree and placed presents around it on Christmas Eve. Yes, our children were a delight and we both enjoyed them. There were birthday parties each year for each one which we planned and I cooked for and the children revelled in. Then they were invited back to parties and I have photographs of them, spruced up and holding the obligatory present ready to depart for a party.

Xavier's second practice was a partnership between himself and his brother Jan, Bob Silk and Victor Magestro. They built a large well-designed surgery. The building must have been financed by the surgery partnership. We both drove lovely cars. Xavier had a philosophy about cars … if a doctor drives a quality, expensive car people think, 'He is doing well. He must be a good doctor.' Whereas if a plumber drives an expensive car people think, 'That plumber must be overcharging to pay for such a car.'

Xavier laid down the ground rules with respect to my behaviour towards our neighbours. I was to treat them as 'other ranks.' If you let them get chummy they would try to take advantage of the situation and expect medical help for free at any time. I was not to be on first name terms with anyone, which was a great embarrassment for a person of my naturally friendly nature. When I introduced myself to my next-door neighbour she offered her hand saying, 'I'm Joan.'

There followed an embarrassed silence when I did not say 'I am Christine'. She must have thought me a right snob and we never became chummy. That embarrassment prevented me from introducing myself to any other neighbours, and if it hadn't been for Beta Sigma Phi, I would have had a totally friendless existence.

However, thanks to Helen Belton, one of my husband's patients, I was invited to an introductory meeting of Beta Sigma Phi and she sold Xavier on the idea because she pointed out that most members were either professional women or wives of professional men so it was the type of organisation that a doctor's wife would be completely at home in. She knew that within this organisation I would have the freedom to grow in my own right.

I was puzzled and surprised when he told me that I had been invited to an introductory meeting and went along with curiosity. When I arrived at Helen's home there was a cocktail party in full swing but there were no men. The room was a bubble of chatter, a sparkle of relaxed conversation between the most amazing and interesting group of women I had ever met, and I was delighted to call them my friends.

This is for me, I decided immediately, and joined the happy throng.

Because Para Hills was a new housing estate, we were to be a new chapter of all new members. Big sisters from other chapters would help us set up and get used to the activities that all Beta Sigma Phi participated in. There was a business meeting to start proceedings. We each had to take turns fulfilling the roles of President, Treasurer, Secretary, leaders of various sub-committees. We also had to take it in turns to produce a program of interest to the chapter for each meeting. The Greek letters stood for Life, Learning and Friendship, and this was exactly what I needed.

Chapter 24   Real life in Para Hills

The women in that first chapter are still my friends (rather, sisters). Most of us were British migrants who had left their families behind and we became a substitute family for each other. I don't think any of them had university degrees, but they were charming, intelligent and capable women, and I was delighted to call them my friends. The two older ladies, Judy and Rita, would have been candidates for university when they left grammar school, but the war had put paid to that. They had worked for the war effort. They had responsible jobs and had married one an engineer and one scientist during that war period and these husbands now worked at Weapons Research Establishment, WRE, out at Salisbury and that is why they were in South Australia. Both had children. Julia Magestro, wife of one of the surgery partners joined our number. She had been at Adelaide Girls High when I was there matriculating, so I already knew her. Two of the 'girls' were nurses Margaret and Ann, also with WRE husbands and children.

I must tell you the strange story of Ann.

When we met each other we both thought that we had met before. How could I forget the brown eyes and red hair? When we compared our life histories nothing seemed to click. I had migrated with my family to Australia when I was 13 and she had only recently migrated with her husband and children, we couldn't see how we could possibly have met before. Then, one afternoon, we were driving to a Beta Sigma Phi function together and she happened to say, 'I was educated at a very swanky grammar school in England called Sir William Perkins School for girls at Chertsey!'

'That's it!' I exclaimed. 'So was I!'

On examining our ages, we discovered that she must have been just one year ahead of me at the school and to have frequently travelled on the same bus, but being in different year levels we never communicated. We went on to talk about the members of staff and I told her how I had idolised Joyce Bishop, my maths teacher, which had led me to become a maths teacher too.

'Old fish eyes! That's what we used to call her.'

I felt hurt on her behalf because I really loved and admired Joyce. Admittedly, she had very pale blue eyes, so I could see how the nickname had come about. No point pursuing that further.

Ann and I became great friends because of our common education. She joins the saga here and later she became the means whereby Joyce and I came into contact with each other again.

Back to the BSP 'girls'. Two held secretarial jobs, Solange and Yvonne, and one, Madge, was an accountant. Only one besides me was a home-body, Maud. She had a daughter who was blind, so a lot of her day was spent reading and discussing schoolwork with her daughter. These women had tasted much more of life than I had and I listened avidly as they recounted their life's adventures. We took the program very seriously, using our library for research and often seeking out help from knowledgeable people in the community. In fact, one of our main problems was keeping the programs to less than two hours.

I was amazed to discover that they juggled family life and a job with some help from their husbands. This was never going to work for me because Xavier refused any domestic duties. Children and home were my responsibility and consequently a full-time job. But these wonderful women lifted me out of my humdrum existence. My eyes were opened to all the possibilities that they embodied. One of the girls, Madge, the accountant, did not bear fools lightly. They were spoken of with an acerbic wit that I found very daring.

She amazed me because she was assertive while I just hovered around Xavier. He earned a good wage. It was up to me to be supportive in all other ways. That is what a stay at home mother did at that time. Well, Madge held the purse strings in her family. Her husband would ask her if they could afford new tyres this month and she would decide. Compare this to me who sat at the table once a month with my husband. He scanned the bills, decided which we would pay, wrote the checks while I addressed the envelopes, folded the check with the account, inserted them in the envelope, sealed and posted it. Things have moved on, I'm glad to say, in most Australian homes to a more balanced situation.

Sometimes the parties were Beta Sigma Phi focused, so that meant all my girlfriends and their husbands were invited. Solange and Gerry became a firm part of our social group. However, Gerry and I frequently noticed that Xav and Solange had disappeared from the party. At first we were miffed and then we realised that an affair was going on. We were embarrassed and hoping that it was not obvious to everyone at the party. We danced together to fill the gap but said nothing about it.

Although such an incident was painful, I never made a scene about it because there was still a lot of happiness in our family.

In 1967, we took a special trip to Melbourne to see *Hair*. We were both party animals and every Saturday evening would find us at a party or hosting one or at the very least taking the kids to a drive-in theatre. Often it was a Beta Sigma Phi fundraising party and Xavier got to know my lovely friends. He flattered and flirted with them, and poor Yvonne, he teased outrageously because when she blushed not only did her face go crimson but her neck and decolletage too.

On very special occasions we would go out, just the two of us, dressed to the nines. We'd go to Adelaide's one and only nightclub, 'The Paprika'. This solitary nightclub was famous for serving drinks after hours in coffee cups. There you could enjoy intimate conversation, whisper sweet nothings, eat a sumptuous meal, drink wine and dance smoochy dancing. Oh, the heady aroma of his California poppy hair cream. However, we had a different take on our sex life. I only had to give Xavier an affectionate kiss and he would interpret it as an invitation to bed. I was afraid of sex unless we were actually planning a pregnancy, or I was pregnant, because I felt sure that if I fell pregnant when it was not planned it would be my fault and an abortion would follow. That never happened after the first time, but it was always there at the back of my mind.

Because Christmas and New Year fall in mid-summer in Australia, many workplaces close down for a long summer break over Christmas and New Year. It was common for each medical practice to throw a drinks party for its associates, and not to be out done, all the specialist practices threw parties for all the doctors who referred patients to them. All very palsy walsy, but it meant that as Christmas approached we were out most evenings attending a surgery for drinks. There were the usual family tensions building at this time. What to buy the children, the parents, the other relatives and friends? When will we celebrate with the Jancariks? When will we celebrate with the

Tailors? When will we spend some time with just our children? There never seemed to be enough time to give everyone their due. And just when your liver was saying 'ENOUGH', along came New Year's Eve.

We loved to go to the Czech club on NYE. It was always a lovely dance party and not our responsibility. We could relax and let our hair down. The Jancarik family was a feted family at the Czech club and rightly so. Three sons had been raised to professional men by a migrant family starting from scratch, something to be really proud of. The sons were adored. The adoration meant that Xavier's flirtatious nature had a field day. One particular NYE, he danced and flirted with every pretty girl in the room and, of course, they all spoke Czech to each other and I felt excluded.

I might as well not have been there. I was devastated. The evening ended with an almighty row between Xav and me and it continued when we surfaced on New Year's Day.

I walked out, leaving him with the full domestic situation to deal with. I do not know how he managed and I didn't care! I walked to the lower reaches of Para Hills where Jan and Anne lived. They were not at home and their house was unlocked. I went inside and lay on the floor in their bedroom where I would not be seen and cried myself to sleep. I needed that sleep and I wanted to worry Him. I had never abandoned my family before. I was discovered several hours later and persuaded to return home. Jan came with me and smoothed the waters. Xav and I grudgingly agreed to forget the incident.

Against this backdrop several events took place.

CHAPTER 25

MORE REAL LIFE AT PARA HILLS

The first event was my patellectomy. My collapsing knees had been a source of concern since my ballet dancing years back in Surbiton. Xavier was seriously concerned whenever I was pregnant that I might fall and lose or damage a child. Now we were in permanent civilisation it was possible for me to attend a knee specialist and get advice.

'The best thing we can do is remove the kneecap.'

The left knee was selected and its kneecap removed. That was much easier said than done. First, and having little to do with my knees, there's the fight between grandmas as to who will care for the children while I'm in hospital. The operation itself was perfectly straightforward. However, that little bone, the kneecap, is vital to knee function and serves as a tethering point for a large muscle in the upper leg. This had to be transferred and fixed to the front bone in the lower leg and held there for six weeks while it grew into place. During that time, I was in a full leg plaster and mobility was difficult. Since Xavier did not do domestic stuff, my parents volunteered to live with us for a while and carry out the domestic duties. That was a very kind of them and I insisted that we give up our double bed for them, as they always did for visitors. However, this meant that Xavier and I and my plaster were sleeping on the foldout settee, and a man was not to be denied his sex no matter how uncomfortable it was for me. Xavier was unhappy with the situation. He decided that my parents had to go. His method was to tell me that we could not feed two extra people and that I had to ask my parents to pay for the food they were eating.

I was extremely embarrassed to have to do this, but Dad, as always, was quick to read between the lines and with regret, my parents took the hint and returned home. A cleaning lady had to be hired. I really could not cope with my two rascals and everything else. Mrs Woolley became a treasured aid.

The wonderful day came when I was released from plaster only to be confronted with the need to teach the knee to bend again. It was agony. I found it easier to run around with a straight leg than to force it to bend.

A dear friend, Lindy Leak, had had some experience in nursing and came to be my live-in physiotherapist to help me force that knee through agony to bend again. When she left it was my duty to continue with exercises, as well as the other home duties. I just did not find time for the exercises and so lived with a limp instead.

Then, with children there is never a dull moment.

When she was about three years old, Kathy fell over with a glass in her hand and collected a very deep gash across her hand. Fortunately, Xavier was home. He wrapped the hand in a tea towel and rushed her to his surgery where he applied all the necessary first-aid and stitched the hand before dressing it. It was my job two days later to replace the dressing. I prepared the swab and the new dressing and had her sit down while I explained what I was going to do. As I sat with swab raised she turned to me and fixed me with a serious stare.

'It's not allowed to hurt.'

Another memorable thing about this young lady was how she learned to hold her breath when she was having a tantrum. This caused her to faint and fall to the ground which sent me into a panic, fussing over her, trying to bring her round, worried that it would hurt her. When I explained the situation to Xavier he said, 'I've heard of cases of this behaviour. When the child falls unconscious, the involuntary nervous system takes over and they start breathing normally. So next time that this happens, just leave her there.'

Well, the whole idea worried me but *he* had spoken. A few days later there came a tantrum followed by a self-induced fainting fit. So, I left her there. She peed on the floor and still lay there. Eventually, she woke up finding herself in her mess looked around in amazement. No one was making any fuss of her.

Chapter 25 *More real life at Para hills*

Eventually, I stepped in with a matter-of-fact manner. 'Well, get up then and let me change your wet clothes.'

In never happened again.

There was one more Kathy idiosyncrasy. She had more energy than I had. After lunch, youngsters and babies should be put down for a nap.

'Hooray!' says Chrissie, *'that's just what I need!'*

So, they were put down to sleep and I flaked out too. Kathy waited until the house was quiet and then got up and went off for her own adventures. Rialto Avenue was empty at that time of day because most residents were out at work, so Kathy could confidently toddle across the road to the O Reilly's yard where she could pick up their tame bantam. With the hen tucked underneath her arm she would wander up the Avenue until she found a bread box on a neighbour's doorstep. The baker would have delivered a fresh, sliced loaf wrapped in waxed paper during the morning. He thought he was delivering it to the householder who had left the cash in the tin. However, Kathy needed that bread to feed herself and her feathered friend so she opened the box and the paper, then took as many slices as she saw fit. When I woke from my well-deserved nap I would find her and her friend picnicking on the kitchen floor and was left to wonder which irate neighbour would shortly descend upon me to exact retribution.

About a year before he went to school, we started sending Paul to a little privately run kindergarten on weekdays. A woman called Margaret would drive back and forth around Para Hills at about 8.30 in the morning picking up her clients. When the last client was on board she would drive the carload of chatting, laughing, screaming children to her own house. Seat belts and regulations on numbers of people permitted had not yet been enforced. The children took their own lunches in their kindy cases and she entertained them for the day.

Paul enjoyed this outing and was always ready early. As soon as I had his lunch packed he waited by the front door. When Margaret appeared and tooted in the driveway, he ran out to jump into her car.

One morning, Margaret arrived and tooted in the driveway. Then she knocked at the door and called for Paul.

'Isn't he there, Margaret?'

'No... can't see him.'

Panic immediately set in. We looked and called and looked again. He was nowhere to be seen. His kindy case was gone too. Margaret joined in the cacophony as we became more and more frantic. Eventually she said, 'Well, I have to go. I have other kids to pick up. When you find him you can bring him around.'

We continued our frantic search in panic mode. We were disputing whether we should call the police when the phone rang. It was Margaret.

'Guess what? When I got home he was sitting on the doorstep waiting for us.'

It turns out he just got fed up with waiting and decided to walk to Margaret's. How a four-year-old had such a perfect sense of direction I'll never know!

Our children were a delight to us both. Xavier adored them and praised my parenting. Small, simple pleasures gave them such delight. How can anyone forget their squeals of delight as they ran through the water sprayed from the sprinkler hose on the lawn on a hot day?

When Kathy was almost two it was time to think about child number three because the doctor had deemed that two and a half years between each child was the ideal spacing and we had set our hearts on a family of four. I was always relieved when planned pregnancy time arrived because it meant I could stop worrying about becoming pregnant at a wrong time, stop taking the pill or whatever contraception method we were involved in and enjoy sex just for the fun of it.

We decided that it would be a good idea to take a holiday, just the two of us, to start this baby. We went to Lake Eucumbene and lived in a caravan. While Xavier fished, I collected mushrooms.

We had a delicious evening meal of mushrooms and fresh fish fried in butter, washed down with red wine. The next day when we were together on a small boat on the lake I emptied my stomach contents into the lake and, feeling very shaky, went to bed for the rest of the day.

During this holiday, I remember Xavier trying to explain to me how to make our sex life more exciting. So, you see he did try to enliven me. He did

Chapter 25   *More real life at Para hills*

not abandon me without trying to rebuild me as a sex kitten. He suggested that sometimes I should initiate the sex play and even try to seduce him. Until then he had always been the initiator of sex play, all I had to do was relax and think of England, as the saying goes. He showed me that we did not have to stick to this habit. At the time, I was perfectly happy with the way things were in bed, and although I tried his suggestions for a while on the holiday, when we returned home everything fell into the same old same old routine. Silly me!

The suggestion of a key party was a nasty shock.

Xavier told me that there were couples who partied together, then as the evening was about to finish every husband threw his house keys into a bowl. Each husband then took a key from the bowl ready to go home. The wife belonging to the keys went home with the new partner who had taken her key from the bowl. She willingly had sex with the new partner when they reached her home. Would I like to go to such a party? Clearly he would! My response was somewhat different.

'No! No! No! A thousand times no! I have sex with you because I love you! I cannot even imagine having sex with anyone else. I would feel prostituted. I'm horrified that you would have sex with anyone else and that you would offer me up in exchange!'

'But it is just sex! It doesn't mean that I love you any less.'

'No, I could not do it. I could not have sex without being in love. They go together.'

Enough said. It was not mentioned again, but it haunted me. Surely most couples are monogamous. It seemed an outrageous request at the time. Surely there was enough sex in our marriage. Why would he want this?

Peter was conceived immediately during this holiday and I became very large with child as I always did. Summer approached and my ankles swelled and I found it hard to cope with ironing seven shirts each week, to say nothing of all the other ironing. We ironed everything in those days, even sheets, pillowcases and tea towels. Maria Paradiso came to my aide. Maria was an amazing Italian neighbour. She could not read or write.

'Where I come from, it is thought not necessary for a girl to read or write,' she said, and yet she worked as a cleaner in a hotel, she maintained her house and garden where she grew her own tomatoes, made her own tomato sauce, made her own pasta. She knitted, sewed and cooked for her family without patterns or recipes. This all seemed so amazing to me because I cooked with a cookbook in my left hand. I undertook to teach her to read. When she saw how stressed I was, she offered to take my ironing. I was so weary that I surrendered the laundry basket to her.

My fatigue did not abate. Our energy levels were out of synch. Xavier had energy, much more than I could ever muster. He could work all day, watch telly into the evening and then want lively sex before falling asleep. While at the end of my day of doing nothing but caring for children and looking after a house I was exhausted.

He insisted that I sat with him through a couple of hours of television before bed and I did not have the self-confidence to suggest we select a different time of day to be our time together. Oh! How I would have loved to have just gone to bed with the children. As a result, I was just a bore. He enjoyed our family life and he loved our children and so when he needed more exciting sex he simply went and found it. I became aware of the situation because some women eased their consciences by confessing to me. I felt powerless to do anything about it. My more liberated friends would have spoken up. I was behind the times because my self-esteem had been steadily chipped away throughout our marriage, so I just accepted it as our situation.

When I was pregnant with Peter I became fed up with all the parties. I just wanted to sleep. On one Saturday night the party was at our place. After I had served supper I thought, I am so tired, I'll leave them all to it. They'll enjoy themselves without me.

Little did I know that Solange was in love with Xavier and he was pursuing Ann at that point. I just went to bed.

At some stage, Solange noticed that Ann and Xavier were both missing from the general party and decided to look for them. She found them in one of the children's bedrooms in a compromising position and she screamed out and made a hell of a fuss, I am told. After all, her own heart was breaking.

'How could he be seduced by this redhead!' she demanded.

Chapter 25   *More real life at Para hills*

I slept peacefully on through the ruckus and do not know what became of the party after that. Talking to Ann later, I discovered that Xavier was merely showing her that she was not frigid as her husband had accused. We all know who the chief mover and shaker was. I remained friends with Solange and Ann because I knew if it hadn't been them it would have been someone else, it's just the way he was and by then I was resigned to the fact.

The moon landing was in 1969 and about the same time Weapons Research closed, leaving husbands unemployed. This affected about half of our Beta Sigma Phi chapter. When the husbands did find work in their area of expertise they often had to move to another state and we lost touch with them.

It was a very hot November and I was overdue by that point. It was my fault, of course, and Xavier and the obstetrician agreed I should simply go into hospital and wait for the baby to come. The usual world war broke out about who should have the children, but when that was settled I simply moved into The Lyle McEwen Hospital at Elizabeth with instructions to keep walking and the threat that if I hadn't delivered within five days the labour would be induced. All I could do was keep on walking. In his own good time Peter was delivered a big and beautiful boy. He knew he was in safe hands. He was a relaxed and happy baby and his nickname became Smiley.

A lot of things happened in this time in my life, but I remained pretty much the same.

I was the mother, the doctor's wife, and not much of a person in my own right. I had let our relationship slip into the dark ages by not speaking up for myself.

CHAPTER 26

ERICA

When we were first married and invincible we planned to have six children, four of our own and two adopted. We wanted to do a charitable thing, but we wanted to see the fruit of our charity. Not just send off money and hope that it landed where it was intended and that it was not siphoned off by some crooked fat cat. So, adopting two children seemed a very sensible way to be charitable. Because of my continuing fatigue, we decided that we should be less ambitious re: the size of our family. We modified it to three of our own and one adopted. Adoption was complicated. It was full of regulations as you might expect from a government department. The child had to appear like a natural part of our family. That means it could fit between Kathy and Paul or between Kathy and Peter or be even younger than Peter. The clever seekers eventually came up with a girl who was just a few days older than Peter so that we could pass them off as twins.

We were thoroughly vetted and jumped through all the bureaucratic hoops and she eventually became our fourth child. She was referred to as 'the child'. 'The child' was from an unmarried mother. Her grandmother had cared for her for the first eighteen months of her life. But as her grandfather's health declined, the child was too much for the grandmother and had to be put up for adoption. We picked her up in an office in town along with a suitcase full of lovely little dresses. She was totally bewildered by all these very kind people removing her from her grandmother and handing her over to us. She wore a tiny gold bracelet with a lock on it and the name Erica engraved on it. Could her father have been Eric?

I recall driving home from town with our new daughter. She was quiet and soft and obedient. She stood in the footwell, her little feet between mine. I steadied her body when we cornered. It seemed amazing to me that this beautiful child had been given over to us in good faith that we would cherish

Chapter 26 *Erica*

her as we did our own. How could anyone be sure that we would? What a risk to take with a precious vulnerable young life?

'Do not worry, Erica,' I mentally said to her. 'We will not let you down. You will be our second daughter. You will be treated as an equal to our existing children. You will receive love and discipline in the same amounts as the other three and you will grow strong knowing that you are safe, nourished and loved, and that you are now secure as part of a loving family.'

There were three very notable things about Erica. She had a quaint habit of following me out to the washing line and handing me the pegs as required. She smiled as though she was holding loose false teeth in her mouth. Thirdly, she was so quiet and ladylike that I gave her the nickname Lady Erica. My parents loved their new granddaughter immediately, but her Czechoslovakian grandmother never forgave her for not being a genuine Jancarik. Indeed, as she grew, Erica told me later, that on several occasions Babichka put her down by telling her that she was not as valued as the genuine Jancariks. Mrs Jancarik senior thought that we should be producing genuine Jancariks ourselves. 'Blood' was everything to her. We could not convince her that the world was already over-populated. We had been reading *The Population Bomb* by Dr Paul Ehrlich and knew that what the people of Earth should be aiming for is ZPG (zero population growth).

In her details, it told us that Erica did not like egg. I was prepared to introduce egg slowly, but Dr Xav said that he would not tolerate picky children. She would eat egg along with the other children and if she balked and spat it out it would be fed back to her until she learned to take it in the first place. Naturally, it fell to me to carry out these orders so I had to find ways around the impasse. She was quiet and obedient in everything else, so she soon became as beloved as the others and was rapidly absorbed into our family.

Peter and Erica became known as 'The Littlies' and were soon as thick as thieves. I resolved that I would have no sex discrimination between them so they both received cars and dolls as presents. However, it seems that the die had already been cast. She soon had both dolls and he both cars. We never regretted adopting Erica. She fitted smoothly into our family. She was as bright as our other children. Today, she is the person I most frequently turn to for an unbiased opinion.

CHAPTER 27

SALISBURY

Xavier was increasingly dissatisfied with the business partnership he was in. He felt that he was working harder than the other doctors, but the profits were being shared equally among them. He therefore decided to leave the practice and start up on his own.

He intended to buy a house in Para Field Gardens, a new housing estate, where he would soon gain a good following. At the same time, he felt that we needed a larger house a little closer to Para Field Gardens, but not in Para Field Gardens. He found a house on a large piece of land that had been built by a builder for himself.

I was taken to see the house in Salisbury, one afternoon, and was amazed at the size of it. It would certainly accommodate our family of six better than our current house. I didn't really like the house because it had point tucking across the front and was a very unimaginative design, with a long passage down the middle. Obviously, an architect had not been consulted.

However, with such large grounds we could fence it off and install a swimming pool in the back garden. Xavier must've organised large bank loans to cover both our new home and the new surgery house, which needed a few alterations to make it into a functioning surgery. A large boat soon filled one of the sheds and the desired pool was installed. We were very comfortable. A gardener kept the grounds in order and the pool clean.

Paul and Kathy were both in school while Erica and Peter happily played on the floor together. Xavier would have his breakfast and rush off to his surgery. He preferred that the children were fed and ready for bed by the time he returned in the evening and so it came to pass. His wish was my commandment. About this stage I remember my mother saying to me, 'You know you are an absolute slave to that man.'

Chapter 27   *Salisbury*

I replied, 'Yes, but I'm a happy slave.'

I did not confess to her the repeated dream that I had concocted for myself in which Xavier suddenly realised what an excellent wife I was and abandoned all his other affairs to devote himself to me.

At about this time he told me why he was glad that I was his wife.

'You are good looking, but not so beautiful that I need to fight off other men. You are intelligent, but not as smart as me. Clearly, I am the brains of the family. And, you are a good mother.'

Talk about damning with faint praise! I was belittled by his comments and something inside me was beginning to rebel. I thought, 'You do not value me, but our children need me.'

Once again, I found myself bored, or perhaps under-appreciated as a housewife, even though I had four lovely children. So, one afternoon I went down to the Salisbury High School to investigate the possibility of returning to work. Did they have need of a science teacher like me? The deputy head was absolutely delighted to see me when he knew my quest. Apparently, a junior science teacher had literally dropped dead during a science class last week. They were in desperate need of a replacement. I asked about pay and conditions because I hadn't even broached the subject with Xavier. I didn't make any promises to the deputy head because I was not sure how my plan would be accepted at home. I intended to use my salary to pay for a house cleaner and an ironing lady who would double as babysitter for the Littlies who were still only three years old.

Xavier was not really happy with the idea because he felt that he would lose the benefit of claiming me as a dependent in his tax return and the children would lose the security of having a mother at home. However, I managed to persuade him that the gain in income would cover this and we compromised on my working half-time only. Thus, I became a member of staff at Salisbury High School, which was only a five minute drive from our Fleet St home. I made new friends there and although I still only merited classes in second and third year maths and science, it was an added interest in my life. Dear Mrs Woolley took over as ironing lady and babysitter and Mrs Wegmann, a fastidious German, did a much better job of keeping the house clean than I ever did.

Female teachers were paid equal pay for equal work, but women were not permitted to wear trousers.

Towards the end of the year, a staff dinner was planned and I booked myself and husband to join the party. We all went to a hotel with a set menu dinner because it gave good value. Xavier perused the set menu with dissatisfaction and despite my pleas to just go with the flow and eat the same as everyone else, he proclaimed that he wanted oysters, which were not in the set menu. Then, after speaking firmly to the waiter and insisting that he would pay for his own oysters, they were duly delivered and consumed while the rest of the party waited for their main course because it would not be served until all the table was ready for it. I was extremely embarrassed by this flagrant showing off of independence and wealth that Xavier liked to exude. But the party proceeded and no one else seemed to mind.

When the school year resumed, anticipation increased as Mr Kite, the senior Maths master, worked out the timetable for the year and allocated subjects. Of course, I still had the same old maths and science with the least interested students. I was not a particularly inspiring teacher. My classes were not particularly interested in Maths or General Science. I felt as if I was just babysitting until they were old enough to leave school. However, I had one inspiration. I asked myself what topic would interest my Year 9 girls? Why, sex of course! I wrote a sex education course with all the physiology, biology and life experience that I had, I only had to search for good illustrations. It was a huge success; they were spellbound and discipline was not an issue.

Drama teachers had still not been invented, so as an extra-curricular activity a few of us got together to produce school musicals. We produced *Oliver* one year and *The King and I* the next. My own children joined the cast of *The King and I* as extra smaller children necessary in the march of the children. They loved it and it saved me babysitting fees.

My household was ticking over nicely with the help of Mrs Wegmann and Mrs Woolley, as the Littlies were perfectly happy in their care when I was away.

By the end of the year, Xavier and I were living almost separate lives. I

Chapter 27 *Salisbury*

had my Beta Sigma Phi, my teaching and my children. He had his own surgery with Carol, a petite, glamorous receptionist, and my friend Madge as accountant. He went fishing on my Beta Sigma Phi nights. He said that he deserved a night off just as much as I did, so a babysitter was hired.

When it came to the staff dinner, I was relieved to hear that he would be away for the weekend at a conference in Sydney. I found out later that this was a euphemism for a weekend away with Carol. So, I felt free to dress in my finest, have a shampoo and set, and go out to enjoy myself with my teacher friends. Towards the end of the dinner people were ordering liqueurs and I mentioned that I would like Drambuie. Ian, senior science master, said he would get me one. It was a calm offer with no innuendo. If Xavier had ordered a liqueur for a lady, he would have offered it with a mocking threat in his voice as if to say, 'you will be paying for this later, in kind.' But there was none of that in Ian's voice. I was taken aback as I made this comparison. So, men can just treat women as friends without the overtones? Then we all adjourned to the home of one of the teachers because we didn't want the evening to end. My babysitter was paid for, so I was happy to go too. While we were there another surprising thing happened. Michael, a history teacher, sat next to me. He was not drunk, but pretty merry, and he said with a great deal of admiration in his voice, 'You are beautiful!'

I was utterly amazed, and asked myself, why am I married to a man who cares little for me if there are other men out there who think I am beautiful and are willing to buy me a drink without innuendo? I really must examine my marriage closely. But there were four good reasons to stay in my marriage: Paul, Kathy, Erica and Peter. Divorce is bad for the children, we were frequently told. The underperformers at school are usually from single parent families. I was desperately unhappy, but not willing to sacrifice my children and their futures. I felt trapped, which only made me feel even more unhappy.

I knew that Xavier was having an affair with Carol and I felt that everyone else did too. As a result, I was offended when he invited her to his birthday party at our home. As usual, there was a merry crowd, plenty to eat, plenty to drink, dance music playing, dancing and chatting, so it was a happy occasion. But the fact that Carol was there was galling to me. When she wanted another drink she would sidle up to him, flutter her eyelashes and ask sweetly for a refill. So, I thought I would try the same ploy to show him that this had not gone unnoticed. He turned to me quite annoyed and so I laid it on thick.

'Pretty, pretty please will you get me a drink?'

He could hear the sarcasm in my voice. He grabbed my shoulders and propelled me to our bedroom where he proceeded to tell me how annoyed he was. I of course retorted with how hurt, embarrassed and ashamed I was with his flagrant display of Carol in our home. His hand came up and he gave me a mighty slap across the right side of my head. This hurt, but not as much as I pretended. I let out a mighty yell of pain so that it might be heard in the party. Everything went quiet for an instant and then the party noise continued. He took me by the shoulders and gave me a good shake.

'I will return to the party now, while you calm down. You must calm down and come out again when you have stopped crying and fixed your make up.'

I did as I was told. I sat quietly in the bedroom for a few minutes deciding that this quite definitely was the end.

He had resorted to violence. This was my line in the sand. I had put up with so much, but this I would not tolerate.

After touching up my make-up, I returned to the party where everyone was behaving as if nothing had happened. I was surprised that no one had come to my aid when they heard my yell. I spoke to Mum and Dad about it later. They told me that when he re-entered the party he had gone up to them and said, 'Nothing will happen from this incident because your daughter needs me for security.'

Madge was my friend and Xavier's accountant. She and her husband Brian tried not to interfere in anyone's private business. However, one evening she felt that she just had to tell me that Carol was pregnant. I was amazed that Xav would let this happen, especially as he had been so fanatical about *his wife* falling pregnant at the allotted times.

How did he intend to continue? Was he going to maintain two households in the one suburb? This was the last straw! The pain was definitely outweighing the joy. I started to think, how did one go about getting a divorce?

I had absolutely no idea, so I mentally scanned my friends and their husbands. There was Roger Smithson, Beth's husband, another of my Beta Sigma Phi friends and I thought him a man of the world. He told me I could go to a lawyer, and gave me the name of one.

I kept all this to myself because I wasn't sure what I was doing. The lawyer told me that blame had to be appropriated in order to get a divorce. I told him that I knew Xavier was being unfaithful and his mistress was pregnant to him. He said that there had to be a third party to give evidence. A private eye had to be hired to follow them. I said we could minimise this because I knew that they always went out together on Thursday nights when I was at my Beta Sigma Phi meeting. Nevertheless, the private eye had to be hired and paid for. Then I had to wait and pretend that nothing was going on. During this waiting period, Xavier and I had a few chats. Meaning that he told me the way things would be in the future. He really felt that our house with its pool and large garden was too big for us and we should move to something smaller. I remained in the character that he had become accustomed to and agreed with everything he said.

One Thursday night after I had returned from Beta Sigma Phi, paid the babysitter and put myself to bed, there came a knock at the door.

'It's me, Mrs Jancarik, Joe Brown, your private investigator. You need to come to identify the parties.'

'But I can't leave the children.'

'It will only take a few minutes, an hour at the most.'

I dressed and went with him to Carol's place. He told me that I had to knock on the door and get Carol to open it, which I did with increasing trepidation and a million 'what ifs' in my mind. Carol opened the door. She was indeed large with child.

'Carol, this is my private detective Joe Brown. May we come in? Is Xavier here?'

'Yes.'

'Can we speak to him?'

'Of course.' She was perfectly calm, as if expecting the whole thing to happen sometime. We sat in the lounge while she went off to tell Xavier that we were there. His shoes and socks were neatly placed before the fireplace. After about five minutes Carol came in picked up the shoes and socks and took them out. I felt very nervous, thinking to myself, what if he should get angry and physical? He's a big man and can have a violent temper.

By the time he entered the room, I was quaking with fear. He was immaculately dressed as if taking a house call.

'Is this your husband, Mrs Jancarik?'

'Yes.'

'Is this your wife, Dr Jancarik?'

'Yes.'

'I think you can go to the car now, Mrs Jancarik. You are trembling. Try to calm down, dear.'

I was greatly relieved to leave the room and sat in the car for about 15 minutes while he did whatever private eyes do. He came out with a paper in his hand.

'All fixed! They didn't deny anything, it was very easy to get statements from them.'

He drove me home and in the warmth of my bed, I gradually relaxed with relief that this deed was done and the divorce would proceed.

Madge reported to me a few days later that Xavier had stormed into the surgery the next morning saying, 'I'll never trust Chris again!'

I had asserted myself! Xavier was angry because I had taken the initiative and moved for divorce. He was sure that my father had suggested it because I would never have had the initiative to think of such a thing!

The law moves very slowly, or at least, that's how it feels when you're trying to end one chapter of your life. Besides the legal side of things, we had to sell the house on Fleet Street, so in the meanwhile I stayed there with the three younger kids. Paul, who wanted to be with his father, went to live with Xavier and Carol. I have two notable memories of this period.

The first was when we had to repaint some of the interior walls to spruce up the house for sale. I remember we played a Beatles record while we worked. The most memorable song was 'Yesterday'. It has a sad haunting melody and you feel that the singer would like to return to his 'Yesterdays'. They were not my sentiments, but I will always associate that song with that job.

Chapter 27 *Salisbury*

One evening the children were in bed and I was preparing lessons for the next day. I had the radiogram playing softly in the lounge while I was in another room working. I thought I heard a noise at the back door, and then in the kitchen, and was quite frightened because I hadn't locked the back door. I crept along the passage to the kitchen where Xavier and I came face-to-face, giving each other quite a scare.

'What are you doing here?'

'I just came to see that everything was all right,' he said with a guilty look on his face.

I said nothing but thought, 'Liar! You thought I was entertaining someone. Judge other people by yourself, Old Chum!'

So, the divorce slowly happened, degree nisi, degree absolute, some things settled out of court. I won't bother you with all the sordid details, suffice to say that in the end Paul said, 'I want to be with my dad!'

I understood. He was ten years old. Any boy his age would choose a strong, generous, manly father over the weak, wishy-washy, weeping woman as I was at that time.

I have three other children to care for on my own, that will be enough work, and his father loves him so he will care for Paul.

Xav gave me $2000 as a deposit on a house and ten dollars per week per child to maintain the children. In today's money that would be a deposit of $10,000 and $54 per week per child. I could see Paul by arrangement and he would have access to the other children on Sundays, time to be arranged.

Mum and Dad wanted me to move south of Adelaide so that they could help more conveniently.

I had been reading *Future shock*, which tells us that divorce and house moving are big shocks to your system and at such times one should avoid as many other shocks as possible. It seemed better for the children to continue at the same schools with their mates, so I decided to stay in Salisbury.

I was shown a small house on the other side of the tracks by a real estate agent who said as we entered, 'You're going to love this house!' It was tidy and clean, had just enough bedrooms, a rather small bathroom, but a big backyard.

There was room for the kids to run around, it was convenient to the shops and the schools. And I did love the house. I settled on it with my $2000 deposit and a mortgage from the bank.

The bank manager who had been handling our affairs was not known to me personally. However, he was aware of our situation and when I applied for the mortgage he turned out to be quite an ally.

'Not many banks will give a mortgage to a woman on her own, but I see you are teaching and I feel you won't let us down. By the way, Mrs Jancarik, we have here as security on a previous loans that your husband took out, an insurance policy against his life. He has not tried to reclaim it and you have an insurable interest in his life, so I could give it to you and if you will continue with its instalments you can be registered as the recipient.'

'I don't know if I can afford that. I will have to talk to Madge,' was my response.

Xavier had handled the majority of our finances and I no clue how to go about anything.

Bertram Bennet 1914

Louisa's family. Back row Louise, Donald, Louisa, Winifred, young Bertram. Front row Ruth and Suzanne

Sue and Ted's wedding

Chris with dog

Jackie with Apples 1957

Ted at Pooraka?

*Dino and Chris,
Silver Medallists*

Enlarged Tailor family Jackie and Denis, Ted and Sue with Xavier and me.

Xavier and Me

Four good reasons for not having a divorce

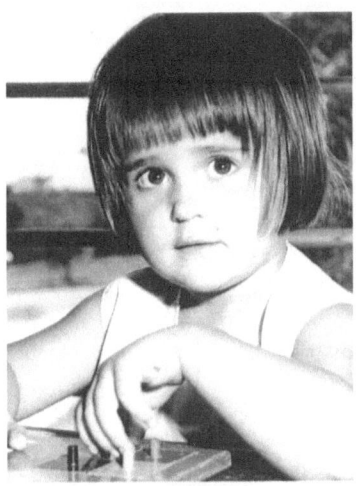

Kathy at four

Paul at seven

The Littlies, Peter and Erica

PART TWO

Between husbands

CHAPTER 28

ABLE STREET

'What am I to do, Madge? This is all new to me. Sue and Ted had a very flippant attitude towards bill paying. They would periodically look at their bills and then put them away saying, "Well, we've looked at them".'

Xavier did not discuss money matters with me, except for telling me that I was spending too much. I wrote the envelopes, he decided what would be paid.

'How am I going to manage, Madge? I have never handled money in my life on this scale. Now I'm responsible for my kids and this house! Can I afford the mortgage and the life insurance policy?'

Madge seemed somewhat bewildered. 'You mean you've never made a budget?'

'No, Madge. What's a budget?'

'Okay. Go to your neighbours and ask them to tell you what your council rates are, what your electricity bill is likely to be, and gas bill and water rates, and when you know all that we will sit down and I'll show you.'

So, she did. We added in the mortgage and the insurance policy, converted everything to its annual cost, added them up and divided by 52.

'Now, is this amount less than your weekly income?'

A sense of relief flooded me. 'Yes, it is.'

'Good. You have to open a new savings account and every week put that amount in. Whatever is left you can use for food and clothes and entertainment. When one of those big bills comes you pay them out of the new household account.'

I was struck by a horrible thought. 'What if they all come along at once and there isn't enough to pay them all?'

'They won't. Believe me, it works,' she said, in her unflappable manner.

I was grateful. 'That's simple, Madge! Thank you so much.'

And it did work! Fear of failure made me very cautious with my spending, so I did everything I could to live within the means available to me. At the end of the year, I was a few hundred dollars in pocket, which enabled me to buy an upright piano and two small air conditioners for the bedroom windows.

There was, however, one small catch.

They say 'buyer beware' and I was the buyer that made a big mistake. The house had no hot water system. There were just two little gas heaters, one in the kitchen and one in the bathroom. The one in the bathroom could not generate enough hot water to bathe my children.

There was only one person I knew with enough money to rectify this situation, so I went cap in hand to Xavier. After all, they were his children too. The bathroom really needed rehashing because it contained only a bath and hand basin and we needed a toilet and a shower as well. When I explained our sorry plight, he came to examine the situation. He gave me a look that said, 'I knew you couldn't manage without me', and said he would see what he could do. He hired a plumber. The whole bathroom was ripped out and reinstalled with a hot water service put in the roof all at his expense. I couldn't believe my luck.

Being in charge of my own life bought three main dilemmas ...

Firstly, how were we to survive financially?

As you see, Madge helped me over that hurdle. So did Mrs Woolley. She had been my ironing lady/babysitter when we lived in Fleet Street and she loved my kids like a second family. Her Sally and Andrew were a couple of years older than Paul and Kathy, so she brought all their hand-me-downs to us. Twice a year, in spring and autumn she would visit us at the weekend for Box Day! We regarded this as a special fun day when I took down two large boxes from the top of my wardrobe. The boxes were full of clothes, which the children would try on. What fitted last year was now too small. So, they had to find things that were just right or perhaps just a bit too big. Mrs Woolley and her pincushion took up or let down hemlines and adjusted sizes. She would take away the pinned up clothes and a week or so later a box of clothes that fitted my kids was brought back. What a gem she was!

Secondly, what to do for transport?

Well, we could walk and we could use the train, which we did quite often. Xavier took pity on us and gave me the family station wagon. However, there was a hitch. He also gave me the paying in book. He had refinanced this car to help him through some financial crisis so the car was only half paid for and I was expected to keep up the payments. I could not afford this, so I had to sell the car to cover the remaining debt. Later, he gave us a fully paid-up second-hand car with strict instructions that it was only to be used to transport the children. They were delighted and we took off to visit Babichka, the children's Czechoslovakian grandmother, and have a visit to the beach. On the way home we were stopped at traffic lights waiting to turn right and I happened to check the rear vision mirror. A car was bearing down upon us at great speed. The young driver looked terrified as if he couldn't find the brake pedal.

'Lie down everyone, and keep down, there's going to be a crash!' I commanded. Sure enough, there was. The car was a write-off. Peter and I were admitted to hospital with concussion while Kathy and Erica were taken to Mrs Button, our neighbour, by the police. She was asked to care for them for the night. Xavier decided that the crash was my fault, so his generosity expired at that point and we were back to walking or taking a train.

Thirdly, how was I to give the children some moral guidance for their lives?

I was a practising Catholic at the time of the divorce and thought that the church community would wash their hands of me. They didn't and I joined a Bible study group and decided that I should try Catholic education for the three children in my care. It really stretched the budget as they had to wear uniforms, but I thought I was doing the right thing for them. That was until Erica came home and said, 'I'm fed up with that school! There is too much bloody religion and not enough education!' She went on to explain how the school day was usually spent and I had to agree with her. So back to the public school they went. We continued to go to mass and Sunday school, which they enjoyed, and I remember taking them to see the film *Jesus Christ Superstar*. One of the nuns who took Sunday school played guitar and taught the children some cute songs. One went ...

I've got joy, joy, joy, joy down in my heart!
Yea! Down in my heart to stay,
And if the devil doesn't like it he can sit on a tack,
Yea! Sit on a tack to stay.

Peter especially liked that one and would often burst out singing it.

Apart from that, they had to rely on quiet talks about right and wrong when occasions arose. I'm uncertain how successful I was because once I remember having a serious talk to Kathy about God wanting her to be a good girl.

She turned to me and in her firm, no-nonsense voice said, 'Well, that's how He made me!'

That firm no-nonsense voice could be used to great effect. Once, when I was feeling very frustrated with Xavier's latest string-pulling exercise I showed my exasperation by saying, 'MEN!' to which she replied, 'Look! He's my daddy!'

I was taken aback and from then on remembered not to criticise her daddy within her hearing.

She also did not hesitate to criticise me. My laughter embarrassed her, so when parent visiting night approached I was told that I could attend but only if I did not laugh out loud!

Xavier's sister Helen was married at about this time and the children were involved as flower girls and page boys. Mrs J senior wanted me to attend. She was hoping that the romance of a wedding would bring X and me back together again. No, thank you!

But that first explosion of *MEN!* was how I viewed that half of our species. Being liberated from my marriage, I was free to be myself and was not going to fall into that trap again. I viewed all men as potential traps. I really did not need them and I could happily go without their company. Friends tried to pair me up with that 'nice divorcee from next door' or 'Roger's brother who had just arrived from England'. I suffered the date or dinner party of introduction. The poor guy knew within the first 15 minutes of meeting me that he was going to get nowhere with this very cold bitch. Yes, I said it. I froze them out.

Eventually, I began to thaw. On New Year's Eve, I was at a party singing

Abba songs with a group of old friends and acquaintances from my pre-divorce days. One chap had been temporarily deserted by his wife, she was on a holiday in Britain, and he asked if I would like to go home with him later. I was flattered, no, more than that, I was delighted. I began to bubble with joy and had to tell someone.

'Madge, a word in your ear.'

'Yes, Chrissie. What?'

'Max has asked me to go home with him.' I was jubilant.

'Okay, Chris. Calm down. Don't tell anyone else. You know it's a one night stand because Beverly is away, and you wouldn't want to rock the boat would you?'

Good old Madge, she calmed me down and told no one else. This first small secret dalliance was just an experiment.

The one night stand turned into a couple of weekends at his place with good food and wine and his favourite music ... Mahler. I was new to classical music and had never heard Mahler before. I didn't find it particularly inspiring. However, it lit his fire, so who was I to complain? He was helping me to put my shattered ego back together. I had no designs on him. He just showed me that sex was a pleasure that perhaps I could indulge in occasionally. We were not in love. We merely enjoyed relaxing together and having sex.

So now I understood. It was possible to enjoy sex without being in love! I was free. No master to be behoven to. Life was good!

For three years I lived at Able Street, Salisbury, with Kathy, Erica and Peter, while Paul was living with his father. I studied Biology 1 while I continued to teach, then Botany and Zoology 2 and 3 full-time at Adelaide University, which, when added to my earlier studies, completed my Bachelor of Science, or BSc. See the next chapter for more on this topic.

Each year, once school and university terms had started, life at Able Street had a pattern to it. At the weekend I cleaned, washed and did a cook up. I cooked meals for the week and froze them in ice-cream containers. On weekdays, we arose at 7 am and by 8:30 am we were fed, washed, dressed, lunches were in school bags, the evening meal was put out to defrost and I was ready to leave for uni. The kids were entrusted to wash the breakfast dishes, lock the house and go to school. If I could not be at home to greet them in the evening, one of my trusted helpers would be there to serve their evening meal and put them through the bath and get ready for bed routine. I would always be home in time to put them to bed.

There were two notable occasions when the routine was disrupted. I came home one evening to an extremely clean kitchen.

'Wow! What a lovely clean kitchen! Have some good fairies been doing some cleaning for me?'

Kathy, ever the straight talker, told me the story. 'Well, Mummy, it's like this. It's Peter's fault. I was just starting to wash the dishes when he said, "I'm not staying around to wipe up! I'm off to school!" Now, that's not fair. Erica and I were not gonna let him get away with it. So, we chased after him when we caught him we bought him back. The kitchen was flooded because I hadn't turned off the taps. We just got all the towels we could find and dried it up. Peter had to help too. It was his fault!'

The second occasion must have been Pinky's fault.

Pinky was a dear little white ball of fluff given to the children by their father, much to my annoyance. After all, I had the children to feed. Didn't he know how hard I was having it? They had her with them when they returned from Xav's access visit one Sunday evening.

'Please can we keep her, Mummy? She is such a sweet little puppy! Daddy gave her to us. Please, please let us keep her, Mummy!'

'She's from a litter that Joan's bitch produced. (*Joan must be the latest girlfriend.*) She's been de-sexed, it's perfectly safe.'

What can a mother do in these circumstances? I would have been considered an absolute cold hearted witch if I had said 'No.' So even though I could not afford another mouth to feed and I knew no extra cash would come my way, Pinky joined the family. Needless to say, about two months down the track, every dog in Salisbury was in our backyard and I realised that I had misunderstood. It must be Joan that was desexed. We took Pinky inside and shooed away the dogs, but it was too late. She was pregnant.

Chapter 28 *Able Street*

Ho hum, one more thing to deal with down the track. Let's hope they are attractive puppies that I can easily give way.

I didn't count the months; I was just too busy. Then, one morning, just as I was about to leave, Peter and Kathy decided that they weren't going to school. They were 'ill' they said. I really had no time for an argument. I had a 9 am lecture.

'Well, be very good. Get some sleep. Don't do anything silly or naughty and don't make a habit of it! I'll phone you at lunchtime to see how you are. Are you going to school, Erica?'

'Yes, Mummy.'

'Okay, see you all this evening. Be good.' Off I rushed. At lunchtime I phoned to check up on the rascals. Peter's excited voice came over the phone.

'Pinky's had her puppies! The black one came out first!'

'Let me talk to Kathy!' was my immediate response. The phone was quickly handed over. 'Okay, what happened?'

'Pinky was in her box in the laundry, she was crying so we went to look. She had them slowly and she cleaned them all by herself. She's had four puppies, two white and two black.'

'Do not touch her or the puppies, she can take care of them herself.'

'Okay, Mummy. Isn't it fun?'

I did not share her enthusiasm. Homes were found for all the puppies and Pinky was desexed as soon as possible. I did not want a repeat of that fiasco.

On Saturdays, the girls had a calisthenics class and Peter played soccer. The girls loved these classes—it gave them a certain poise and confidence and we all loved the concerts with their bespangled costumes.

Peter's soccer game was a hoot. While the soccer mad fathers raced up and down the sidelines, the ball moved in a random way around the field while small boys chased it, trying to get in a kick at it whenever possible.

Saturday lunch was a very casual affair. Our favourite was bananas mushed onto bread and sprinkled with sugar. Saturday evening was a revelation to me. At first I felt lost and lonely because me and Xavier had always had socially busy Saturday nights. But I gradually began to appreciate it as a quiet time when I could catch up with lecture notes and essays while the rest of the world was out earning Sunday's hangover.

Sunday was access day, so the kids were cleaned and dressed in their best by whatever time Xavier had dictated was pick up time. If they were not ready in time there would be hell to pay and threats of my losing that week's maintenance filled the air. However, he did not feel the obligation to arrive at the decided time—it was the doctor's waiting room principle.

Once they were gone, the day was mine. I could settle down to some uni work. The student side of my life was so happy. It was the something for me and the way to a brighter future for us all.

So, once again, I was learning, and not just my university studies. I sang the Helen Reddy songs and really felt them. I was strong! I was invincible! I was woman! I loved to read *Cleo* in idle moments. I was learning what wonderful people my parents and friends were. They rose to help wherever they could. I was learning that I had strengths. I had the strength to discipline and organise myself.

Yes, I thought, life really is a learning experience.

CHAPTER 29

BACK TO UNIVERSITY

There I was, back in the cloisters adjacent to the canteen at the Adelaide University. I was back in the hallowed halls of learning, ready for two years of study to complete my degree. The quadrangle was still the same, but everything else seemed to have grown.

The refectory building was enormous with a lovely bistro upstairs, but the prices weren't cheap. Xav had been ordered to pay me $10 per week per child and I was receiving the single parent pension which meant that I would be bringing my lunch. But it was great to be back. This time, my focus was the botany and zoology departments.

Ever since Sir William Perkins School for girls I had become an education snob. I judged and valued people from the level of education they had achieved. I was in for a big lesson.

My first zoology essay, something about flies tasting with their feet, was returned to me with red circles, crossing outs and underlines through the first paragraph, and a note written large in red that said, 'This is dreadful! Six spelling mistakes and three grammatical errors in the first paragraph! I can read no more!'

I was gobsmacked. I had put a lot of effort into that essay and I was sure it was a good essay, but obviously my command of English had let me down. I nursed the grief for several days, telling every sympathetic ear that I could find. Yvonne, one of my Beta Sigma Phi friends, yes, she of the blushing decolletage came to my rescue. Educated at a commercial school, she was proficient in shorthand and typing and her English was impeccable. She had risen from the typing pool to become a personal private secretary and she made me a magnificent offer.

'If you get your handwritten essay to me a week before the due date, I will type it out for you and make the necessary corrections as I go. If there is anything in the essay that I do not understand I'll ring you.'

She did this for me for the next three years, getting me through my BSc. and Dip Ed. I don't think I would have made it without her help. With no grammar school education, she saved my bacon. What a friend!

Clearly, my thoughts on education needed revising. Judging people by their level of education is too facile. After all, I have always considered Ted to be a wise man and he left school at twelve. If we are wise our education does not stop when we leave school or university. If we remain aware LIFE will continue to teach us.

That was not the only help I needed …

Since I was 20 years older than the last time I attended university, I needed another mature-aged student friend and there she was: Kate.

I sat next to Kate, and although she was a mature age student, she was not quite as mature as I. She had started teaching before completing her degree and had reached the stage in her career where she would soon be promoted to senior. She decided that a completed degree was appropriate, so she had settled down to two years of work to finish a degree before returning to her spot on the promotion ladder.

We sat together in the front row of the lecture theatre. We took our notes for rewriting that night while it was still fresh in our brains. If anything couldn't be recalled precisely, we could ask our buddy the next day, and we worked as a pair for the practicals.

Then there were the tutorials. Anything that we didn't quite understand in the lectures or pracs could be discussed at tutorials. I went through my notes and had a list of questions ready for each tutorial. When all my questions were answered, I sat back and waited for the few questions that came from the others.

After three tutorials the tutor took me aside. 'It is good that you're thinking things through and come armed with questions, but the tutorial is intended to help ALL students. Could you hold back a little and let the others ask a few questions before you start your interrogation?'

'Fine, yes, I understand.' She was not trying to put me down, she was just asking me to share the time with the more timid students. They were backward in coming forward, but all my questions were eventually answered.

The tutors were people who had their degrees, they certainly knew a lot more than us mere undergraduate students. David was a tutor. He was helpful, generous with his time and had a good-natured, even amusing, manner. I admired him. He was clearly knowledgeable but did not have a distant superior academic attitude.

At the end of the first term, came the end of the Vietnam War, and the Keith camp. This camp, under canvas, was intended to show students what botanical fieldwork was like. We all paid a small fee to cover the food, but the running of the camp and the lectures were supplied by the tutors.

Kate had a car. She drove me and a few other students out to the camp. The boys were sent to dig the latrines while the girls erected the tents around the permanent shed where we would have our lectures and meals. We soon began to realise that this experience in fieldwork, learning the names of plants on site, gathering data and specimens, was as much for the benefit of the tutors as for ourselves. The experiments and the collections were planned by tutors so that the results could be used in their PhD papers. We were slave labour to collect and classify samples of material for them. But it was fun and the privations, like rationed water and smelly latrines, became jokes. For me, it was a week's holiday away from all my domestic responsibilities while Mum and Dad manned the home front.

Because I was studying botany and zoology, words like environment, niche and ecology were creeping into my vocabulary, and we were frequently reminded that loss of habitat was leading to species extinction. Holes in the ozone layer were blamed for excessive UV rays reaching Earth and causing more skin cancers in humans. Hence, forward looking scientists were urging us to reduce, reuse and recycle. I did not need urging because that was the economical way to live, and although my children laughed at me, I would wash and reuse even plastic bags. In third year zoology, our professor recommended that we all read Vance Packard's *The Waste Makers*, take it to heart and spread the word amongst our friends. It was the beginning of the realisation for me that mankind was wrecking Earth.

A plan was crystalising in my mind ...

When I finally start to earn money, I will buy land and have a small farm producing all that my little family needs. We will be self-sustaining.

I was becoming a greeny.

CHAPTER 30

DAVID

One afternoon at the Keith Camp in the main shed, David was marking papers. He called me over to discuss my paper.

'Can you come over here, Mrs Jancarik, and tell me what you mean by this?' We had our little discussion and again he emphasised my surname. 'Thank you, Mrs *Jancarik*.'

I was curious, when it hit me.

Aha! He is enquiring into my marital status.

'What's with all the "Mrs Jancarik" stuff?' I asked him. 'Aren't I usually just "Chris"?'

He didn't have much of a reply, so I took a chance.

'Actually, I'm divorced, but I keep the Mrs Jancarik "moniker" for the sake of my kids. They feel happier having a mother with the same surname as they have.'

He grinned back at me cheekily. We both knew what he was really asking and I was delighted that he had asked. He was interested. He had made the initial step in my direction.

Back in the lab, a week or so after the camp, I was gathering up my stuff to make a run to the train when he offered to give me a lift to the railway station.

'Let's go to North Adelaide, its closer to my home,' he suggested. We drove there and sat in his car talking for a couple of hours while I missed train after train. Fortunately, there was a babysitter in place at the other end so I knew I could indulge myself in this time alone with him. I brought him up-to-date with my current situation and he gave me a potted history of his.

He hadn't liked school, preferring to wander the bushland and study plants and animals firsthand. Then he became a truck driver. I wondered how on earth had ever become so well-educated.

'I thought all truck drivers read Plato,' he said, explaining how he had self-educated during his truck driver years.

'Isobel, my wife, realised that I was not the typical truck driver. After we were married she encouraged me to go to university to get my degree. We conceived and lost our child at about six months, which was a terrible blow to her. But I felt that there was something genetically wrong with me and the natural abortion had been nature's way of rejecting the child. Isobel had such a bad depression that she was in a mental hospital for a while. I dutifully visited her there, until I realised that she was just clinging onto me. As long as I visited, she would remain ill so that I had to keep visiting. So, I decided that the relationship was over. I would not be clung unto. She just had to pull herself together and get on with her life.'

He wanted to be sure that I understood he did not want a permanent relationship because he felt that women clinging onto a man held him down and back.

Well, I thought, at this stage we didn't even have a relationship. We were just talking in a car.

We discovered that we both liked theatre. He was a member of the State Theatre Company which meant he had two tickets for every production through the year. Would I like to dine out and go to the theatre on Friday? Would I ever!

And on that note I caught the next train home. As he saw me onto the train he said, 'You have a wicked eyes, woman!'

Wow, wicked eyes! I do have an attraction. This was an unexpected complement for a girl who dressed down from necessity and didn't seek compliments. So, he admires the wicked eyes. Will he enjoy the woman?

He visited Able Street on a Sunday, while the kids were with their father, and was introduced to The Woman and the waterbed and he was satisfied with both.

From there, we moved to visits to the theatre, always preceded by a lovely Chinese meal. That was his favourite and it soon became mine. He introduced me to the delights of lychees and ice cream. There was plenty of time to chat, discuss the play and the deeper thoughts that arose from it

Chapter 30 *David*

as we travelled back to his room in Seventh Avenue. He had a mattress on the floor, a desk and books—a veritable student's room. We usually went to the theatre a weekday and he drove me into uni the next day so there was plenty of time for my Philosophy Lessons. He was always questioning the accepted point of view, accepted attitudes, things that most people just accepted as the status quo.

Until this point, I had felt that life was carrying me along like a paper boat on a stream. Divorcing Xavier had been an act of desperation because I was so unhappy and getting back to uni to complete my degree was an automatic follow on from that, but David made it clear I could and should be looking ahead and consciously steering my own boat. Until that point, my brain was set on conventional lines. I had to think about my situation and alternatives. Teaching was an excellent career for a woman with children because of the working hours and holidays. I also wanted to attract a husband to give my children a conventional and reliable home life. Although David was adamant that he did not want to be dependant or have anyone dependant on him, I could not shift these two main goals; that is, to become a teacher (hopefully of Matric Biology) and to attract a husband as adorable as him.

Mum and Dad babysat when I went out on these dates. They helped me so much through these years.

David proceeded to open up my world both psychologically and geographically. His PhD required visits to Arkaroola in the Flinders ranges. He knew the owner of the station, Reg Sprig, a geologist who allowed us to sleep in the shearer's quarters and eat with staff while we were there. I served as his field assistant. Until then, I had only experienced Adelaide and its suburbs. The Flinders Ranges were magnificent, a vast mountainous wilderness that was all geology and botany. David had aerial photographs of the areas that we visited for his study. They all looked the same to me, but he could pick the dominant species on this hillside and that peak.

One morning while in the shearer's canteen, we were planning our day's activities when we had a spat. He stood up and marched towards the door. I called after him with a pleading, panicky tone in my voice, 'Xavier!'

He laughed, realising that he had triggered an old fear in me. It gave him insight into my relationship with Xavier and defused our row.

He was such good company, so thoughtful and considerate, but it didn't stop my thoughts theorising on his inner self.

Does it seem that way to me because, after Xavier's self-centred personality just a modicum of consideration feels like a lot, or is he just a kind person?

David proclaimed himself to be an atheist. I'd never met one before. When I said that, he commented that most people like to have two bob each way! He was very honest, perhaps he is as honest as one person can be to another. We all have our ulterior motives, myself included. I argued with myself. Eventually, I decided to go along with his expressed desire to remain a solitary being, but I liked him so much that I would have been over the moon if he proclaimed that he loved me.

In my heart, I realised that was what I was angling for.

Yes, I was in love with him.

On the downside, I was a practicing Catholic and he was an atheist. I thought that if I prayed diligently, perhaps God would help me to overcome this impasse.

He told me some of his impressions of me and women in general.

'Women think that because they are weaker than men they have to use more effort to shut a car door and inevitably they slam it too hard.'

(*Guilty as charged. I'll have to moderate that behaviour.*)

Other positive ones I hold on to and cherish. For example, he thought me intelligent in a practical way. (*I cut bread in vertical slices and improvise when I do not have the perfect tools at my disposal.*) He says that I am an enjoyable woman. (*I hope he means as a companion as well as in bed*).

He talked of self-awareness and consciousness.

I tried to understand him because I was very impressed by him and really enjoyed his company. I would like the relationship to grow. So, as I understood it at the time ... run of the mill people, that is, most ordinary people are unconscious, they just follow the herd, do what society expects of them. While conscious people think for themselves and do not necessarily follow a conventional life plan. At present, I am unconscious. I see the fact that we

Chapter 30   *David*

enjoy each other's company and have great sex together leading to a romantic attachment and marriage in a few years, when we have both finished our studies. However, he continually reiterated that he was a solitary animal and did not want to be dependent or have anyone dependent on him.

During my second year at uni, we spent a lot of time together. All my leisure time was occupied with him. There were theatre and dinner dates, trips to Arkaroola (all at his expense), while Mum and Dad took care of my children. They did this gladly. I daresay they thought, as most parents would, that they were assisting a romance that would lead to the conventional conclusion.

By the end of that year, I was beginning to have some thought of my own about topics that concerned me. I kept records of some.

For example:

> Say what you like about liberation and equality of the sexes, I have my own opinion. Men and women are born equal of that I am convinced, but in childhood no matter how carefully a parent can be the social pressures get to work and part of the female brain usually shuts up shop. Then when she marries, usually to a man more intelligent than herself, or she lets him think he is, for they all love to lord it over someone, she is shackled to the commonplace of home and children leaving all the really stimulating thinking to him. Hence more brain shuts up shop. This is the status quo because men inform sons better than they inform daughters. So, in general, men are better informed than women about most things.

Lucky for me, my father had two daughters, and took the attitude that girls were every bit as intelligent and valuable as boys.

Then there was Kangaroo Island, locally called KI. David owned a property there jointly with three other academics and needed to visit occasionally to do jobs. We'd fly out in a light aircraft to a landing field near the property where they kept a utility van to carry us to the property.

'Would you like to come to KI this weekend? I need to build a cattle yard. We will be flying out.'

Of course, my answer was 'yes'. Mum and Dad were delighted to babysit so that I could have a holiday on KI. Mum insisted that it warranted a new outfit and I insisted that it be something practical, so denim jeans with a matching jacket were purchased and I had my hair cut at the hairdressers, thinking this was going to be so romantic and glamourous.

It certainly was exciting flying in the six seater aeroplane, but all the glamour evaporated when the car wouldn't start and I had to push. The accommodation was another shock. It was a big shed with a bed at one end and a kitchen sink at the other and a table in the middle with cupboards along the sides that stored tinned food. I spent most of the weekend cleaning up, trying to get rid of the smell of mice, while he was busy welding the new stockyards. In the evening we concocted pleasant meals and made full use of the double bed. It was a strange set up, but I really enjoyed my weekends there. There was a particular smell when you opened a window and smelt the hay and the mustard weed. I used to sing 'Mockingbird Hill' out loud. It expressed my joy.

With our meals came more philosophy. Philosophy was new to me, and I was totally bamboozled by both it and him at first. I wrote down a lot of his dissertations and tried to understand them and apply them to myself. He recommended and I read *The Island* by Aldous Huxley. It is a great book about self-awareness and an idyllic civilisation.

There is no doubt that the self-confidence I gained and the ability to think for myself are assets that he gave me. They are not to be forgotten.

But other issues came with the growth of my mindset, including a greater understanding of who I was in relation to him. I suppose I was his mistress. That's probably how he saw it. I saw us as boyfriend and girlfriend, sweethearts even ... and despite everything he said, I still saw us walking hand-in-hand into the sunset in my imagination, even though he avoided meeting my children and constantly gave me talks about how he saw his life as a solitary being.

Since those years, I have read and observed a lot and realised how unattractive a single mother with four children must be to a single man. That he dated me at all is amazing. That he did not want the friendship to develop into a romance is understandable. When I realised that I was in love with David I made another realisation. Only a fool makes the same mistake twice and I had done it! I had fallen for a man that I greatly admired, thereby making myself subservient to him.

About this time, I began doubting my religion. There are many contradictions in it and David was so convinced of there not being any God out there. When he wanted to provoke rain, he would cry out to the sky, 'Bring it on, Hughey!'. It was just as effective as me praying for rain.

There are worthy and unworthy people in the Church. There are worthy and unworthy people outside the Church. The answering of prayers could just be your brain working on a problem while you sleep. I was confused and ambivalent.

He said that he felt free because he could sense when people were trying to pressure him into conformity and since he had no ties, no one had him cornered. He could escape any type of pressure by recognising it and resisting or escaping its influence. One evening, David and me and Lorna, another botany tutor, with her husband, happened to go to the same theatre production. Lorna and David could not stop talking to one another. They were obviously wrapped in each other, while her husband and I just hung around feeling useless. The Lorna–David relationship continued for a few months and then they decided that they really must stop because she was in love with her husband. David talked to me about it with genuine tears. He really thought she was marvellous but beyond his reach.

I wrote in my Thoughts Book:

> Incidents like this make me a lot more secure as a friend. But am I valued? Will next year be Sue Watson's year or Betty Brown's? He will not change; he will fall in love only to find that they have feet of clay or he is unable to commit himself. This gives me confidence that our friendship will continue if I can bear his sporadic falling in love. This makes me a second class citizen, because he will never be committed to me either. My search for a mate should exclude him. I think I prefer to lead my own life, parts of which are shared with him unless someone with desirable qualities and willing to commit himself to me turns up. David is just Xavier in a different set of clothes.
>
> What am I to him?

A friend with benefits? Yes. He was enjoying sex without connecting it to love, while I was telling myself that because we were having regular sex we must be in love. No, Chrissie! Love and sex are separate entities. If they occur simultaneously for you, you are very lucky.

Life is a continuous lesson if you will let it be. Here are a few lessons/thoughts that I cherished. Know thyself. Be willing to work. Be willing to learn. You need to think and store life's lessons as you travel.

I did not think about LIFE and its lessons until I was 35. I just let myself be carried along by external forces. Then, when things went very wrong, I was forced to think about my life and where it was going, and my children's lives and the necessity for change.

What a pity that our life has to be in crisis before we stop and think.

CHAPTER 31

ONE MORE YEAR

Madge told me of a little drama that had unfolded at the surgery. Xavier was fond of doing minor surgery at his practice in Parafield Gardens. He did vasectomies and any stitching up that was necessary in his surgery, thereby saving his patients trips to hospital and giving himself more kudos and cash. In 1975, he discovered an unsightly mole on his forehead and asked his medical partner to remove it for him during their lunch hour. The partner did as requested, and Xavier spoke so lightly of the procedure that the partner was about to throw the section away when Xavier intervened.

'Oh, we must send that off for a biopsy!'

Unfortunately, the biopsy showed that it was a melanoma and had not been completely excised. This means that melanoma cells were floating free in his body and could settle anywhere.

In 1976, came Xavier's threat. When Xav and I were somewhere between decree nisi and decree absolute, he had come to pick up the children for his Sunday access and told me to get into his car, he had something to tell me. He told me that the mole that he had had removed from his forehead was a melanoma and had been incompletely removed.

This was a death sentence for him, and he knew it.

As a consequence, he wanted me to take Paul back under my care. He did not want his son to witness his decline. Xav planned also to sell his surgery, take himself to the Philippines for a cure, if that really was available there, then move himself from Brenda (his current girlfriend) to Carol (his former girlfriend) because she had some nursing experience and would be better equipped to care for him if and when he needed it. He said that melanoma was brought on by stress and that I had caused him stress by filing for divorce. He was certain that I would not have had the courage or brains to move for a divorce and that my father had put me up to it. He'd come to the conclusion that he wanted to make my parents and me suffer. He said, in all seriousness, that he intended to shoot Ted dead. Since he was on death row himself, The Law could not really touch him. He would not kill Mum or me, because someone had to look after our children. The death of Ted would make us suffer enough.

I was shocked and horrified and did not know how to respond. To have me show these feelings was probably what he wanted. But I had changed. I was no longer that girl who went along with his every idea. I was the Woman who'd had the courage to leave.

I would not give him that satisfaction.

If I put on a big bravado and said, 'You wouldn't dare!' this might add fuel to his fire. Instead, I said, 'Is that all?' in as flat a voice as I could muster. I then calmly got out of the car, went inside and brought the children out to him, while maintaining a quiet, thoughtful demeanour.

When they had gone, I burst into tears and did a panic scream to get it out of my system as much as anything, then I settled down to some quiet thinking.

This was a threat. It was intended to scare Mum and Dad and me. It had already scared me. Would telling Mum and Dad help the situation? Would being forewarned really help? I thought not. Although Xavier was dying, he would not want his children to remember him as a murderer. If anything, I was sure I could count on his self-image to not go through with such a threat.

I said nothing about the threat to anyone.

That was the best thing that I could have done. Mum and Dad lived on and helped me raise the kids, giving them some lovely holidays and firm advice over the years, lovingly given which endeared them to all.

Xavier, meanwhile, lingered on, the cancer within him slowly taking over.

When it came to receiving my degree in December 1975, the graduates had the choice of having it sent by mail or attending a graduation ceremony. Although I am not one for pomp and ceremony, I knew that I would have to attend the ceremony so that Sue and Ted could come and feel proud of me and of themselves for all that they had done to make this dream a reality.

Mrs Woolley turned up too. She was also justifiably proud. In fact, I knew that this degree was not mine alone. I had so much help with the kids while I studied, and they all deserved their dues.

I did not return to teaching immediately. I discovered that teachers are paid not in accordance with their ability as teachers, but in consideration of their academic qualifications. This meant if I spent a year acquiring a Diploma in Education I would be better paid in the long run.

So, we moved to a rented flat in Tonsley Park, near Flinders University, where I studied for the Dip. Ed. Distancing myself from David seemed like a good idea, and I hoped my absence would make his heart grow fonder, or I would grow to live life without him. I let my house in Able St to a young couple so that the mortgage would be paid off. My three children went to nearby primary schools and all performed well. Xavier, thinking that he was in remission, took Paul back to live with him. I assumed that he was being a caring father to Paul and giving tough love when it was required, performing all parental services to him as I was to my little charges.

So that I would not be totally brainwashed by David, I read some self-help books. They suggested that I try some self-examination so I did. This is what I came to:

> I am smarter than the average woman. Not a brilliant one, as those who go with depth and fullness into their studies. In short, those who do not have children to support. I am warm, witty, compassionate, quite sensitive to the feelings of others and able to take the slings and arrows of most adverse events. I have been through the worst. No man can crush me like that again. However, I can improve in awareness there is so much to learn. Learn it! Don't just let it float by unexamined.

I plunged into university life at Flinders University. I attended the lectures and tutorials, read the prescribed texts, wrote the required essays, and sat the exams, getting a pass result, but what did I learn about teaching? A few crumbs of wisdom like, 'Know your subject!', 'Do not smile before Easter!', 'Get to know your classes and adjust your methods accordingly!'

What methods? I had never had methods. I was all at sea when it came to how to persuade thirty disinterested teenagers to sit quietly while I explained the finer points of our 'study'. I could only hope that I would learn as I go.

Matric Biology was my aim. I really knew my Biology and Matric students were really serious students. They wanted to pass their all-important exams. It'll be fine, I told myself.

The year rolled along pleasantly enough. David would pop up occasionally and I learned a way of dealing with my emotions. If we said 'bye' without fixing a date for our next rendezvous, I would think to myself, *'I may never see him again, but it was fun wasn't it?'* Then when he turned up again of his own volition I was very happy. There was no reason to hide my affection for him. That would be dishonest, but I tried to keep it low key. As a result, our trips to the Flinders Ranges and Kangaroo Island continued. Sue and Ted willingly took on the children as necessary and I had welcome breaks from my student life.

Perhaps I had embodied the Serenity Prayer and learned the serenity to accept the things that I could not change. I had the courage to change the things I could, and hopefully, the wisdom to know the difference.

CHAPTER 32

MURRAY BRIDGE

January came. We were full of anticipation. Where would the Education Department send me? Weeks passed. Other teachers were moving into position preparing for the year and still I was given no posting by the Education Department. I was worried so I contacted the Department.

'Oh, Mrs Jancarik, you are a woman on her own with children. We do not like to send you out unless we can supply a house and we cannot supply a house.'

'If you give me a posting, I will find a house,' I implored them.

'Very well, there are three primary schools at Murray Bridge. We will surely be able to find a posting for you at one of those.'

I was immediately concerned. 'I am a high school teacher.'

'Sorry, there are no high school postings left. You will have to teach primary school if you want a posting. As I said, Murray Bridge is your best opportunity.'

Naturally I talked this over with Dad.

His response was as pragmatic as ever. 'Well, let's go find a house in Murray Bridge.'

We took off that very day and went to the real estate agents in Murray Bridge, asking for a house to rent. We found a pleasant house on the other side of the river from the town. It was on a dirt road, and although the soil was sandy, there were sunflowers growing opposite and the rent was reasonable. I still had tenants in my Able Street house, so now that I was going to be a teacher with a proper income I could afford to rent. I then notified the education department that I had a house and they gave me a posting at the Murray Bridge Primary School. It seemed better for the children to be enrolled at different primary schools to where I taught; however, Peter proclaimed that he'd rather be at the same one as his mummy. So that's how it went. Our furniture was duly installed and we moved in just in time for the start of the school year.

I was given a Year 7 class. The Year 7 room was of the new open plan design. This meant that there was one large room with teaching areas in each corner. There was Miss West, Mr Young and Mr Farmer. We each organised the corners in which we would do the majority of our teaching. We then conferred with each other to decide how best to use our areas of expertise. Miss West delighted in drama, I was the science guru, Mr Young took most of the PE, and Mr Farmer most of the English. For other subjects, we each took our home class. We organised our timetable to accommodate these considerations. This worked quite well, despite the different teaching personalities in each of the corners.

It was always fine and warm in Murray Bridge because it was in the rain shadow of the Adelaide hills. This meant that washing dried readily, children could play outside most days, and a cardigan was only needed on rare occasions.

Despite those positives, I found life in Murray Bridge boring at the least and annoying most of the time. It had the disadvantage of remoteness and the disadvantage of the largeness. It was not a cosy country village where you could get to know everyone, and it was so far from the city that there was no entertainment. I asked the staff what they did for entertainment and I was told there's 'The Club.' The headmaster introduced me to The Club. It was a drinking hole. It provided no other entertainment. It was more pleasant than the average pub, but its function was the same; that is, sit, talk and drink.

A couple of times a year a big show would come to town and everyone would attend, but that was all.

But there were compensations. Since I was earning I could afford a brand new car. I brought a Toyota 120Y, white. It was a dream to drive and absolutely reliable.

We could escape at the weekend. I designated days during the week for housework, shopping, washing, a visit to 'Pick your own.' This was a market garden where we could pick our own fruit and vegetables and pay for them as we left. I leave you to imagine what went on in the strawberry patch. I organised piano lessons for Erica and horse riding lessons for Kathy. I did my lesson preparation and marking after the children were in bed.

Frequently, Peter would appear just as I was getting settled.

'Mummy, I've got a headache.'

'Oh dear. Do you need an aspirin or will it get better if you go into Mummy's bed?'

'Mummy's bed.'

'Okay, off you go.'

'Thank you, Mummy.'

I never minded.

The children soon had school friends who visited occasionally. Kathy had a friend, Marie, living on our street, whose mother was a Girl Guide leader. Kathy joined the Girl Guides, having loads of fun at meetings. Marie and Kathy became such firm friends that whenever she was not at home I knew exactly where to find her.

Meanwhile, Xavier's cancer spread and he became weaker. Babichka insisted that I visit him now that he was dying in hospital. The children were not allowed to see him, but I was coerced into his room. He was unconscious and breathing through a respirator. His body was emaciated and quivering.

It was curious moment for me. I still remember my thoughts at this moment.

> So, this is what remains of the man that had impressed me so much. He had been strong, lively and intelligent. This is the man that I had admired, loved, adored, respected, and, finally, feared. Did Babichka expect me to be heartbroken at this sight? Sorry, Babi, I can understand your grief. You have invested so much of your life into his, but you did not see his dark side.

The best I could give her was a smile of regret as I left.

Paul must have been feeling his father's slow demise very strongly. He was shuttled around the Jancarik family, mainly living with Babichka or his Uncle Jan, so he would have been aware on a day-by-day basis of the deterioration in Xavier's condition. My suggestion that he returned to me was firmly rebuffed.

Xavier died in March. I took a day leave from school and took the children to the funeral. I wanted them to get his demise firmly fixed in their minds, and I was glad to be putting a full stop to that period of my life. Having attended Mr Jan Jancarik senior's funeral only last year, I was prepared for the cacophony, the loud outpouring of grief. The coffin, open in the middle of the lounge was visited by each mourner before they collapsed onto Babi's shoulders with their messages of condolence and added their wails and tears to hers. As a stiff-upper-lip Brit, I could only wonder where she found the energy for a fresh outburst of crying as each mourner approached her. Perhaps they were so spent by the end of the funeral they were purged of grief.

Kathy, observant as ever, said, 'That coffin is too small for my daddy. He is a big man.'

I thought that finally my son might be returned to me after the funeral, but the family decided that Paul should stay with Jan junior for the rest of the year.

I was very pleased that Xavier was gone. While he was alive there was always the chance that he would find some way to unsettle me. Even though he was gone he had burnt a deep hole into my psyche and continued to haunt my dreams. The fear that he would find some way to unsettle me took a long time to fade.

A few days after the funeral, Peter asked me, 'Are we Christians, Mummy?'

I was having trouble deciding where my own faith lay. What was I to say to this innocent question?

'If you believe that Jesus is the son of God and came to earth to save you from your sins then you are Christian. It doesn't matter what I believe or Kathy believes or Erica believes, it's what you believe that matters. So, you have to ask yourself "Am I a Christian?"'

David was still on the scene occasionally, but I was trying to look elsewhere for 'Mr Right'. The experiences of both Xavier and David had to be replaced by something better. Mum and Dad encouraged me to go on dates at the weekend, when we could escape Murray Bridge and visit them.

One Saturday night, towards the end of first term, Peter asked his grandma if he could watch *Willy Wonka and The Chocolate Factory* on TV. Mum and Dad actually wanted to watch something else, but they finally gave in to

Peter's enthusiasm. Halfway through the show, he turned to grandma and said with his irrepressible grin, 'It's good, isn't it, Grandma?' He was such a bright little boy.

Peter had a girlfriend and was overheard saying to her, 'I love you even more than I love my mum!' I thought that it was wonderful that he measured love by how much he loved me.

With school holidays approaching we needed to make plans.

One night, David appeared and we spent a lovely night together and he invited me to Kangaroo Island for the second week of the holidays. In the morning, I had to get off to school with the children. I suggested that he stay in bed until we were out of the house. He agreed to the plan, so I carefully shut my bedroom door behind me. The usual crazy run around ensued to get everyone fed, dressed and ready for school. We got to the stage of 'Everyone into the car!' and Peter could not be found. After shouting and searching, he was found in my bedroom having a friendly chat to David. I was embarrassed and delighted.

I had intended to keep David a secret and just whisk the children off to school, so that he could make his escape as he had never expressed the slightest interest in my children. Yet here he was, having an amicable, heart-to-heart with my inquisitive, cheeky son. They were both relaxed and obviously enjoying each other's company.

There was not time to investigate the situation further, and the less I fussed the less the children's curiosity would be aroused.

'Come along, Peter, we will all be late. We have to get to school and David has to go to work!'

Wouldn't it be wonderful if Peter had made a conquest and changed David's attitude to dependents!

Off to school we went and when we arrived home David was gone. Perhaps we had all imagined him.

CHAPTER 33

MAY HOLIDAYS

I wanted to go to KI with David, but this would only be possible if I could find accommodation for the children during that second week. I suggested to the children that they invite a friend to stay with us for the first week if their friend's parents were agreeable to accommodate them for the second week. They teed up the families and I phoned the parents to clinch the deal. I had a house full of happy, active children for the first week. Peter invited Tom, Erica invited Ella, and Kathy invited Marie. I attempted to prep my lessons for the first week of next term at the same time as caring for my enlarged family.

Our sensations of time are strange, aren't they? Some days fly peacefully by and leave only the faintest of memories, while others I can recount frame by frame.

This was one of those days.

Kathy was at Marie's place, but the four small fries were playing outside, thanks to the mild Murray Bridge weather. At lunchtime, they were excitedly telling me that they had found a cave just up the road.

I was relieved, as there to my mind there were infinitely more dangerous places in the area. 'Good, so you are not playing down by the river. The river is very dangerous you know.'

They scampered off after lunch—Peter, Tom, Erica and Ella—keen to investigate this cave and promising to stay clear of the river. They were so happy!

The kitchen was cleaned after the lunchtime invasion and I was just settling down to work again when Tom knocked on the front door. Erica was behind him, bouncing nervously from foot to foot.

I immediately knew that something was wrong.

Chapter 33 *May Holidays*

'Mrs Jancarik, the sand has fallen on Peter and Ella and we can't get them out,' said Tom, wringing his hands.

'My goodness, you kids always getting into some kind of trouble! I'll get the spade from the shed. You show me where they are.' I didn't understand the urgency of the situation. I thought it was simple sand pile, a quick spade job.

We trudged slowly up the hill to where they had been playing. Peter's legs were sticking out from the roadside bank but nothing else.

I could not see my little boy's face.

The spade was useless. I dropped to my knees and started to use my hands.

'Erica!' I screamed, digging madly. 'Run down the hill to the first house you can find with someone at home and ask them to phone for an ambulance. Tom, you keep helping me to dig while I pull. Where is Ella?'

'She is further in,' he said desperately. 'We were making the cave bigger and longer.'

I pulled Peter free of the bank and did my best to clean sand from his face, his eyes, his mouth, so I could breathe life back into his lungs. A car came up the hill and I put my son down to wave it down.

'Can I help?' asked the driver.

I picked up Peter and carried him right over to the car. 'Yes. Please drive us to the hospital.'

The diver understood the issue immediately and took us at breakneck speed to hospital. When we arrived, I laid him on the pavement as two nurses ran out.

'Please resuscitate him!'

One of the nurses looked up at me. 'Is he from the cave in on Thiele Road?'

'Yes, a little girl is still buried there!'

The nurse directed me to the waiting truck. 'The ambulance is about to leave. We will take the boy. Will you go to guide the ambulance?'

'Yes,' I said and I climbed up beside the ambulance driver. I didn't want to leave Peter, but there was another child who desperately needed help, and Peter was with the best possible help that he could have.

'Over the bridge and turn left,' I directed the ambulance driver, hoping that someone had tried to get Ella out in my absence.

The rescue squad quickly took over and dug out Ella and took her into the ambulance. A small crowd had gathered in my absence and one woman known to me saw that I was beginning to fail under the strain. Peter ... Ella ... it was too much.

'I'll walk you home, dear,' she said. 'You can phone the hospital to find out how Peter is.'

I dialled the hospital with shaking hands. Their words burn me even today.

'We were unable to revive him.'

'No! No! Hospitals can always fix an accident!'

Sobs welled up inside me like some internal motor that was firing unevenly. They shook my body and squeezed out tears.

Peter was an imp, a rascal, a nuisance and a pest to his teachers. He was always the class clown and mischief-maker, a lovable rascal, my lively nine-year-old boy. He cannot be dead!

There was no 'stiff upper lip' Brit now. I was a mother who had lost her son.

I phoned Mum and Dad told them what had happened.

'We're on our way,' was the immediate response. Then I called David. He was dumbstruck and I said I'd get back to him later. The friendly neighbour phoned the parents of Ella and Tom and was doing her best to soothe me with a cup of tea when a policewoman came in. Investigations had begun.

'Mrs Jancarik, I'm afraid we have to ask you to come to the hospital with us to identify your son. You can tell me how it happened on the way.'

I tried to keep calm, but how could I? Peter was dead, I knew that, but part of me was saying, 'no, it can't be true'. He still had a chance when I dropped him at the hospital, didn't he?

But there he was, cleaned up, lying on a bed with no sheets or blanket, eyes asleep, fingers curled into a gentle fist.

'Peter! Peter! Oh my dear boy! No! No! You can't be dead!'

I lay across his passive body and the tears and moans and shakes began again. The self-recrimination began almost immediately.

Oh God, so this is my punishment! I was unmoved by Xavier's death so you dreamed up this to really make me suffer! You Bastard! It is kinder to not believe in God at all than to believe in an almighty presence that concocts such

Chapter 33 *May Holidays*

a punishment as this!

A doctor took me aside and gave me sedatives. By the time the police had returned me to home, Mum and Dad were there and I was zonked out by the sedatives. I was put to bed and they looked after Kathy and Erica. I wafted it in and out of consciousness for two days while Mum and Dad organised everything. I remember hearing Madge's voice saying she would take Erica until everything had settled.

Good old Madge, where did she come from? How did she know?

Then it was back into oblivion.

Soon, there was a male voice I did not recognise. 'I am the undertaker. Could I have something clean to dress Peter in? For children, most people give me a pair of pyjamas.'

'His pyjamas are in his middle drawer, Mum,' I said in my haze, before slipping back into oblivion.

I remember there was a small white coffin. There was a crowded chapel. There were graveside words. There was a sea of sympathetic faces looming out of a mist. There was another small white coffin being buried in the Anglican section ... Ella hadn't survived either.

Another man showed up.

'I don't know that man. Who is he?' I asked my mother.

'He is from the Education Department, dear.'

'Why? Please just let me go back to bed.'

'No, now you must pack, dear. Tomorrow you're going to Kangaroo Island.'

'Really. Why?'

'David rang while you were asleep and asked if you still want to go. We decided it would be good for you to get away and relax somewhere quiet, so we said yes.'

The trip out to KI was hazy. Upon arrival we sat in the kitchen and he gave me his usual talk about how this does not change anything between us. He is still a solitary being. I sat and listened again for the nth time thinking to myself, *No, David, of course I understand. The last thing you want is a dead child and a weeping mother, it's Isobel all over again. I'm over all of this. I am not in pursuit. I just want to sit on the beach and howl with the wind.*

So, I did just that. I cried myself dry each day, not caring too much about his wants or needs.

I began to think of my other children. How was I going to find the strength to support them with my weak, jelly-like ego?

I remembered a conversation that I had with David a few months earlier.

I had said, 'If an ego had material form mine would be jelly.'

David had replied, 'Oh no! I think you will find there is a rod of iron in there.'

I had to find that rod of iron. I had to go back and be a teacher and mother again.

It was cathartic that trip, despite being in the worst pain of my life. I recovered enough to get myself functional, to be there for Kathy, Erica and Paul, but I was still jelly.

The rest of the year was survival through the kindness of others. The staff at Murray Bridge Primary had got together and altered the teaching load and timetables so that I could teach science to every class in the school, thereby giving each class teacher one non-contact lesson per week, and I only needed to prepare one lesson each week. The lesson only needed slight modification to suit each year level. There were a series of science TV tapes which the children liked to watch. After the TV, we would discuss the tape and sometimes follow up with an experiment suggested in the tape. It was extremely easy. I glided through term two. I fed my girls. I kept house. I taxied them around. I cannot remember being mentally present much at all. I just maintained the status quo.

Term three was easier. My little girls were still there, full of happy bounce and an interest in life that I struggled to share but didn't fail to encourage in them.

Kathy's school was organising a debutante ball for the Year 7 students. She disliked the beautiful dress I had made for her, and she thought that all the boys were just so immature. But she went through with it and must have enjoyed it somewhat.

I needed to recover from the death of my dear son and my clinging love for David.

One of my favourite songs at the time was Bette Midler's song 'The Rose'. The first verse tells how much love hurts and didn't I know it! The second verse talks about a person who is not committing themselves and consequently misses out on much of life. To me, that summarised David's holding back. And the last verse tells us not to give up hope because the smallest germ of life will eventually blossom again. I hoped on through my darkest hours. I also loved 'Puff the Magic Dragon' because a dragon lives forever, but not so little boys!

I had little moments, all the time, such as remembering the way Peter used to always go to the toilet when it was time for him to wipe the dishes, the way how he wore his socks until they felt like cardboard, and he always put too much salt on his boiled eggs.

What did he teach us?

Tragedy happens! Sometimes it happens to you and sometimes to someone else. When it is your turn, you just have to put one foot in front of the other and keep walking.

Or to put it more poetically, I will quote Adam Lindsay Gordon.

In this life of froth and bubbles, two things stand like stone,

Kindness in another's troubles, courage in your own.

CHAPTER 34

MCLAREN FLAT SECTION 761

I needed a new start. I was numb and struggling to just keep going. I needed to leave Murray Bridge. I still wanted to be in the country and Kathy wanted a horse. I could not afford agistment for a horse so a small country property is what I needed. All of my family and friends realised this. Paul had been living with Jan and Anne since Xavier's death and I wanted him back in my care. With this in mind, Jan kept his eyes open for a suitable property near his own. He found part section 761 through the local grapevine. It was fifteen acres of land with a very run down hundred year old stone cottage.

Bazza Smart had been living there with his new lady love, a Mrs Williams, his children, her children and their child, a toddler, when Bazza's father died. This meant that he could move back into the family home next door and he could sell off his cottage to pay for the holiday that he wanted to give to his huge family.

Jan told me about the property and I told Dad. We visited the property with great anticipation. Dad had just retired and wanted to help me to resettle. The house really was a handyman's delight and he was a handyman par excellence.

'Well, the price is good and the basic structure sound. It's filthy dirty, so we'd better not bring your mum here yet. We need to clean it up, then I think I can fix this. Do you still have the $16,000 from Xavier's life insurance? I'll need that for materials and some specialist workmen, but I think we can make this into quite a cosy cottage.'

'So, I'll buy it then, Dad?' I was thrilled because I also wanted to test out my ideas on sustainability that I had picked up at university during zoology lectures.

'Yes, I think it'll suit you down to the ground when I've finished with it.'

Chapter 34   *McLaren Flat Section 761*

Jan was pleased to have us near. He wanted to keep his avuncular eye on us because he was the trustee of the children's inheritance.

Dad was happy because there was something that he could do for me.

I was glad that perhaps there was a light at the end of the tunnel, a new life for me and the kids. Paul would be placed back in my care, and it was a way to impress David.

Why must I keep on trying to impress him?

And then there was fifteen acres! I could manage that, I said to myself, with more bravado than I actually felt.

Mum and Dad were encouraging me to go out on dates at this time, so I read the newspaper and replied to a few ads and sometimes had a date on Saturday night in the city.

I don't know if my heart was really in it.

While I was still teaching at Murray Bridge and Dad had started work on the cottage, I would bring the girls down to McLaren Flat at the weekend. We camped in the house as it was being remodelled and renovated. We helped Dad wherever and whenever we could. That way I was on hand to discuss the modifications and could go out for a Saturday night date while Kathy and Erica had a sleepover at Grandma and Grandad's.

Since we were doing nothing with the land, the grass grew long and verdant. Jan pointed out that if I cut the whole place to hay and had Paul, who was still living with him, collect it and stack it in the sheds, I would have a valuable asset to sell because dry-shedded hay was top price. Paul was therefore hired at a dollar per bale. He must've borrowed a truck or trailer and collected it after school, a bit at time, until my sheds were full to bursting with beautiful fresh hay.

The money earned from hay sales was invested in fences. Bazza fixed our common fence while I paid for the materials. The caretaker of the nearby waterworks fixed our common fence with bits and pieces, at no charge to me. We had to fix the road fence and internal fencing ourselves and materials were expensive. I hired a local man to hang gates in new positions. We agreed on a price before he started work.

One of my outings was to a party at the Para Hills home of friendly couple from my married days. I moved among the guests, trying to strike conversations with new people, but I preferred chatting to old friends. We were catching up with comfortable conversations because we knew each other's past history and attitudes. Auntie Anne and Dr Jan were there in the company of a strikingly good-looking but not matching couple who they were introducing around. The girl, Sally, was elegant with brown eyes and honey blonde hair. She was fashionably dressed, a little over-groomed by my standards. While the young man had a solid, strong frame, his eyes an obvious blue, his hair coal black. He was dressed neatly and cleanly but with no attempt at fashion. He looked as though he had been scrubbed up just for the occasion. Anne referred to him as Bruce. The girl was visiting from Melbourne and he was a farm labourer living in McLaren Flat. They were youngsters more interested in each other than the rest of the party. After making a small attempt at conversation, I left to them to seek another drink and another comfortable conversation.

On other dates I met Ian, a plumber, and Sam, a carpet retailer. I would only date single men, bachelors or divorcees. These were both divorcees.

I knew from the start that Sam was not the man for me. His short tubbiness did not appeal to me at all and I could see that his ultimate goal for us was a prissy, conservative suburban bungalow. However, he was persistent and I enjoyed outings with him. We would go clubbing—places where you could eat, drink, talk and dance. They were places where the music did not override conversation. He was a hard-working self-employed carpet salesman. One of the annoying things about him was that wherever we went he looked carefully at the carpeting and if he thought he had a chance of selling new carpet he would seek out the manager or owner and try to make a sale.

Once we went up to Arkaroola and stayed in the motel. After taking the recommended walks and making love, we lay on the bed with the air-conditioner humming away and talked. He was delighted with this intimacy and I realised what a lonely man he must have been, even when he was married, if he found that sort of relaxed intimate, honest conversation so novel. He could afford holidays like this, and that was a treat for me, but he was not what I was looking for.

I suppose I just wanted David without his hang-ups.

It took a while to work out Ian. He was quite a looker and liked to dance, eat and talk as a precursor to returning to his flat for hot stuff. He had left (or been booted out) of a family situation and so liked the idea of taking up with a woman with children.

When I told him about my loss of Peter he said, 'I could give you beautiful sons.'

I felt stung!

No, no! There is no replacing Peter, I thought, and started to look for other faults. This became one of my essential dating bi-laws.

Look for their faults and ask yourself, 'Could I live with these faults?'

He dressed exceptionally well and thought highly of himself. I settled on vanity as his chief fault and thought that if I was married to such a man, I would resent the amount of money he would spend on clothes. I was dating to put some pleasure into my personal life and in the hope of finding a mate to share this new life that I was establishing.

And while the dates continued, my time in Murray Bridge was ending. My farewells to staff at Murray Bridge Primary School were full of sincere thanks for help and support. They all wished me a brighter future, and the Education Department staffing showed that it has a heart as well. I was asked where I would like to teach next year and when I explained about the McLaren Flat property they found a posting at Meadows Primary School, just 20 minutes away.

CHAPTER 35

HILLBILLIES

Part section 176 Scenic Road was a 15-acre block situated at the northern most end of Scenic Rd at the junction with Quipp Rd. These two roads were L-shaped and together created a rectangle. Inside the rectangle was mostly Dudley Wiseman's place, and other neighbours inhabited the outside of the rectangle.

During these years Paul, Kathy, Erica and I were a family. We developed as a whole and as individuals. I call them our 'hillbilly years' because we grew with a foot in each camp. We were part of the civilised world, we attended schools, we watched television and joined in activities which were part of that civilised, suburban life, but we also lived a life separate from that when we were on the property, which I named 'Attention'. We were free spirits and each grew in our own way. I like to think that this is what enabled us to develop as unique individuals with our own sets of values. The name 'Attention' was from the book *The Island* by Aldous Huxley.

When I bought and named 'Attention', I wanted to raise everything. Everything would work in peace and harmony and I would be the conductor. It would all be self-supporting. I was full of university theory and idealism. I thought myself very knowledgeable on ecology, biology, botany and zoology, but could I grow our needs and keep livestock? I knew very little of the practical side of farming, so there were a few hitches along the way.

When we moved from Murray Bridge to McLaren Flat, the house was not ready for occupancy. A few vital jobs had to be done as cheaply as possible. The walls of the stone cottage remained and a new roof was resting on those sturdy walls, the next step was internal walls and ceilings made of gyprock. Floor coverings and some internal fittings were still missing.

As the summer holidays were with us, it was easy to live in a caravan parked near the shed to supply us with electricity. We carried the water we needed from a tank by the house to the van.

Also, since Paul was to return to us, Uncle Jan thought a family holiday was in order and could be paid for by the children's trust money. Mum and Dad said, 'Go! We will fix the gyprock while you are away.'

We had a fly-drive holiday in Tasmania. However, the kids soon became bored with the things that interested me.

'Ruins and forests, ruins and forests that's all you want to look at!'

When we reached Hobart, for a change of pace, we stayed in a hotel. Erica was fascinated by the lifts. 'When I grow up I want to be a lift lady.'

On Saturday night, the kids went to the pictures and I went to the casino. Dressed up to the nines and taking $20 play money I soaked up the atmosphere and moved amongst the wealthy gamblers. As I moved from table to table, winning on some and losing on others, I remembered Dad's advice to 'quit when you're ahead'. I left with $20 still in my purse. I thought this quite an achievement.

Sam phoned almost every night. He was helping Mum and Dad to put up the gyprock walls and ceilings. All three were short people, but they got it done with the aid of long-handled brooms. Mum and Dad encouraged Sam to continue to press his suit, while I wanted to shake him off. On our return he made an offer that I could not refuse. He would carpet the house. He sold me the carpet of my choice at wholesale prices and he laid the carpet himself at no charge. I was very grateful but not grateful enough. I still wanted to drop him. When the carpet was down, we put a quick lick of paint on the walls and we were then able to move into the house.

Dad had made large hollow beams to run across the living room/kitchen ceiling. We had planned for and ordered Stramit, straw panels, in between the beams as the ceiling material. It was very slow coming. Throughout that first year, which included a very cold winter, we could not use the front of the house. We used the back playroom as our living quarters and the laundry as our kitchen. Once free of Xavier, my self-confidence returned. I was the original Christine again, and because I was I could do anything!

CHAPTER 36

HOW TO SETTLE INTO A COUNTRY PROPERTY

First, get to know your neighbours.

In our first couple of years, I had a lot to learn. My children seemed to land on their feet in a new environment. Paul knew McLaren Flat because he had been living there with Uncle Jan. He already played football, Australian rules, with the Flat Club, and pretty soon Kathy was playing netball for McLaren Flat, so they were well on their way to being accepted by the local community. Erica made her friends through the Meadows Primary School. Her buddy there, Elizabeth Smart, is still a friend to this day. I gradually got to know the locals and learnt to be a farmer by interaction with them. They were an interesting bunch.

Bazza Smart and his partner were living diagonally across Scenic Rd and were very friendly. She had been a country woman all her life and was full of good advice as to how I should manage things. She showed me the bulk buying shops and told me where I could buy stock for the place. She would buy all sorts of stock when she thought the price was good, keep it on Bazza's farm to improve in condition and sell it on at a profit. I was just getting used to turning to her for advice when she told me that she was leaving Bazza. She just wasn't happy. The next I knew she did a flit, taking some of the children and his furniture with her. She had also sold on some stock before paying for it, leaving a debt that farmers laid at Bazza's door. Bazza simply came home one night to an empty house, no goodbyes no explanation. As you can imagine, he was upset when he told me what had happened. He was left with her debts and an assortment of boys, some at high school, some already working. As I already knew, when you have children you just keep going, and he did too. He disliked farm work because he had been overworked on the farm as the only child of a farmer, but he liked living where he was. His solution was to put beef cattle on his land, as that was the easiest thing for him to farm, while he worked as a mechanic. He was a totally self-taught mechanic and had all the ingenuity of an Aussie cockie. He could fix anything with an axe and a piece of bailing twine. When I complained that my cows were leaning on my fences and getting in wherever I didn't want them, Bazza explained, 'Well, they've nothing else to do all day. If you've got some old hay that you want them to eat best thing to do with it is to put it in the middle of the paddock and put a fence around it. Then the silly buggers'll eat it.' He also warned me that if you have livestock you are going to have deaths, so be prepared. He for-warned me that my fussy city kids would probably not want to eat the beef I was producing.

The waterworks caretaker was also a mine of information and taught me this very elementary fact. 'If you wish to move your animals around your farm, it's best to give them some additional feed in the same place at the same time each day. Then they become accustomed to you and the food. When you want to move them, you arrive at the usual time and place with the food but you don't put it down. You slowly walk, still carrying the feed, into the new paddock and they will follow you. You go right into the paddock before you put down the feed and then you calmly return and close the gate.' I remember how delighted I was the first time I achieved that. I felt I was becoming a farmer.

I met Mr Quipp, a fig farmer and dairy man over an accident. It was his habit to tether calves that he was weaning at the side of the road to nibble on the roadside grass. One of these broke free and ran into the front of my car as I was descending the hill past his house. I wanted recompense for the damage to my car and he wanted recompense for the injured calf which he probably shot and ate. I remember us having very heated words, but I can't remember how we resolved the issue. He and his wife had a large paddock of fig trees. In the season they hired pickers to pick all the figs which she converted into excellent fig jam. This they sold at weekends from their garage. It was a lot of work, especially for her. They had been city dwellers and the farm was his dream. When he died some 15 years later, she had all the fig trees pulled out and simply stocked beef cattle.

Then there was Theo Thompson, who grew many varieties of apples and sold them from his garage, which held a cold room, at weekends. Every Saturday, I would go to buy our apples, it usually took about an hour because he always had some gem of information to impart, tales about the weather, the price of things, and bits of his life history was given away free with every kilogram of apples. His wife used to say, 'If you put a hat on a post he would stop and talk to it.' When he knew I wanted to start a vegetable garden he showed me how he dealt with snails. He picked them up off his lettuces and cabbages and threw them onto the road.

'It's totally organic, I give them a fighting chance, you see. If they can get to the other side before they get run over they deserve to live.' He later visited 'Attention' with a hand-held rotary hoe and ploughed up a big patch of land on which I could start my veggie garden.

At the end of February, I met other neighbours, Max Wiseman and sons, the family who occupied the eastern side of our dirt road rectangle. We had very early opening rains. Warm, wet westerly winds in winter were expected, but this wind sprung from the south-west and felt as if it was blowing off the South Pole. It raged and ripped through the trees and was indiscriminately tearing off branches. This is nature's way of pruning off the weaker branches so that more light can reach the younger saplings beneath.

When I found a bough over the road I would stop and drag it off and onto the grassy bank if I could. I realised that out here on the dirt road, we rely on each other. Whoever comes to a blockage first clears it. It's no use waiting for 'them' to clear the road for you. One day there was a fallen branch over someone's fence. I worked out that it belonged to the dairy people, so I called in on them as I passed the dairy. There were two young men working there.

'Hello, I'm Chris Jancarik, I bought Bazza Smart's cottage. Did you know that there is a large branch over your fence up in the top corner of that paddock?'

'Yes, thanks. Bazza called by a few minutes ago. When Scott and I have finished milking we will take off with a chainsaw and see to it. Thanks for calling in.'

Although Bazza had passed on the intelligence before me, I was registering myself as a caring neighbour and before long I was a regular caller, and like most of the locals, bought my milk there.

Finish the building

Fences and grids were constructed by a variety of workmen. First, there was the fencing contractor who named his price to do the described job and then, when he was halfway through the job, put his price up. We concluded this fiasco in the Small Claims Court and he was ordered to finish the job for the first agreed price.

Then there was a plumber, who had not learned elementary science, or refused to acknowledge it, and told Dad that it was not possible to run pipes from the hot back on the woodstove and the solar panels into the hot water storage tank.

'He is a plumber, Chris, he should know best.'

'I am a Bachelor of Science, Dad! I know how water behaves when it is heated. He just has to put incoming pipes at the bottom and outgoing pipes at the top. He does not know more just because he is a man! Why bother to educate a girl if you will not listen to her!'

I was really angry. So, he talked to the plumber again and they decided that he could put in enough pipes to accommodate both the solar heater and the wood stove heater. What a clever plumber.

Another troublesome worker was Mr Roko, hired to build retaining walls. He was a very good stonemason, but from the outset I told him that I could only afford $400, so please build the walls within this budget. He replied that he worked for a set rate per hour, so when he reaches $400 he will stop. When he reached that point he stopped and asked for his cash. There was still one wall missing. I could not afford more and he would not work for any less than his stated price. Paul came to the rescue. He finished the job. Nowhere near Mr R's standard, but job done!

CARE FOR YOUR ANIMALS

I wanted livestock immediately. I bought Foxy, Jet and Silver, an assortment of coloured sheep for fleece, then a few 'ration' sheep for our own meat supply. I learnt how to cut feet, give injections, crutch the filthy back ends of sheep, castrate male lambs and to recognise the dopey look of a fly-struck sheep. In the process of my learning, a couple of the ration sheep died of flystrike. Shearing and dipping was a hassle because we had to take the sheep to a shearer in the car and then physically dip them in a bath of sheep dip.

By the way, if you ever need to transport a live sheep in the back of your car or ute, you will need to lay the animal on its back and tie its legs together. The real trick to this is to tie the font two legs together and then add one, and only one, of its back legs to the leg-bundle. If you tie all four legs the sheep will panic and kick and struggle, but if you tie only three it will lie still.

Two full grown brown cows were purchased—Mama and Big Sister. One of them was 'coming in' the farmer said, so they were a bargain. When Mama delivered a black and white calf we called her Panda, and realised what 'coming in' meant.

Erica was given a feral doe goat called Flopsy, which was happy to join the cows and seemed to think of herself as a cow. In due course, Flopsy was taken to meet an angora ram and in the fullness of time she produced twin kids. Goats can be very troublesome because they can tiptoe over grids and will eat anything. To prevent this, we tried tethering them, but when one of the kids strangled itself with its chain Erica decided that she would give up animal husbandry. She gave Flopsy away and recouped her stud fees by selling the remaining kid.

Kathy had a horse. She saved hard so that she could buy equipment to use him at The Pony Club. When we found out how much it cost for worming, shoeing, supplementary feed and the pony club, we were dismayed. Her $35 a week pocket money would be easily consumed by the horse. Nevertheless, the horse stayed.

I planted some young trees of the fruits not already represented in our orchard. These were mulched and each was surrounded by a strong wire guard to keep the animals off. Every tree had to be protected by a tree guard which had to be continually repaired because the cows used them as back-scratchers, and as Bazza had said, anything inside a fence is more delicious and tempting to our four-legged friends than whatever is available on their side of the fence.

It was beautiful, organised chaos.

CHAPTER 37

HOW TO SETTLE INTO A COUNTRY PROPERTY PART TWO

DO YOUR JOB WELL

We relied on my income as a teacher at Meadows Primary School where I taught a class of Years 3, 4 and 5 students. Yes, the school was so small that there were only 3 classes. Harry Ruggles taught Years 6 and 7, so Erica spent two years in his class. Miss Penny Little taught the preps, with Grades 1 and 2, and we had the luxury of a headmaster, Jack Sames. Each morning, I drove Kathy, Paul, Erica and sundry Smarts and Williams children to the McLaren Flat Post office, where high school students, including Kathy and Paul, caught their school busses, while the younger children stayed on board for the trip to Meadows Primary. In the evening, while reversing the procedure, I could pick up my mail and any grocery items that I needed because the post office was also a general store. The post office staff knew all the local gossip, which they willingly passed on with the mail. The grapevine was as reliable as the post. I realised that I had to keep my amorous adventures in the city or I would soon become the subject of local gossip, a scarlet woman!

KEEP YOUR CHILDREN IN LINE!

My children, aged 15, 13 and 11, were not exactly under my control. Paul would shrug off my requests for work in his relaxed way. 'Yeah, yeah, I'll get around to it when I can.' His attitude was the initiation of the fireplace incident. Kathy would throw tantrums when she disliked my instructions and Erica, although she was quietly obedient, worried me the most because I was sure that she was up to something behind my back. In fact, we had a joke about my control: *'One word from me and they all do exactly as they like!'*

The fireplace incident went like this. A feature of the front lounge was to

Chapter 37 *How to settle into a country property part two*

be an open fireplace set in a rough sandstone wall. I bought a 'heat form', a special device that surrounded the open fire, trapped the hot air and recycled it into the room rather than allowing it to go up the chimney. Dad knocked out the stones from the wall to accommodate the heat form and roughly put stones back around it. However, the rest of the wall, although built of the local sandstone, was still plastered and this old plaster had to be removed before we could have the whole wall grouted to give it a neatly finished stone wall effect. I chipped away at that plaster for an hour each night while the kids did homework or looked on. Eventually, I became angry with the large teenage boy sitting and watching in his usual relaxed attitude.

'You could help me, you lazy lump, instead of just lounging around watching!'

'Okay,' was Paul's angry reaction. He took up a sledgehammer.

Wham! Bang! Wallop!

He swung the sledgehammer over his head and bought it crashing against the old plaster which cracked and crumbled and flew about while the whole wall shook. A monster had been unleashed. Frustrations were taken out on that wall. In five minutes, most of the remaining plaster lay on the floor.

'There! Happy now?' he demanded, as he threw down the sledgehammer.

'Marvellous. Now I only have to remove the bits around the edge.'

Kathy and I had loud emotional arguments. One night she stormed out into the dark night to get away from me and, naturally, I was worried. I went to Paul who was already in bed.

'Paul, please get up. Kathy has stormed out into the night and I'm worried about her. Please go and get her in.'

'Oh, Mum, she'll come back, don't worry. She'll get cold and want her warm bed. Just leave her out there and go to bed.'

A few minutes of thought made me realise the wisdom of his attitude. If we showed our concern by going after her, she could lead us a merry chase. If I left her in the cold she might come to regret fighting with me and being so melodramatic. So, I went to bed and the ploy worked.

Erica, not be out done by her siblings, did create one major problem at a most inconvenient time. Meadows Primary School took their senior students away on a one week bus tour and camp every other year. Both Erica and I were to participate. The tour was to be taken in the north of South Australia. It would include Port Augusta, Silverton, The School of the Air, and the Flinders Ranges. It was an eye-opening education for these children of dairy farmers and apple growers. The parents' livelihoods were cleverly used to bring costs down. All parents were asked to contribute to help feed the party. Boxes of apples, litres of milk, cheese, a side of lamb, home grown vegies, homemade cakes were dropped off to school in the days prior to our departure so our quartermaster could plan our menu around these gifts and buy a few groceries to complete the food store. Erica and I would be fed for a week, but I spent the weekend cooking and freezing meals for Kathy and Paul to defrost and use while we were away.

Suddenly Erica rushed into the kitchen with a horrified expression on her face.

'Oh Mum! I've swallowed a pin!'

'Oh my goodness!' was my panicked response, or words to that effect, and were followed by comments about her limited intelligence! 'How did you do that?'

'I was just sewing a dart into my shorts. I took the pin out of my shorts and held it in my mouth while I finished off the job. I went to bite the end of the thread and oops I swallowed the pin.'

'Well, thank Heavens we have an uncle who's a doctor. We can get this seen to immediately. You will probably have to go into hospital and miss the camp.'

She found this more distressing than the internal pin. After a trip to Jan's surgery and an x-ray, we came home with the advice that she should eat cotton wool soaked with honey. She could still go on the camp and we just had to wait for the trouble to pass. Another x-ray would be taken when we returned from the camp to determine if she still had the problem. Keeping a watchful eye on her throughout the camp distracted me somewhat from enjoying the outing. However, the follow-up x-ray revealed that the problem had passed without damage to Erica.

Working as a teacher was my means of keeping us afloat financially, which meant that I could not be *the little woman*, attending to cleaning, laundry, shopping and taxiing, so the kids each had home duties over and above what most children of their age had to do. As compensation, they had a private tutor/slave/driver at their disposal.

Erica judged the distribution of labour as usual with, 'It's not fair! It's not fair that Kathy and I have to do the washing and housework! Paul doesn't!'

Paul's angry response was, 'I have to help with all the blasted farm work! So don't you complain!'

And that's not the only issue that drew her ire.

'It's not fair that girls have to have periods. Why can't *they* have them instead?'

'Some things cannot be changed,' I replied. 'We just have to put up with them.'

Her 'It's not fair!' eventually drew a different response from me.

'Life isn't fair, Erica! Just get used to it!'

Paul, Kathy and Erica all attended school for our first year. Paul, however, insisted that he had no interest in school and just wanted to be a motor mechanic. Being a motor mechanic was not a career I wanted for my son. Surely, he could do better than that! After much arguing, he finally persuaded me to let him become an apprentice, but I thought that he would soon discover that it was not to his liking and that he would want something else. I could not let him leave school and become a drifter, so I mustered up all my strength of character to say, 'If I let you do this, I will not tolerate a change of mind. If you start, this you must see it through! You must become a qualified tradesman.'

When he first went to work, I really felt sorry for him. He had to leave the house at about 7 am, dressed in his heavy work boots and overalls, as the rest of us were just waking up. He folded himself into his Mini for the drive to the far side of Adelaide. He returned utterly exhausted at about 5 pm. This little boy of mine had been keeping school hours only the previous week. To his credit, despite many unhappy incidents, he served his four years and grew from a boy to a young man.

An important project that the children helped to build was our 200,000 gallon water tank to serve as our main water reservoir. It would be situated on the hill behind the house. Water would be pumped up to it from the small tank collecting rainwater from the house roof. Gravity would feed water to the house. It was David's plan and consisted of a cement base with uprights around the circumference, a metre apart. Fencing wire was then wound around these up rights. Close to the bottom where the water pressure would be greatest, the wires were very close together and their distance apart increased with height. Then all was clad in chicken-wire. The children and I did all the wiring. Finally, the cylinder was rendered inside and out with cement. This took a cementing specialist like Toni. He had done several cementing jobs for us. Toni trusted cement more than he trusted the wire framework, so he put in twice the recommended amount of cement to build that rainwater tank.

During all this building his wife was in hospital, and he begged me for the occasional date. He overcame my 'No married men!' rule because we knew it was to be a secret one-off affair due to his circumstances, and he was being very generous towards me with his work. Unfortunately, she was kept in hospital for longer than anticipated. On one cold winter night while we were still living in the back room doing homework, he visited, asking me to take a car ride with him. I was most reluctant.

'I cannot leave the children just like that!'

'Don't worry, Mum, I'm here!' chirped up Paul, who had been listening. He clearly understood what was meant by a car ride. The pair of them persuaded me that everything would be fine. My 15-year-old son had apparently joined the men's club and was sympathetic to a fellow sufferer. When I returned home the house was quiet, homework finished, children in bed. There was not a mention of my absence the next morning, we just rushed around as usual getting off to school.

Keep your old friends

My Beta Sigma Phi membership continued. I served on the city council and attempted to form new chapters. Not always successfully. On one occasion after a new chapter had failed, I announced my failure to council and

Chapter 37 — *How to settle into a country property part two*

recounted where I had gone wrong. During the tea break a member came up to me and said that my announcement and admission of fault was an admirable character trait which had endeared and elevated me in her opinion.

How I had the energy for all this, I do not know. I can only say I was young and silly. I turned 40 in the first year of our residence at 'Attention' and that was celebrated with a large party. I invited all my neighbours, all my Beta Sigma Phi girlfriends and husbands, all my current boyfriends. It was a beautiful party, and the rafters rang.

CHAPTER 38

FRIENDS AND LOVERS

I went on dates in the city and sometimes stayed out all night. Mum thought that I should tell the kids that I was staying with them, but I decided against the notion. They would eventually find out and I did not want them to feel deceived. I did not concoct stories and they did not ask questions, we all just accepted each other for what we were without being judgemental.

Because of my brother-in-law Jan's generous, company-loving nature, and Anne's inability to curb and direct this aspect of his temperament, their home was like a hotel at weekends. Happy friends were entertained to barbecues, drinks and an endless stream of dirty jokes and gossip about other friends by the head of the household, accompanied by brief but noisy interjections from his spouse.

I visited one Sunday afternoon and while the children played up on the hill, the chops sizzled and the brandy flowed, I was entertained by Anne with a recital of the events of the previous day.

'Remember Sally? You met her and Bruce a few years ago. Sally was visiting again and Bruce had come on a wooing visit. However, he had met and been quite taken by Carol. Yes, Carol, the co-respondent in your divorce. Well, you know how petite and attractive and what a man-trap she can be. Sally, in a jealous huff, took off on Jan's most spirited horse in a dramatic bid for attention and was thrown off just a little way down the drive. Bruce did the gallant thing and rushed down to pick her up and carried her back to the house for medical attention. Jan deemed her unbroken but possibly concussed. Bruce carried her to bed, kissed her with a 'sleep tight' and shut the door. She was left alone to listen to the continual merrymaking in the lounge and to imagine how superlatively her beau was being won by Carol's flirtatious eyes.'

Chapter 38   *Friends and Lovers*

Sally visited Adelaide when she could, but this could not be every weekend. I was not surprised to find her beau drinking alone in Jan and Anne's lounge one weekend. I was waiting for Jan to discuss a family matter and decided to wait inside rather than join the inevitable party around the barbecue. Bruce started to talk to me. We spoke in generalities, but he gradually swung the conversation to myself and began singing my praises and moving closer. I was stunned, my thoughts running wild.

This extremely attractive youth was making verbal passes at me! He was lonely for Sally and tipsy. He didn't know what he was saying. Such rosy adamant phrases must stem from some positive feeling towards me. I had done nothing to provoke his attention.

I decided to put a stop to this. 'Hold on there, boy. We've hardly spoken more than three sentences to each other!'

Too late, she cried, I thought, as gentle but firm arms entrapped me and I was being kissed to stop my protestations. I pushed him away.

'This is all very flattering, but you're at least ten years my junior, and I'd be highly embarrassed if anyone should walk in on such a scene, especially my children who are just outside.'

'Bugger them, it's you I'm interested in, so soft and warm and lovable.' His words were merely covering for his arms, hands and lips which were wielded skilfully and seductively. There was clarity in his actions that his words could never express. I was being swept away by him like a cork in a tidal wave.

It was delightful, but it had to stop! I had not been flirting with him.

At that moment, Anne passed through the lounge, travelling from kitchen to barbecue. I looked at her for help. This was her guest. I had to be rescued. She must've noticed my look of mingled pleasure and embarrassment, as I extracted myself from him saying, 'What can be done with him?'

She merely smiled back and said, 'Enjoy yourself.'

I was very ruffled, yet growing more attracted to this sexually powerful man, but I could not permit myself to be embarrassed in front of my children. The sweep of his advance had been interrupted and I managed to become indignant and pointed out that he was tipsy, that this was virtually a public place and thought it best that we forget the incident. He smilingly shrugged and withdrew to his neglected beer. Although he physically moved away, he smiled and said, 'Some other time.'

Eventually, I managed to get time with Jan. He had been left in control of the children's trust fund. Both Carol and I had to go a-begging if we were in financial straits. I'm sure that Xav had instructed his brother, 'Don't let Chris or Carol get their hands on this money! It is for the children. The more they take, the less there is left for my dying gift!'

That was all well and good, but Carol and I had to feed, clothe and generally care for his children, at least until they were 18 and could inherit his precious gift. This time it was shoes for the children that were giving me anxiety. Jan finally decided to give me $40 per month and I still had to negotiate when other expenses came along.

But Bruce ... he didn't leave my thoughts.

Paul went on a trip to Coober Pedy with Jan and a pack of his drinking buddies over Easter. I was worried by the drinking and driving situation. I leapt up when the phone rang.

'Chris?' The deep, warm and friendly voice was unmistakable.

'Well, what can I do for you?' I answered, attempting a handoff, business-like sarcasm in my tone.

'I'm bringing Paul home for you.'

'Are you sober?'

'As a judge.'

'Well, thank you then, I'll be grateful. It'll save me a trip. I'll wait tea till you get home.'

'See you.'

'Cheerio.'

Wow! I thought. This could be exciting. I planned to make the best of it. The meal must be good, but not ostentatious. I must look attractive but not dressed up. The children must not know how elated I feel. He must not know how elated I am.

I hugged my boy as soon as they came in, while over his head the man with the blue eyes smiled at me.

'Is this some other time?' Bruce asked.

Chapter 38 *Friends and Lovers*

'Yes.'

A noisy happy family meal with adventures recounted followed, then dishes were washed and children packed off to bed.

Finally, peace, finally, and I was sinking, floating, swimming, carried away by a forceful, youthful lover. We both realised that we revelled in a lusty pleasure of hearty physical attraction. In the warmth of the afterglow cuddles we talked more freely. I praised his technique and self-control which had extended our mutual bliss, for I was beginning to realise that it takes talent, intelligence and consideration to make a really enjoyable lover. We told each other of our first encounters. When he was seven years old, his older sisters, anxious to improve their knowledge of male physiology, had taken him in hand and played with him to his great delight. The resulting sibling intimacy led to frank exchanges about what pleased each sex. So, from the tender age of seven his knowledge of this two-sided pleasure had been building.

'Young women are silly. They hold off from sex as a means of getting a man harnessed. They are not such fun to be with as a more mature woman.'

Fortunately, I was regarding this encounter as a purely sexual adventure. Had it been otherwise, I was being told where I stood.

Our parting conversation was, 'I'll come again, Chrissie. Now, you be good while I'm away.'

'Don't be silly. I don't make such demands of you, so you may not make them of me. But I'll be glad to see you again, you're terrific.'

A few weeks later I visited Jan's bacchanal again. Sally was there. She was on the brink of tears. 'Please come outside, I must talk to you.'

If she wants to accuse me it would be best done in private, so I'll hear her outside.

As we walked through the cold soggy paddocks, wind swirled about us. She unburdened her heart to me. 'That bitch Carol has got him! We've written to each other and things were mending between us so I thought I'd visit again. They've gone! They borrowed or stole the red convertible that Jan was lending her. Taken her children and gone to the Northern Territory. Chris, he knew I was coming. How could he prefer such a slut to me? She stole your husband, didn't she? Some women will stop at nothing. What shall I do?'

And so she raged on and on, only needing a sympathetic ear. It would not have helped her to tell about his other adventures. Her heart was broken. She was betrayed, she was rejected. Her pride was injured.

'Some men are easily led,' I consoled her. 'It's better to find out now before you marry him.'

'Yes, you're right.'

'Chin up, then. There are plenty more fish in the sea for a young attractive girl like you.'

A little more walking and talking and the only tears left were those that the wind was whipping into the sides of our eyes.

Jan had the police recover his car and the affair was short lived. Carol and her children hitched a ride back to Adelaide, leaving him working as a barman. He liked the warmth of Darwin.

Spring was returning. There were fewer cold, wet westerlies. Sunshine encouraged the grass to grow rapidly. There was no more need to feed hay to the cows.

On my way home from the general store one Saturday morning, a lumbering, rock-carrying truck approached. I glanced up to salute the driver as was the country habit.

'Bruce!' I looked back. He had pulled off the road and was leaping down from the cabin. He raced back as I pulled off the road. I emerged from the car to be picked up and hugged and whirled around 'Great to see you. What have you been up to?' He gave me a quick resume of the jobs and girls that had tumbled through his life in the last few months and then said, 'We must go out next weekend. I will call around one night so we can make plans. See ya!'

He was sprinting off to the truck again and I wondered, *How long he will be here this time? Hey ho, enjoy him while he's here.*

And yes, he visited and yes, we went out. We giggled and messed around during some senseless movie, it was juvenile behaviour. Blame it on the bottle of rough red we consumed with those delightfully rare oversized steaks in some cheap barbecue place on Hindley Street. He was fun. Stupid, but fun. He visited us often through the spring and summer. He would watch a bit of telly with us, tell us about his latest job: driving, potato picking, hay carting, fencing, on the dole, labouring for a builder, then he would tease my girls over some trivia, and arm wrestle with Paul. He was almost part of the family, like a noisy big brother returning home to liven us up from time to time. But when they went to bed, so did we. We were no longer just a clumsy lad and a middle-aged mum, but a man and a woman who could grant each other bliss of the highest degree. At one stage he almost lived in. He was on the dole and did a few jobs for us, not that it didn't come with a few issues.

'Running a farm is not really a job for a woman and three children!' he would say. He built an incinerator and a compost area and mended a few fences. He certainly fulfilled a few needs for me. I almost asked him to stay.

Almost? Why not?

Well, to put it bluntly, beer. Local lads who could afford booze would drive their jalopies to a spot by the river a few kilometres past our place. 'Drunken Dip' I think they called it. There they would drink and yarn and drink themselves paralytic. They made themselves physically sick, sometimes for a few days. I could never understand such blatant masochism. On his return to sobriety, we discussed this quirk in his nature. But, try as I may, I could not understand or sympathise with this need he had for male companionship of this type so heavily loaded with booze. I would usually conclude my little tirade with, 'If you can't enjoy each other's company without being pissed it doesn't say much for the relationship.'

He only visited me once while under the influence and although I cherished his friendship I had to be absolutely resolute in my refusal of his amorous advances. Drunken lovers are repulsive to me. They are frightening because their strength could be uncontrolled and behaviour unreasonable.

Although sorely tempted, I would never ask him to stay permanently and he would never ask to stay. We understood. We had pleasure together, but we knew our characters, backgrounds and goals were miles apart. Eventually, the days grew short again and so did his casual jobs, so he headed north like a migratory bird. And like a migratory bird he returned with the spring and visited our lives occasionally. I think my children liked him more than any of my dates, probably because he would fool around with all of them, just like a big kid. He rarely took me out. I think he would have found it as difficult to explain to me his drinking mates as it was to explain drinking to me.

The time for the Compass Cup was approaching.

Bruce intended to participate with his football team and suggested that I take the kids for the day out to see this unique event. It takes place at Mount Compass and is the only Cow Race in Australia. There was fairy floss, watermelon, barbecues, beer, pony rides, calf races and finally The Cow Race.

Early in the day, each cow was auctioned to the various visiting football clubs. Then, at 3 pm, each team put up one jockey and three urgers, all suitably inebriated. They could exchange roles as necessary. How the cow was moved from start to finish was their business, but one of the team had to be jockey, in position, as she crossed the finishing line. Dairy cows can be cooperative and regular as clockwork when it comes to strolling to the dairy at milking time, but as obstinate as mules when it comes to a race. Much urging, falling off and remounting was necessary. A surge of action by a cow for two or three yards would be followed by a tug-of-war accompanied by colourful Australian language for a few minutes. Each cow would stop at different spots, so the action was all over the field. Finally, one cow got fed up with the whole affair and took off with her jockey and urgers in hot pursuit. They tossed a jockey onto her back as she crossed the line and the thousand dollars was won by the Euchunga Urgers! The teams laughingly returned their cows to the stalls and went back to their team tents for more anaesthetic to soothe their bruised bodies.

'Are those men going to drive home in that state?' Erica asked. 'Bruce could be killed in a car smash if he goes around with blokes like them.'

'Yes dear, that's the chance he's prepared to take.'

You never really dwell on throwaway comments like that. A few weeks later I heard on the grapevine that he had died in a car crash. I didn't pry into the details. I knew that he was dearly loved by his family and I was not an integral part of his life.

Chapter 38   *Friends and Lovers*

Keith Tylor I met through an agency. He was a man looking to make a fresh start. He was interesting because he was a reformed alcoholic. There was a roughness about him and his appearance that accompanies a life of too much drinking and smoking. But he had found Jesus, who had helped him to change his ways. He attended his AA meetings and was feeling the health benefits of abstinence. Now he wanted a lady in his life, but living in Port Adelaide meant he was repeatedly meeting women who fitted his old lifestyle. I was not the lady for him, but I could not tell him that I was now an atheist and my reasons for turning so. Jesus had done the trick for him and I could not be so cruel as to remove the main prop that was keeping him sober and happy. We became platonic friends and he visited 'Attention' a few times. He thought the home and property were lovely and found a way to help around the house. He was a painter by trade and set about painting all our internal doors. Eventually, he found the lady he had been looking for and had no more spare time to visit us. Good on you, Keith! I hope Jesus keeps on working for you.

I maintained my membership in Beta Sigma Phi by attending meetings of my old chapter in the northern suburbs. It was a long journey to make twice a month, but these were a wonderful group of women of varying backgrounds and attitudes whose company I enjoyed and whose advice I frequently took. Amorous adventures were not related at meetings because I knew I would offend some members.

However, there was Ann, yes, she of the explosive Party back in Para Hills. We were both single ladies having similar adventures. My dad called her The Captain. If a new situation arose he would ask, 'What does The Captain say about that?'

'Don't screw the workman until the job is finished!' was one of her favourites. Another was, 'I wouldn't know where to start!' She used this when asked to do a job (usually of a handyman nature).

I could not use this line as often as her, because I was frequently alone on the farm and a job just had to be done. Consequently, I thought it necessary to learn how to change a wheel on the car should I get a puncture in some remote spot. Fortunately, my flats always happened on bitumen and although I immediately set to work with jack and nut spanner, I must praise the gallantry of local farmers by telling you that I never completed the job unaided.

Not all my friends were lovers. Some were families like the Smarts and the Tothills. I loved and respected them as a couple, besides I had a 'no married men' policy. Even some single men remained just friends.

The Smart family, Tessa and Frank, was Meadows 'high society'. When they met he was a dairyman and she a teacher fresh from college. They had the intelligence and the ability and the local knowledge to work out a plan to prosperity. They bought a dairy which involved working early and late in the day and enabled them both to have a day job as well. Money accrued and was invested into land, beef cattle and beef futures. When I met them they had two lovely daughters at the Meadows Primary School. Meredith was in my class and Elizabeth in Erica's. Elizabeth became a lifelong friend of Erica's. I encouraged her to have sleepovers and other visits to the Smarts. I wanted her to see what normal family life was like. As a consequence, I was also invited and we spent a couple of weekends at their remote cattle property, Yungaburra. Here, I saw how they rounded up their cattle using a car or motorbike. They had recently built a luxury house on their Meadows property with a large indoor swimming pool and spa. He was the only person I knew who did not seek tax minimalisation. He thought the tax system perfectly fair and just and willingly made his contribution to government coffers.

I met the Tothills on parent visiting night and discovered that they lived the lifestyle I emulated. They were almost self-sufficient on a small acreage. Mrs T stayed at home, and spun and knitted the fleece from their flock of coloured sheep. She baked for the local market and did preserves and jam for their own use and for sale. He worked, so there was some regular income, and he was the handyman to keep the farm in good repair. I supported their enterprise by commissioning chocolate-coloured jumpers for Erica and Kathy and enough homespun wool for me to knit myself a jumper. There, at least, we looked the part even if we were far from self-sufficiency. Mum and Dad saw what my aim was and bought me a Fowlers preserving outfit and helped me to put down preserves as well.

These settling in years were very busy. Later, I managed to halve my time in the classroom by finding another primary schoolteacher prepared to share-teach with me. Jack, the headmaster, disapproved but bore it for one year. At the end of that year, he pointed out that I was much more suited to high school teaching and that there was vacancy at McLaren Vale High for a Science/Maths teacher. I applied and was successful.

Thanks, Jack. It was a win-win move for us both. I could confidently move on. I had regained myself. I had overcome the pain of loss and was rebuilding the real me.

CHAPTER 39

MY MAN PAUL

One summer in the early eighties, Marilyn and David Farmer invited me to lunch and because it was school holidays their three children were there too. I noted how although they were the same age as my independent mob, they still behaved as children. They maintained the picture that one holds dear of a normal family around their lunch table, telling each other of their latest adventures, but always deferring to their parents.

My children were a pleasure and a pain, they were maturing and being more outspoken. They hated the health drink that I made for them daily, calling it 'yucky stuff.' The girls attended to our laundry and house-cleaning while Paul helped me with the farm. On a typical Sunday, I started with lighting the woodstove and cooking Paul an English breakfast. I then put on a joint to roast, and Paul and I went outside for a day's work. We attended to the fencing, cleaning out the chicken shed and sheep shed, any new project that I had in mind and eventually, when I learned how, prepared vegetable beds. I thought that 'Attention' would look so much nicer if we had native eucalypts growing alongside our long driveway. Sheep and cows have no such aesthetic appreciation. Food had to be protected from them, so we needed tree guards. This would be an added expense. However, when I took our rubbish to the dump each month I noticed that some useful materials were being discarded by other farmers. What was too short a length of barbed wire or sheep mesh for them to use in a long fence was perfect for a tree guard. So, over time, it seemed that I brought back from the dump almost as much as I took in. I invested in a drip system for native and fruit trees and installed old baths as drinking troughs in two paddocks. When it grew dark, we finished, tidied up and came inside to complete and eat the roast dinner. Paul lit the fire and we sat by the telly to watch 'The Muppet Show' followed by a Sunday night movie. The kids would slip away to bed when they felt tired. I relaxed and slid blissfully to sleep where I sat. But it was all bearing fruit. We had a side of beef and a hogget butchered and packaged in our deep freezer.

I employed a professional fencer to upgrade several fences and I worked out a system with the butcher whereby he kept offal and skins in exchange for slaughtering and butchering sheep.

Early each year, a neighbour's bull visited my herd of five mature cows. When the neighbour came for his bull, he also drenched my cows. I decided to try to stick to this routine annually. Five healthy calves all looking like their father were born to my hotch-potch herd of dairy cows. By using the combination of dairy cow and Hereford bull, we produce beefy calves which were well looked after by their dairy mothers.

The light appeared at the end of the sheep tunnel. Beautiful sturdy lambs were born each spring. I 'marked them myself. When summer brought on the shearing, I found a shearer who would shear a small flock at the weekend in his own shed. This meant that I could be present to skirt and bag my own fleeces, even though we had the problem of dipping. This we solved by yarding the shorn sheep and spraying them heavily with sheep dip. It took the entire family but we managed.

School and the apprenticeship seemed to be going well for the kids, but it was extracurricular activities that worried me, like boyfriends and marijuana. I was so worried that I turned to my source of wisdom, my father.

'I really don't know what to do, Dad. One word from me and they do exactly as they like! How can I control or guide them? I really feel like just abandoning any idea of parental guidance.'

'No, Chris, you must not give up on them. You are the parent. It is your responsibility to talk seriously to them. You must deal with each one individually. You must sit them down and say something to this effect, "Please listen carefully to what I am about to say. I am only going to say it once because I don't think repetitious nagging has any effect. You are really taking a wrong turn when you do this or that and if you continue, you will slip into a very bad habit or get a reputation for being something nasty that I know you are not. Such a reputation will be hard to shake off, so give it some serious thought. I have told you now. I have given you my opinion. If you continue to behave in this way it will be your own fault. You must take responsibility for yourself because I cannot be with you all the time to guide your decisions and interests".'

It was good advice. 'Thank you, Dad,' I said. 'I will use your advice to give it another try.'

I had those serious talks with each of my children. There was no obvious immediate change, but I think they each began to take responsibility for themselves. Didn't we all?

Paul was a motor mechanic apprentice and happy with what he was learning. He had dates with girls and talked with me about them in an open, frank way. We also conferred about our motor vehicle situation, and heaven knows I needed someone to help me decide what to do in that department. I had swapped my new Toyota with Dad's old Ford as a 'thank you' for all the work he had done on the house, and because it seemed a shame to age my new car prematurely by driving it over our rough dirt roads, so it remained his on paper but mine in fact. However, the Ford always seemed to need some major repair. I couldn't sell it while it had a major fault so Paul fixed it, then once it was fixed I just kept on driving it.

'What we need, Mum, is an old farm ute. We need an extra vehicle for emergencies and with my current knowledge I can keep an old car running.' That was good advice from my teenage man. We could use the ute for farm chores. Later, he said, 'Mum, the old Ford is dying again. There is only so much I can do without giving it a complete, expensive overhaul. It is not worth what it's insured for. We really need another smaller sedan for getting you three to the school bus stop and for your trips to town. Do you think Uncle Jan will advance you some money?'

I snorted. 'No way! That would be helping me personally and your dad's money is designated for children's use only. Am I right in thinking that what we could get for the insurance would be enough for a small sedan in working order?'

'Probably,' he admitted.

Chapter 39   *My Man Paul*

'And we always leave the keys in the cars overnight to make for a smoother take off in the morning,' I mused, an idea coming to me.

'I reckon most farmers do that and every now and again cars do get stolen from country properties,' added Paul.

We exchanged a significant glance. 'Best we don't let the girls know that we've had this discussion,' I told him. 'If the Ford is stolen and wrecked it'll be a big surprise to all of us.'

When it was stolen, we had to go to the school bus stop in the old ute and Dad had to report its theft to the police because it was his car on paper. He was most distressed, but he did claim the insurance and we were able to buy a secondhand, four-cylinder sedan which Paul continued to maintain, thus keeping our head just above water as far as cars were concerned.

He really was becoming the man of the house. I remember one evening we came home to find a very shaggy ewe had fallen into the underground well. To rescue her, Paul had to reach over the well. He had to lean so far over that we had to hold onto his feet. He grabbed the saturated animal by the fleece and hauled her out. What strength and effort that took!

Later, when Paul had struck out into the big wide world and was living in a share house with some mates, he appeared at home on his birthday with a bottle of wine. We spent the evening with the bottle, talking like old friends. He told me of his experiences with housemates. He was learning how unreliable young men can be. He was appalled by one lad who had to be spoken to very firmly because he ate other people's supplies from the fridge.

Then, he dropped the bomb on me, please could I appear in court with him over a traffic infringement.

'It looks better if you have a mother! They go easier on you,' he insisted.

We chatted on about cementing jobs needed on the farm and the inevitable car maintenance. Then came the birthday present, since I had bought him nothing, so why not forgive his current debt? Yes, he had been borrowing off me, just as I was always borrowing from Dad. The difference was I repaid my debt before asking for the next loan. Naturally, mellowed by the wine and the amusing conversation, I forgave the debt.

I often mused on my treatment of my son over the years.

Why do I feel that I owe Paul something over and above what I owe the girls? Is it because he suffered most through the divorce? Is it because he's a boy, the Oedipus effect? Is it because being a male he takes longer to establish himself and get his life in order?

Or did I just like being needed?

CHAPTER 40

KATHY THE COUNTRY GIRL

Kathy had a gelding and was given a young mare. I saw a not-to-be-repeated deal. An Appaloosa stallion was about to 'stand' for stud, but he was offered at a reduced rate during his first year to prove himself. The stud fee was still expensive, so I offered it to her as two Christmas presents. For the first Christmas, I would pay the stud fee and we would take the mare to stud. For the second Christmas, all being well, she would receive the foal. She took out books from the school library about delivering foals, which worried me, because she kept telling me about the possible complications and how she would deal with them. Fortunately, we came home from school one evening to see a leggy foal gradually stand beside his mother. Kathy did not need to intervene. We just gazed at the little miracle. It was a colt, which incurred another fee for he had to be gelded for everyone's safety. She called him Zardos.

I was amazed to see how she played and trained that lovely foal. He ran with her around the paddock like a puppy with a small child. He was so frisky I was afraid she would collect a careless kick but that never happened. As he grew, she would lean against him and sometimes put a blanket on his back. He did not mind. The affection was mutual. She gradually introduced him to a halter and of course the day came when I looked out to see her riding him. Wow! Kathy has broken in a horse! She also realised that the expenses incurred by three horses were too great for a schoolgirl budget. Something had to go. She dealt with the problem herself by selling off all the horses, except Zardos.

The farm progressed in a less haphazard way because McLaren Vale High School had an Agricultural Department with serious agricultural experts teaching there. I could take problems as they occurred to the men in this department and always came away with sound advice. They taught me tailing and castrating by the knife. I worked out an efficient way of butchering chickens alone.

Our main hassle was the small, leaky, dilapidated chicken shed. It had to be cleaned out regularly. We kept the chooks on a deep litter of sawdust. Shovelling wet, stinking sawdust from a shed in which we could not stand upright was no joke. We didn't even know what to do with the mess once it was out, so we left it in smelly mounds over what was going to be the garden. I tried to start a garden. The soil was hard and weeds abounded, especially dock and couch. Gardening books confused me. So much super, lime and urea should be dug in six weeks before planting. So much blah, blah, on planting and even more chemicals added as each plant grows. The Agricultural chaps at school recommended that I go to a course called 'Organic Gardening' which was given by the Soil Association. As a result, I learnt a lot and joined the Soil Association so that I could continue to learn at their monthly meetings. Finally, I knew how to use that heap of chicken mess and the garden was launched.

When she was in Year 11 at high school, Kathy broke her Achilles tendon. The cure was rest with an elevated foot. While the rest of us rushed off to school or work, she reclined happily on the sofa with instructions to do schoolwork and to hop over to the kitchen to get lunch or drinks for herself.

While she was indisposed, I can't remember checking what work she did. We were a busy crew. When we arrived home we scoffed bread and jam to give us energy to do the evening jobs. When Kathy had her leg in plaster there was one less hand on deck for the jobs. Then I prepared the evening meal, did my lesson preparation for the next day, while the children did their homework.

By the time third term rolled around, her schoolwork was slipping behind and she was developing a lackadaisical attitude toward school which she hid from me.

One evening she made a request.

'Mum, can you come up to the school and try to persuade the deputy to let me drop History? I'm not getting on with Miss Juet, she is a bitch and always picking on me. If I dropped her subject, I could have more time for my other more important subjects.'

It sounded very reasonable to me. Kathy was inclined towards the sciences, so dropping History did not seem like much of a loss.

'This will mean I have to take time off from school. I'll talk to the head about it and see if I can make an appointment with your Deputy.'

Everyone was co-operative. After all, Year 11 is the run-up to Year 12, matriculation year, and a mother is justifiably concerned with her daughter's success at this critical stage.

'Mrs Jancarik, we are so glad that you could come,' said the deputy as he ushered me into his study, where two teachers had already gathered. After I had been introduced to the History bitch and the class teacher lamb, he looked at me very sternly and said, 'We need to talk about Kathy's work and behaviour.'

I was shocked to the core by what I heard. Kathy was not working; she was flippant and careless. I could only reply that the Kathy I knew was hard-working and diligent and that I was anticipating great things from her.

'Unfortunately, you are misled, Mrs Jancarik. The probable outcome for her is that she will be promoted to our internal Year 12 class next year, which means she will not sit the matriculation exams at the end of the year.'

Wow! What a come down!

'No! no! This is not Kathy. She is a very bright girl. She will be going to university. She is destined to a brilliant career!' I insisted.

'I'm afraid not. It's Year 12 Internal for her.' My brain was in a whirl. There had to be a way around this impasse. I finally came up with a different scenario.

'What if she repeats Year 11? I will see to it that she works. With better results she will progress to the matriculation class the year after that.'

'The department policy is for every student to be promoted each year, except in very exceptional circumstances.'

I was becoming angry, angry with Kathy, angry with these teachers, and angry with the Education Department.

'I insist that this is a very exceptional circumstance. I know she has the potential. I will see that she fulfils it!' I demanded.

They were convinced. They agreed that she should be given this chance and wished me luck.

After the jobs were done that evening, I talked about the decision with my recalcitrant daughter.

'You have been deceiving me, Kathy, and I'm very cross with you. They say you are not pulling your weight and that you will go into the internal Year 12 next year. I can't have that! Surely you don't want that? It would mean that you won't matriculate and you won't be able to go to university. That would be terrible! I've persuaded them to let you repeat Year 11.'

The look on her face was mutinous. I could see she was gearing up to defend herself, but I beat her to the punch.

'Don't give me that look! You brought this upon yourself! There's more to come. You will study Year 11, and I mean study diligently. I don't want to hear any complaints like "I've done all this before!" If you've done it before then you should be top of the class. And if you do not work and come very high up in your final class list Zardos will go!'

She knew that I meant it and did not argue. From then on we had a very studious Kathy. She loved her horse. Needless to say, the following year she passed Year 11 with flying colours and did well in matriculation the year after.

Another interesting association that I joined was SACSOS, the coloured sheep society. Here I met with a big surprise. Their secretary was Jean! Yes! The lady-friend Xavier had bought to Holsworthy to help me settle at home after the birth of Kathy. We recognised each other but said nothing about our previous encounter. That all happened 16 years ago, I thought it best to let bygones be bygones. I had finished with all the anxieties that Xavier had caused me. She was married to a sheep farmer and had children. Clearly she thought 'least said best mended'. SACSOS taught me about breeding sheep. It also enabled me to sell my coloured fleeces at markets and they also had developed a scheme to take our coloured fleeces at a reasonable price to have them converted into naturally coloured knitting yarn which all members endeavoured to sell.

I developed a couple of ploys for sheep management. By feeding them in a small shed and trapping them in there I was able to check for flystrike and so reduced its incidence. Also, during the lambing season, it was wise to keep

Chapter 40 *Kathy the country girl*

the whole flock enclosed in the shed overnight to protect the lambs from foxes.

Daniel was Kathy's current boyfriend, a typical country lad. They didn't take education seriously because they knew that their future was on the farm and that in due course they would inherit the farm and just keep it going as their parents did. Their preoccupations were: footy, girls and cars. Indeed, his nickname was 'Revhead'. Some farmers sent their sons to agricultural college so that they were educated to become better, more up-to-date farmers. Not so with Daniel. I remember he was offered some savoury biscuits sent from Japan. He obviously did not want to try them. He was so suspicious of this foreign object, but he knew that we would tease him if he did not try them. So, he took the tiniest nibble to show willing. I had my concerns.

Remembering how my parents disapproved of Xavier had made me cling to him all the more. I controlled my urge to point out his small-minded attitude and lack of interest in anything outside of McLaren Flat. However, I could not hide my feelings from Kathy. A few days later she said, 'You don't like Daniel do you?' I was taken aback by her forthrightness.

'Daniel is a good-natured boy, just not quite what I would have chosen for you. But you are a free agent and may choose your own friends.'

I congratulated myself on my diplomacy. *Phew! I think I got out of that alright.*

Well, no more was said on the subject and over time Daniel ebbed away, to be replaced by a variety of likely lads, some I liked more than others. Uncle Jan was also keeping an ear to the ground and one day he suggested that I put Kathy on the pill. I was furious!

'How dare you interfere in such a private matter? Kathy will talk to me if she feels the need. Do you know something that I don't?'

'No! I just hear the local gossip,' he protested.

It was rash of me to be so sharp with him. He was being a caring uncle, but I shared the conversation with Kathy so that she would know what the gossips were saying, and to regulate her behaviour accordingly. She did not throw accusations back at me about my own exploits, as she may well have done. I felt happy to leave the subject there knowing that she would come to me if she felt the need.

Meanwhile, the 'Attention' was bursting at the seams. Denis Wiseman, the butcher, told me that my little farm was a four cow farm, and if I want to keep sheep as well I needed to calculate that four sheep eat as much as one cow. I realised that 'Attention' was grossly overstocked. Did I really need so much stock? To supplement my wages and pension, I was already selling the coloured knitting yarn from SACSOS, my surplus eggs, and sides of beef to friends and acquaintances. Less stock would mean less meat to sell, but I did not want to degrade my property.

CHAPTER 41

ERICA AND HIROMI

Erica took to high school like a duck to water and seemed to be particularly talented at Japanese. Her Japanese teacher was organising a student exchange programme with a Japanese school. Would I like Erica to be involved? Of course, I would like her to be involved! I did not know how best to help Erica until this opportunity came along. I did not have the cash for her airfare, so I had to go cap in hand to Jan and beg for an advance for her because this would be a wonderful opportunity. My pleading was successful and she went to Japan to stay with a Japanese family, the Tanakas. Their extended family ran a kimono business. Their daughter Hiromi became a fast friend with Erica. Later, Hiromi visited us.

The weather in spring in South Australia was unpredictable and fickle to say the least. The warmth and rain combined to grow the hay and we had it baled into rectangular bricks. It had been a good year and about 120 bales lay in neat rows ready for collection. We had to stack it into our sheds before the next onslaught of rain. Paul would be getting it in at the weekend.

However, on the Wednesday evening as I was driving my girls home from the school bus the clouds were gathering and we could see farmers out with their trucks, trailers and muscular sons tossing their bales onto trucks and driving them to the safety of their sheds.

Paul was still at work. It would start raining at any minute. That hay had to be in a shed or it would spoil.

'It's down to us, girls. As soon as we get home I want you to change into jeans and come down to the bottom paddock to help me get in the hay.'

'Oh, Mum, how can we manage that?'

'Erica is too young and weak to lift a bale of hay, so she must drive the old ute while you and I, Kathy, pack the bales into the back.'

'I can't drive, Mum!' protested Erica.

'You can learn! Now get a move on before it rains,' I said, shooing the girls into action.

Erica was installed in the driver's seat with cushions shoved behind her back so that she could just reach the floor pedals.

'Now, that's the clutch, that's the gas and that's the brake. Turn on the ignition. Right, now engage the first gear while keeping your foot down on the clutch. Good. Now as you gently release the clutch, you give it gas and you will move forward for a few yards. Then you press the clutch again and you will glide to a stop.'

'Oh, Mum, I'm scared. What happens if it takes off?' she asked, looking at me with imploring eyes.

'That's the brake pedal,' I told her, trying to give her some confidence.

She need not have been worried on that score. It was a matter of start, try to release the clutch, jerk forward, stall, repeat, while Kathy and I loaded the nearest bales. The aim was for the vehicle to progress slowly between two rows of bales of hay so that the loaders could walk to the bale of hay, pick it up then take a route perpendicular to the travelling vehicle, lift the bale into the back of the ute, thus minimising their walk. However, Erica's jerky progress meant that she was either ahead or behind us and Kathy and I walked extra complaining miles, as each bale grew heavier than the last and I frequently returned to her window to repeat the coaching instructions.

Meanwhile, the sky darkened and we could see Bazza and his sons working smoothly and efficiently, loading a large tray truck in their adjacent paddock.

As we turned to return along the next avenue of bales, we would have our backs to our efficient neighbour, but it didn't matter because they had finished loading and were heading back to their shed to unload. We continued our weary, spasmodic effort to get the hay in. How Bazza and his boys must have been laughing at our puny effort.

We laboured on with the frustrating, tiring endeavour. We just had to succeed or our hay would be ruined. Suddenly, a tray truck carrying Bazza and his boys came down the drive and into our hay paddock.

Chapter 41 *Erica and Hiromi*

'Do you need some help? Come on, lads, we'll soon get these in for Chris!' he shouted.

Were these scruffy country lads or knights in shining armour? They achieved in minutes what would have taken us hours.

'Thank you so much, boys,' I said gratefully.

Bazza grinned at me with a humble shrug. 'Agh, it's nothing. What are neighbours for? Best we all get inside now before we get soaked through.'

What a wonderful neighbour he was.

Erica was always a self-contained girl. She tried hard, and she kept most of her problems and thoughts to herself. She was not really happy on the farm and did not like farm chores. When she returned from Japan she was motivated and became even more self-possessed.

'I'm going to get a job! Save up! And go back to Japan and other places! On my first trip to town, I will put my name into John Martin's employment department for casual work. I can work Friday's late-night shopping and Saturday mornings!'

She helped more frequently without being asked. But she was still a little girl. She loved her little knick-knacks, tiny dolls, tiny shoes, pictures. She adorned her room with them.

She took a course in self-defence in Blackwood one weekend. To return home, she could catch a bus to bring her to McLaren Vale, then she could phone home from the public call box and I would come and pick her up by car. On Saturday morning the phone rang.

'Hi, Mum, its Erica. I'm here in McLaren Vale. Can you come and pick me up? There's a man on the other side of the road looking at me. I hope he tries to attack me so that I can practice my self-defence!'

'Stay right there, I'm on my way!' I shouted. I was out of the door, into the car and driving like mad to pick her up in record time!

Hiromi was to visit us. To accommodate her, we rearranged a few cupboards in the big back playroom to create a bedroom for her. I questioned Erica about the suitability of this arrangement for a Japanese girl.

'This will be fine for her. She must have some private space. She will find us rather free and easy.'

When Hiromi visited us, I wanted to show her South Australia's most spectacular sites, at least cost to the household, so in conference with Sue and Ted, I decided a camping holiday for Hiromi, Erica, Kathy and myself in the Flinders ranges fitted the bill. Sue and Ted would swap cars back for the week so that we could drive the reliable Datsun 120Y station wagon. I borrowed two 2-man tents, four camp beds, a Primus stove and various other bits of camping gear from the local girl guides. Each girl was permitted a small backpack of clothes and necessities. To this, we added an esky of fresh food and a box of tinned food. Ted reviewed the kit.

'Don't forget water.'

'Right.' I took a large container of water and each member of the party had a water bottle of her own. I did aim to bring us all safely home from our adventure. A Datsun 120Y station wagon is a small car, but we managed to pack everything in.

I knew the way to Arkaroola, having driven food and equipment up for David in my student years, but decided Wilpena Pound, which was 420 km north of Adelaide, would be far enough for this adventure. This way we could set up camp in an official campsite at Wilpena Pound and go out on day trips to the places of interest.

I don't know whether the 540 million year old landscape impressed the girls, but each morning they happily prepared for the day's trip. We went to Bunyeroo Gorge. What a beautiful gorge it was, lined with magnificent old red gums. The river that carved out this gorge was no more, but the riverbed was marked by water smoothed pebbles and an occasional water hole.

Climbing St Mary's Peak, or at least going over The Saddle, is a must when staying at Wilpena Pound. St Mary's Peak is the highest mountain in the Flinders Ranges. I remember returning from that walk very hot and weary and sitting outside the store, gratefully licking an ice-cream.

At night we could see millions of stars in the clear sky because we were so far away from the light haze of civilisation. Another interesting day without driving was walking around in the Wilpena Pound, a natural amphitheatre, to see the old Wilpena station. Very little remains, but it made you imagine what the pioneer life must've been like. There must have been shearing sheds and shearers quarters when everything was in operation, but now all that is left is the derelict stone building in the middle of the amphitheatre, which had been the boss's house.

One really big day out was to Parachilna Gorge and Blinman. The girls beautified themselves before getting into the car and I must admit that we started out looking very neat and clean, but it was so hot that we had to open all the windows. We were quite prepared to clean the car out later. It was also deemed necessary to stick arms or feet or heads out of the car to catch the breeze. Because the road was dusty, everyone's hair became dusty and windblown. We soon looked like dust-coloured scarecrows.

The Blinman Pub is the one place on earth where I will partake of a beer. No matter when you visit, you arrive with a mighty big thirst that only a cold beer will satisfy. I was pleased to see that they had a small swimming pool adjoining the pub, but we had no bathing costumes with us. The girls were coy, but that didn't stop me. I just stripped down to my underwear and plunged in. It was marvellous! All they would do to keep cool was pretend that I was not with them and drink lemonade. I was the coolest with a cold beer inside me, and when I'd finished swimming I put my clothes on over my wet underwear and off we drove.

After cooking each night, dishes had to be washed and Hiromi, anxious to do her share, happily took the dishes in a bucket to the laundry. Her English was not good enough for her to read the sign saying,
CAMPERS ARE NOT PERMITTED TO WASH THEIR DISHES IN THE LAUNDRY. My girls thought it a joke and fortunately she was never accosted for breaking this rule.

We all relaxed and laughed a lot during this holiday, and I had time to think while the girls chatted.

Looking back into the evolution of society we could say ... Man, the adventurer, the hunter, supplied meat for the family at home, cared for by his woman. He saw all the action while he is out in the big wide world and had a world of love and care when he returned to the nest. Woman's smaller world was the home. This need not be so nowadays, because many families have two breadwinners and hopefully they are equally appreciated for their contribution to the table. As to my own life, I am both husband and wife. My life is as fulfilling as any man's, and love can become of secondary importance. Really, this attitude creates a better balance of things for a woman in my position.

So here I am with children to love and raise and an irrepressible joie de vivre. I love them and I love my life. I enjoy sexual encounters without all the other baggage. Isn't that how men love? Life is good. I am in control of my own life.

When we returned from the holiday, the kitchen was a mess. Dirty dishes were everywhere. I had left Paul food, but I had expected him to clean up after himself. After asking him to clean up and getting no response, I put all his dirty dishes into a bowl and cleaned the kitchen so that I could cook. Later I asked again. Still, he gave no response.

The next morning, I placed the bowl of dirty dishes on his bed so that he would find them in the evening. When he came home, he carried the bowl of dirty dishes down to the kitchen and when I came home I returned them to his bed. This went on for several days.

Finally, Saturday morning arrived and Paul washed his dirty dishes.

CHAPTER 42

AM I STILL SEARCHING FOR MR RIGHT?

In one of the May school holidays, I wanted to prove to myself that I could survive alone so I travelled to Kangaroo Island. I took a backpack of food to last me ten days. Walking in was tough with my heavy backpack, but living there in splendid isolation was marvellous. I walked a lot, wrote the Bruce story, did some knitting and fell asleep each night to the sound of the roaring waves on the nearby beach. I was really happy there and realised how little I needed to be content. The happiest people are not those who have everything, but those who make the most of what they do have.

My buddy Ann and I had lunch one day. We were both single women with active lives. The difference is that she was city-girl while I was the country bumpkin. We constructed our own rules for relationships. She now had the dilemma of a lover who wanted to leave his wife and move in with her. She felt that he just wanted to jump from one 'ship' to the next to ensure that all the comforts of home were maintained. She came to a decision. He must first leave his wife and live alone for six months. If he had the courage to do that she would then take him in. She put the proposition to the lover and he decided that he could not comply. He remained unfaithful to his wife, but with a different girlfriend.

'Hey, ho,' said Ann pragmatically. 'Next?'

I doubt that I will ever see myself in that situation. Her children were gone and she lived in a city apartment. I loved my farm and children with all their complications. What man would ever want to take on a woman with my drawbacks?

Anyway, my uterus was misbehaving, so I decided I could do without it. The medical profession, however, had different opinions and I had to turn to Jan to find me a surgeon who would not go through the usual circus of, 'Suppose you want to have more children, Mrs Jancarik? We do not like to do an operation that you will regret later.'

I had made up my mind and I just wanted the job done.

While I was in hospital recovering from the hysterectomy, I had time to think about what my attitudes were to men in particular. I thought …

First of all, David. Why is he always foremost in my thoughts? For years I have been wallowing in wasteful daydreams. How shall I tackle this problem? We are friends, nothing more! Get that into your head, Chrissie! I have had other lovers who are now good friends. Friendship is what endures. I know that even when I accept my situation with my brain, it will take time before my emotions accept it. But mental acceptance is the first step in the right direction.

Meanwhile, the surgeon was pleased with his work, saying, 'Yes, I have precisely removed the nursery but left an ample playroom.'

How would I use the playroom? Was I still looking for Mr Brady? In only dating bachelors and divorcees, the dates are scant. I was not just a woman in search of a husband. I was a complete package, an educated woman with a professional job and a mind of my own. I like living on my hobby-farm and I have three assertive teenagers, each presenting their own set of problems. No man in his right mind would dream of taking us on and becoming the husband/father/farmer to this gang of hillbillies!

I'm giving up on Mr Brady! I'm not looking for a husband. My family is complete in itself.

I still want outings with men and sex, but I'm uncertain about wanting to fall in love or marry. Therefore, I can embrace married men as well as singles. I have no intention of taking a man away from his existing wife and family. If he has an unhappy marriage or an open marriage he is fair game. I need not sift through the candidates and have rules about married or not. I am free to enjoy the company of anyone I choose, which would broaden my scope when selecting from the Saturday 'friendship' pages.

My thoughts were turned into action when I met Fred, a married man, on King William Street not long after I healed from my operation.

'Shall we eat while we talk?'

Chapter 42 *Am I still searching for Mr Right?*

'Sure, where would you like to go?'

'The Pancake Kitchen is just around the corner,' I told him.

Fred laughed. 'When I take a lady out to lunch I usually expect her to choose something more "expensiff", a flash hotel or restaurant.'

So, this chap has played this game before and he is clearly of German origin. I really like the 'Cherman' accent.

I shrugged. 'Well, I like that sometimes, but the Pancake Kitchen is close and I really fancy one of their vegetarian pancakes with all those lovely mushrooms and sour cream. I'm sure you'll find something that you like on the menu.'

Between delicious, inexpensive mouthfuls we exchanged stories.

He was a German immigrant with a wife and two kinder (children!), worked as a welder at Holden's and had friends in the German community. His wife had a lover who was one of Fred's German mates, which meant that he was free to have a girlfriend. Many couples in the German community had this arrangement. Here was a clear case of separating Love and Sex. However, his wife was a bit jealous of Fred's pleasures, so he thought he would like a girlfriend outside the German community.

I accepted this. 'Fine, if you don't tell, I won't tell either. Besides I live in the country and we are most unlikely to meet with anyone who knows her. How did you get on during the war?'

'I was in Hitler Youth.'

I was disappointed. *Oh no! I was just beginning to like him. Now I'm going to discover that he was a Nazi. This is a quick route to dropping him.*

Fred shook his head. 'I was forced to join. You had no choice. I hated it. I hated the uniforms, marching and brainwashing. I became a saboteur.'

'What did you sabotage?'

'Well, I was only a kid so I could not blow up bridges or meddle with cars, but when we went to Hitler youth camp I would remove the bolts from the boys bunks so that they fell apart when they went to bed. I had some friends who dismantled plumbing to create floods, stuff like that.'

We were soon laughing together! *Oh boy, a rebel! That's more like it!*

'It continues! When we were caught we had our uniforms confiscated and had to walk in disgrace at the back of the parades. That was our punishment.

What fools the leaders were. We were delighted to be without uniforms and not marching in the neat lines with the others.'

By the time we had finished our pancakes and orange juice, I had decided that I liked him so I asked if he would like to visit 'Attention' the following Wednesday.

'Definitely! It sounds most interesting,' he replied.

As we reclined in the afterglow on the waterbed, I thought he performed very well as a lover, if only he wasn't so damn clean. Clearly to prepare himself for this event, he had scrubbed himself and deodorised himself until he no longer smelt like a man.

Do I tell him or do I simply accept that this is what Fred smells like?

Wishing to endear himself to me, he proclaimed he was quite a handyman and could see that I needed one. He had not always been a handyman, he explained, but when the price of carpenters, electricians and plumbers became exorbitant he decided these jobs couldn't be too difficult. If he took his time he could work out how most things work and fix them himself. 'They can get "schtuffed"!'

That was one of his endearing sayings, and soon enough, within our family he became known as 'Get Schtuffed' Fred.

He became a regular visitor to 'Attention'. We built a stock yard and ramp, designed by David and built mainly by Fred, which greatly facilitated the handling of animals.

We had a special annual date on Christmas Eve. Because my children were welcomed to their Czechoslovakian grandmother's home (that's Babichka) for Christmas Eve, and the workers at Holden's had their Christmas break up party on Christmas Eve, Fred and I always had a great night out. He even booked a hotel room for us. He thought it highly amusing to book the whole event as 'Mr Bond'.

When I went out with men, they paid the bills. We lived on a tight budget and I would not have been able to afford the dinners, dances and theatres in any other way.

Once I went to a 'find your partner' agency. They asked an interesting question.

Chapter 42 *Am I still searching for Mr Right?*

'What are you looking for in a man? Is it wealth, looks, an interesting lifestyle?'

'Hold it there!' I said. 'I need a week to think about that. I'll come back next week.'

My answer was NO to most of their suggestions because each of the positive traits that they mentioned is usually accompanied by a downside. I realised that personality was more important than any of their suggestions. What I was looking for was someone who was well-balanced and well-adjusted, intelligent and capable but also accepting. Looks and wealth come a poor second to a well- adjusted personality.

They paired me up with some men. All were happy to comply with my need to have a good time out, including sex. This way I met Cyril Hill. He knew quite a few people in the swinging scene.

'What was that?' I was curious, thinking 'swinging' sounded familiar, but I couldn't remember from where.

'I'll take you to a party, if you like. They do prefer couples to individuals. But the couples are not clinging to each other. They have come to meet other like-minded people. During the party you may have sex with two or three or even more partners. You are asked or invited, as you might be invited to dance at a regular party,' Cyril told me.

'And you accept or refuse as you please?'

'Sure'

'Are these married couples?'

'Mainly. Yes.'

I was amazed. 'And this does not disrupt a marriage?'

'No, the couples have talked and thought about the idea and realise that it is better to be open and frank when they seek variety than to sneak around deceiving their partner to get extra-marital pleasure.'

Wow! This is almost what Xavier wanted 20 years ago. Except with the key in the basket system no one had any choice. We were just out of sync, weren't we? I hated the idea then, but I am ready to join in the fun now.

So, I met Marie and Max, Christel and Charles, Lynne and Lloyd, Harry and Honey, Frank and Freda. They were just the basic crew and were at most parties. Others drifted in and out of the scene and a few unaccompanied males attended when they could escape their usual life problems. Thus, I met Phil the Pharmacist and Alan the Academic. They provided a lot of uncomplicated pleasure for me. I went to parties nearly every month. It cost me a plate of party food for the supper table. Nothing more, and I was obliged to no one. It could really be called Free Love. Fortunately, we were all also free of any health issues that you associate with such seemingly wicked behaviour. We were all contentedly unashamed of our situation because we had come to terms with our sexuality as separate from our love.

Summer holidays meant a wonderful time for R and R. Christmas Eve was spent with Fred and friends, Christmas Day was spent with Sue and Ted and my kids, then New Year's Eve I deliberately spent at home alone so that each January 1st I woke early with a clear head and time to pause for thought.

'What have I learned over these four years at 'Attention'?'

If anything can go wrong it will.

Children do not live on food alone. We would not survive if I gave up my part-time teaching job, much as I would like to. The four of us are working together as a team. We will pull through.

CHAPTER 43

IT'S RAINING MEN

Most of the married men that I met needed someone to listen to them. They had given their all to wife and family. They loved them and worked for them but were gradually taken for granted as a husband and father. They felt that they were only required as a provider. This seemed to me to be totally different from Xavier's dalliances which were continuous, ongoing ego boosters. I will never really know because how can a woman fathom the workings of the male mind? Maybe for all of them it's just a case of the grass is always greener on the other side of the fence?

What was it with men? Did I give out a pheromone? Of course, I expect a come on from the men I was dating.

I was like the young girl from Kent,
Who said that she knew what it meant,
When men asked her to dine on partridge and wine
She knew, oh she knew,
But she went.

But in this particular year, I seemed to attract them like the proverbial moth to a flame. Even the Apple man found an opportunity to try for a kiss and a cuddle with a seemingly sincere 'You are so nice!'. I had to use all my strength to extricate myself from his grasp and laughed it off. I liked him. I looked up to him, as an ancient sage. We did laugh it off and remained friends.

I decided to use a local mechanic in a nearby village. After giving my car a very good service and advice on matters automotive, he let me know that his domestic situation left a lot to be desired. His wife spent most of her life in hospital. Would I be willing to visit him occasionally or allow him to visit me?

Well! What is a girl to do? Spit in his eye?

There was only one man in all my experience that I ever mistrusted. He invited me to lunch at a hotel and asked me to wear a bathing costume so that he could have the pleasure of removing it. There was nothing particularly strange about that. It was just our general conversation that made me feel that he was inventing it and saying what he thought I wanted to hear. I am no psychologist and I don't know what it was, but it spooked me, and needless to say I did not accept a second invitation.

Another one that didn't last very long was George the Greek who I met one Saturday while at the races with Dad. We had a brief conversation when suddenly he asked, 'Do you have a man?'

'No.' I explained I was free, and we had a few encounters at the farm. Although he was an excellent lover and satisfied my curiosity about the Greek style being a little different, his ego was too much to bear. He asked if I kept any liquor in the house because he liked to have a drink after sex. I explained that this household did not run into such a large expense. His interest waned as did mine.

One evening I was on the phone to Fred.

'Oh Fred, why do I try to find myself a special someone when I have friends like you who are so good to me?'

'Well, it's good to have friends, but such a lovely person as you should not be alone. I would hate to lose you, but I wish for you that you have someone of your own. When will we see us again, tomorrow?'

I smile at his odd phrasing. 'Yes, wonderful! I had lots of jobs planned, but I will gladly lay them aside to spend some time relaxing with you.'

When I met Karl, I was 44. I thought that Mr Brady had finally arrived. We seemed to click immediately. He was a delightful personality that I met through the newspaper ads. He was overweight and loved cooking and obviously eating what he cooked. His eyes lit up with glee when he smiled or saw a humorous point in the conversation. I realised that once the weight was under control he would be a very attractive man. He had been in the German merchant Navy as a fitter and turner and had a truck driver's license. He had lived with a 60-year-old widow of a professor in Germany. She loved his cooking and his company. One of her friends had criticised her for taking up

Chapter 43 *It's raining men*

with a 35-year-old truckie. Her reply had been, 'A 35-year-old truckie does more good for me than a dead professor!' However, she was wealthy enough to take cruises and a friend told him that she had a lover in every port. So, he cleared out.

Another woman he had known had cheeky children and she would not discipline them. 'Love me, love my kids,' was her refrain. His was, 'No thank you.'

So, he is a single man looking for a permanent relationship. Maybe he'll do me?

'Well, my kids are not angels, but they are amenable to discussion.' I had better apply the fault test. His fault was an over fondness for cooking and eating. This struck me as easy to bear because I was a foodie myself.

Karl loved theatre and opera. I booked theatre tickets in anticipation of his company, and I was excited about his coming visit. We did one of our mammoth clean-ups as was our custom before visitors. We tidied the veranda, returned the tools to the shed and mowed the 'lawns'. He phoned during the week and Paul, who was present on a brief visit, mistook him for Babichka because of his heavy accent. Then on Friday night, feeling tired, I phoned him to check that he was still coming on Saturday.

'I am not coming. I do not think I would be comfortable there.'

I did not know what had upset him.

'Well, it has to be your decision.' I started to explain about a Czechoslovakian grandmother, but stopped. I was thinking …

I will never force, push or even nudge anyone into my company. They have to be here because they really want to be. If they don't find me attractive enough to overcome whatever it is that offends, or worries them about my home situation, so be it.

'I will not try to persuade you. The decision is yours.'

I was hurt and flopped onto bed for a little weep. The house seemed very quiet. Erica came in and asked what was wrong. I repeated the essence of my feelings and hurt and she sat there for a while, and then Kathy came in and asked the same, whereupon I repeated the summary of my hurt feelings.

'I'll make you a cup of tea. Erica, show Mum your kimono,' Kathy said, and so the healing process started thanks to my two wonderful daughters.

The girls were growing up into sensitive human beings, but I really had to learn 'Love to a man is a passing thing, 'tis women's whole existence'. I would not get sucked into LOVE again. I always end up hurt! Oh well. As Ann said, 'Next?'

A month or so later, I found a Saturday ad interesting. It was offering 'fun times', so I met its author outside the post office on Grenfell Street. He was a skinny chap with hollow cheeks and large brown eyes. When I suggested we have lunch together to talk he seemed embarrassed. He had already eaten his lunch sandwiches but would happily buy me a lunch at a nearby cafeteria. This wasn't making a good impression on me, but as our conversation developed he became very interested in me. When I said, 'Sex is just an appetite, like a hunger for food or any other human need,' his interest grew and he complained of the lack of interest at home as other married men had done before. We both agreed that sex was good for the ego and good for our whole physical wellbeing. Nothing to be proud or ashamed of.

He looks unhealthily skinny. He must be very deprived.

He was a planner for the South Australian government and worked in a nearby government office block. I thought that the people we elected to government governed us and I was quickly informed that they are only politicians. It is the civil servants that actually govern the people and he governed the western suburbs of Adelaide to ensure that all buildings complied with the State Planning Act. Very interesting; I'm always learning something.

Anxious to take our relationship to the next level, he explained that he could escape from the office for prolonged lunch hours if he planned for it. Or he could escape from home of an evening to attend fictitious Council meetings. We arranged to meet at Mum and Dad's unit the following Tuesday.

This is how I met Neil Alexander Scott.

He was very eager, and the most ready, willing and able lover I had ever met. I put this down to his meagre rations. On this first date I learned, while we shared his vegemite sandwiches, that we had been born within 20 km of each other. I was born in Lewisham, London, while he was born in Gillingham, Kent.

Even more surprising though, both he and his wife had been virgins on their wedding night! Wow! That was the first time I had heard of such a situation. She was a Lutheran, raised by a maiden aunt, which explained her virginity, but why was he? He was wary and conservative and had heard stories of how young men could be caught in the tender trap of pregnancy, then coerced into marriage. However, it turned out that he had been trapped by sympathy into loving Paula.

She had contracted TB in the middle of their friendship and was confined to hospital for a year.

He visited her frequently and she was grateful, but because of her strict upbringing she was adamant that sex was for after marriage. She was also adamant that the wedding celebration should be dry.

Neil's father took exception to this idea and set up a bar outside the church hall from the back of his ute. Neil wondered what was amiss at the reception, as the numbers slowly dwindled, especially in the male population. Even his best man, Doug, was missing. He stepped outside to discover the other half of the wedding reception. He returned to his proper reception after briefly imbibing, which made the formalities bearable until he could spirit his bride away.

Now he was wrapped in the full catastrophe—three daughters, cats, mortgage and government job.

This all suited me because I was not in love and had no intension of becoming so. We decided that sex was an appetite we could satisfy for each other, in his extended lunch hours, without upsetting the apple carts of our mainstream life.

Quite a downpour wasn't it?

CHAPTER 44

NEIL VISITS

Christmas seemed to tug at December and make it go faster than any other month.

At school life was hectic with reports to write and parent visiting nights to attend, besides keeping classes occupied with something interesting and on topic. Students just want to slope off and do nothing, which was chaotic and noisy. Then I had to attend parent visiting nights at Blackwood High to find out how my girls had performed. Kathy had worked well as she repeated Year 11 and would be promoted to the Matric Year 12 class. Erica never put a foot wrong and had found work at The Magic Mountain. She was ready to start work as soon as she was released from school.

Farm life was just as frenetic. Finally, I had a shearer who would come to 'Attention'. As he did the shearing, I could skirt and bag the fleeces. The dags would be used as mulch. He also drenched and sprayed them all with sheep-dip. Everything was done in one afternoon.

Then we had to do the preserving and cooking for Christmas. We had to have homemade cake and pudding! Mum's friend Eileen made the best mince pies, so competition was not considered, but I still needed to pick them up and do Christmas gift shopping. Beta Sigma Phi had an end of year celebrations and I attended the swinger's Christmas party and the Spinners and Weavers Christmas party. The Smarts were giving a fundraising breakfast for the Liberal party. Not my political sentiment, but I attended to help Tess serve.

I had a date with Neil at Mum and Dad's flat and learnt a little more about him. He had attended Adelaide Boy's High School just before I had. One evening cycling home after school, he had stopped to watch the trains run under a bridge and there he met a young man about five years his senior also train watching.

Chapter 44 *Neil visits*

'Do you like trains too?' initiated a life-long friendship. This was Doug. He was legally blind but could see well enough to be a brilliant photographer. They were each other's confidant, best man and travelling companion, frequently taking trips together to photograph railway infrastructure and rolling stock. I gave Neil a map to guide him to 'Attention'.

Erica was away at work on Dec 22nd, so Christmas decorating was left to Kathy and me. As always, we went out for a drive around the neighbourhood scouting for a Christmas tree. They grew like weeds along the roadside. When we found one about the right size for us, we chopped it down and carted it home. We were about to trim it to size and put it into its bucket of water when Neil arrived with a large box of apricots.

'We have two apricot trees and they bear prolifically,' he told me. 'Our kitchen cupboards are full of apricot preserves and apricot jam. I do my best to remove as many as I can before Paula starts on this year's crop.'

I was chuffed. 'Oh, lovely! We don't have an apricot tree, and I can always use fruit. Are you any good with a saw? We are about to erect our Christmas tree.'

'Yes, I can saw a Christmas tree to size and even erect it for you. Where is it going to stand? In general, I am not a handyman, but I have been dealing with Christmas trees for a few years.'

He adjusted the size and positioned it securely with Kathy's help while I made tea for all. Then we sat on the front veranda to drink because it was a hot evening.

'This is a beautiful place you have! It must be lovely to live here away from the hustle and bustle!' he exclaimed, looking around with enthusiasm.

If only the reality was so! 'Well, the bank owns more than I do! I may have to sell. Or work full-time at teaching, but then I would not have time to care for the farm. Nothing is ever as easy as it appears. You made it look easy, fixing the tree. Thank you.'

'As you say nothing is quite what it seems. I am the world's worst handyman. This was all due to an incident when I was about 5 years old.'

'Do tell.'

'My father was a bricklayer and building contractor. He had built the row of houses where we lived overlooking the dockyards at Gillingham. He was building a fishpond in our front garden and I watched carefully as he mixed the mortar and laid it between the rocks to make the walls of the fishpond. I thought that it looked quite fun and easy to do. So, when he decided to take a little stroll to the pub, I jumped into the hole of the 'to be fishpond' and continued the building where he had left off. Needless to say, my five-year-old attempt was nowhere near as professional looking as my father's work.

'When he returned nicely relax from his sojourn at the pub, he saw my attempts to emulate him and was furious! He called me the most wicked, contemptable and useless of boys, saying I would never amount to anything. From then on any attempt by me at manual construction had scorn poured upon it before I lifted the first tool. I also noticed that men who worked physically to earn their crust seemed to work twice as hard and earn half as much as those who wore a smart suit and went to an office. I therefore decided that I would be one of the latter and that I would pay other men to do the manual work.'

Sorry to say that his tale had a detrimental effect in my eyes. *Well, that seals your fate, chum. You would be no use to me on my farm.*

Christmas eve, Christmas day and New Year's Eve were spent in my traditional manner.

Despite his lack of handyman skills, I met up with Neil a few times during the summer holidays and learnt little more about his life, like how he had become a planner.

When he reached Year 12 at high school and calculus was introduced to him he found it so abhorrent that he left school and took a job with a real estate agent. He collected rents and gradually learnt the real estate business, eventually establishing his own real estate business and added a travel agency into his office. He realised that the two big airline companies, Qantas and TAA, were keeping airfares up by mutual consent or price-fixing. So, he and a colleague arranged a return flight from Melbourne to London, charging their customers much less than the big companies. It took a lot of organisation and was a huge risk, which led to a nervous breakdown for Neil, but because it demonstrated that flights could be organised cheaply the large

Chapter 44   *Neil visits*

airliners dropped their prices, so it was not necessary for them to repeat the feat.

At about the same time, Neil realised that he no longer wished to be a real estate agent. He disliked the tactics of fellow agents and decided that he wanted to be a town planner. He read the state planning act and applied to the South Australian government planning department for employment. He did not have a degree, but he had such a good grip of the planning act that he eventually landed the job and was one of the last to get such a job without a degree. The process was not as easy as it sounded. Indeed, he was unemployed for several months and the family had to dig into their investments in shares to see them through.

During the holidays, Neil gave me 20 young native trees that were left over from a project at the planning department, 'The Greening of Adelaide'. I invited all my friends from the Soil Association and Permaculture to help me plant them.

Although he was no handyman, Neil was obviously a thoughtful man and he knew what would please me.

CHAPTER 45

THE LETTER

David decided to make Kangaroo Island his permanent home and planned to build himself a cabin from the local limestone. However, it also needed some other building materials. When he had gathered them all together, his ute as well as a small van were full. He needed another driver and a helper. Since it was the January school holidays, I took the job. As usual, the time was laced with philosophical argument. On my return, I wrote a definitive letter, which I hoped would summarise my feelings for him and close a chapter of my life. Here is some of it.

> From 'Attention', January 1984
> Dear Plato,
>
> As the ferry drew into Cape Jervis, it was cold and windy, but huddled in a tartan blanket were Kathy and Pinky. Eyes lit up on seeing me, a grin spread over her face and the tail wagging became so vigorous that Pinky could be held no longer. There was no co-driver with Kathy. Since she had not passed her test she should not have been driving alone. She explained cheekily, 'Joy phoned and said she couldn't make it at the last minute. So, I put the L-plates in the boot, drove Erica to her French lesson and came for you.' Pinky leapt about our feet, not knowing whether to advance along the jetty with us or jump up at my legs to show her pleasure at my return.
>
> As we drove home, Kathy filled me in on all the week's happenings at 'Attention' and a relaxing warmth spread through me.
>
> *Ahh! I am back where I am acknowledged as significant. Was it so painful being with David? Yes, in many ways it was very painful, and I don't think I will repeat the experience.*

Chapter 45   *The Letter*

As we parted, you said, 'I think I could stand it again'.

Yes, but the question is, could I?

In the few days that have followed, I have tried to work out why. As time soothes the pain, this letter seems less necessary, but I feel that you should have more insight into other people's mental workings and feelings.

While I was on KI, you set the scene as an intellectual battleground and I steadily lost ground. Perhaps because of my humility, perhaps because my cerebral processes are slower than yours and I was not quick enough to pick up on the flaws in your arguments at the instant you were bullying on. A letter gives me a chance to rave on uninterrupted.

True, I have been guilty of loving you off and on through the past nine years, and rose-coloured glasses have been used to view you on numerous occasions, but this January I managed the step that I knew would come if I worked at it long enough. One evening a part of me said, 'He is just a man!' and the other part did not argue with me as it usually does when I try to mentally cut you down to size.

Love was converted to a friendship. But what is a friend? To me it is a significant person whose opinion and company is sought and valued. To you, what?

Nothing! Now I can say exactly what I think and if what I say offends you sufficiently for you to sever our relationship, I will not feel too great a loss and you will feel nothing.

I have defended myself against several of the criticisms you have levelled against me, mainly about my ability to think, and I will not bore you further with all the details.

You said, 'It will be different without you'.

How you damn with faint praise. Or perhaps it is laughable. Your life will feel nothing positive, nothing negative, only different, obviously.

Why do you strive so hard to be different from the rest of mankind? Are we so low and defiled to not have traits of value in your estimation? Personally, I have a dilemma with my attitude towards mankind. I feel abhorrence towards him in general, although I love many individuals.

Man is a communicating animal and a community-forming animal. You connect yourself to his communal brain by reading and the use of technology invented by your fellow man and yet you reject him, in general, as a bit of a twit. Whether you like it or not you are a man, homo sapiens, with the same number of genes, chromosomes, arms, legs, capabilities and needs.

Do I hope in vain that you will allow some modifications in your attitude towards mankind? Be honest with yourself. If you do not want a friend, why bother even being civil?

If you take the time to read all this and to reply, or if you reappear at 'Attention', I will take it to mean that you have some respect for this old friend.

Your friend (by my definition), Chris

I came to the conclusion that in going to live on KI, David was not only building himself a cabin but also his own Ivory Tower. I had to leave him there, close the book on David and take time to think about my own future.

In another year, I would no longer be eligible for the supporting parent's pension. Because I still owed money on my mortgage, I didn't own the farm. I would have to work full-time as a teacher, Heaven forbid! That would leave only the weekends to work on the farm and my social life. I really dreaded the thought of working full-time. I realised that my worries were being exacerbated by the heat and my fatigue, so I put thoughts of money into the 'too hard' basket. After all, I still had another year in which everything would stay as it is. Then Kathy would take out a HECs loan and go to live somewhere closer to university. Of course, her horse would stay and she would come home to visit every weekend, but basically, there would only be me and Erica and some cash income generated by the farm, so perhaps it wouldn't be too bad.

CHAPTER 46

FUN TIMES WITH NEIL

In February, when school started and Mr Kane was planning the timetable, I made a decision to simplify my life and his timetabling somewhat. It was difficult for Mr Kane to squeeze my subjects into three days. If I were to attend school every day, which meant I could ride on the school bus, there would be slabs of time when I was not in the classroom. If I used that time for preparation and marking, I would never have to take schoolwork home and this would be a blessed relief.

The girls were working well at school and Kathy excelled at Biology. At one stage, she had to design her own experiment on animal behaviour and she decided to run statistics on the pecking order in our chicken shed. She sat in the chicken shed and identified each chicken then noted every time A pecked B or B pecked C and so on. She sat there for an hour every evening for about four weeks to gather enough data. She was then able to work out the pecking order for our flock. I knew her teacher personally from having taught with him in Salisbury, and he was so delighted with her effort that he telephoned to tell me.

Mum and Dad offered me their home as a venue for trysts. I only had to give them one day warning and they would take themselves off for a picnic and leave the key under the mat. Fictitious Council meetings and days out with 'Doug' increased for Neil during 1984, but it didn't seem to stress the Scott household. Neil and I frequently used Mum and Dad's unit, and on other occasions the kids were happy to leave me alone on the farm. We met on almost a weekly basis where we had sex and talked. I learnt he was fanatical about public transport, trains, in particular.

Neil grew to the age of nine during the war, living with his mother in the house overlooking the dockyards. From his lofty position, he witnessed quite a few air adventures and, as most young boys, considered it all great fun. He was living in 'bomb alley' and frequently witnessed 'our boys' returning from bombing raids in Germany. Once, he even saw a German pilot crash into a tree. The pilot was marched off by the locals to the authorities.

In the early 50s, Australia needed builders and Neil's father, a builder, hated the cold English climate after serving in the Middle East. The family migrated to South Australia, living, at first, in hostels and then in a home, built by his father, in Glenelg.

We found each other intriguing. I was now so liberated and he was so confined. He loved to hear about the swinging parties, but he could never get away for one. I was intrigued by his straightlaced wife. I could see that I had been like her some 15 years ago when the children were small and I had been too tired to go along with all of Xavier's ideas. I had gone along only grudgingly with Xavier's requests and had put a firm line in the sand over what I considered outrageous demands. To some extent I sympathised with her, or at least understood her. Hopefully I was doing her a favour by taking the pressure off her. It would have been good if Xavier had had a discrete mistress, giving me time to mature fifteen years ago. Perhaps, given a break, she could recover her strength and eventually cope with this sexually demanding man.

The barriers must have been overcome at some point because the union produced three daughters. Unfortunately, one suffered from cystic fibrosis. They must have both been carriers of the faulty gene. Neil's parents were not helpful grandparents and the couple had to manage their family alone. This was no mean feat when you consider the extra work that caring for a chronically sick child involved. She needed postural draining and regular dosages of medicines to keep her going. She missed a lot of schooling, but she was a charming, non-complaining, bright personality, loved by her siblings, parents and others who met her.

His wife was always unresponsive to Neil's attempts at seduction. He tried various measures to try to enliven their sex life, but her care of the children always overrode or interrupted his advances. He even tried not making advances, thinking that she would eventually turn to him, but no. She was happy being left alone. Eventually, he tried a totally different tack. He would stay up late until everyone else was asleep then he would draw the women of his imagination and enjoy their company.

He told me how, realising that their marriage was definitely lacking, they had consulted a marriage guidance counsellor. They had been interviewed together and separately and then a verdict had been given to each of them in private. He was told, 'Well, your marriage seems to have reached an impasse. There is no way your wife's behaviour is going to change. The only advice I can give you is to get a mistress.'

Neil was surprised by this broad-minded advice.

You may notice that this married man was not treating me to lunches, dinners or theatre outings. He once offered to buy me jewellery. This was not my style, so I politely knocked back his offer.

However, one day he came up with an idea that was my style. The public transport enthusiast fraternity, TESSA, was in the habit of travelling to Melbourne for a weekend every year because Melbourne's transport system was more advanced than Adelaide's. Doug and Neil usually joined the other enthusiasts for this beano. Would I like to ride to and from Melbourne on the express in a sleeper and to spend two days with him in a motel? He was willing to meet all expenses and even hire a car so that we could do some sightseeing.

Oh yes! An all-expenses paid holiday! That I would willingly accept!

CHAPTER 47

A WEEKEND IN MELBOURNE

The Friday night arrived. The kids were given instructions to have fun without wrecking the house. I had borrowed a couple of pretty dresses. Mum and Dad came to the Adelaide railway station to see us off. Neil, being the gentleman that he was, bought drinks for us all from the refreshment car and we stood around drinking and chatting on the platform. While he stowed my luggage in our sleeper, I was left chatting to Mum and Dad and remember saying, 'He's a funny sort of a chap, quite nice and is being generous enough to take me away for the weekend, so what's not to like?'

They agreed. They were happy for me to be getting a break and were ever hopeful that this would be the real thing, bless their hearts.

Once the train got underway, I began to feel sick. I explained to Neil that this used to happen to me as a child. I got excited about something like a birthday party and would become ill and not be able to go to the party. Perhaps a good night sleep would see me settle down. He kindly agreed and he put his things on the top bunk, so that I could settle on the lower one. He then took himself off to the refreshment car to have drinks with the boys and I had my good night's sleep.

The next morning, I was still a bit shaky and apologetic because this was not how we had planned the weekend to proceed. However, he remained sympathetic and we took a taxi to the booked motel. We then went out to pick up the car and enjoy a casual coffee in the sunshine. On returning to the motel, I was feeling fit again so we made good use of the accommodation rather like the girl on the train ... 'not once, but again, and again, and again'. Then Doug phoned to let us know that we were expected to dine with Ray, their mutual Melbourne railway enthusiast friend.

Blast, I thought, *I didn't expect anything like that. However, I suppose time spent behaving ourselves will make us appreciate our private time even more.*

We still had the rest of the day, and I fancied a little variety, so I suggested we go to the Melbourne Art Gallery and have lunch nearby.

We took the car then a tram to the gallery. I was trying to keep him away from the motel room because I thought he would wear himself out and not continue to rise to the occasion. That would spoil the rest of the weekend.

Over lunch we were in jovial conversation and he asked what I thought of him. I could see that he was fishing for some praise or adoration and to my mind that just led on to love. I was determined to not go there again. My light-hearted reply was that he was the type of man that no one ever noticed.

'If I bought a 10 gallon hat would you notice me?'

'No. Let's face it, Neil, you are the most insignificant looking man I have ever met. You remind me of Phillip Humphrey—boring, square, conventional and assumed cold Englishman. His wife says he is hot stuff however, so perhaps you have something in common. You certainly are extremely sexy without advertising it!'

We took the tram back—to the car. He was well into hand-clasping, eye-gazing, *here we go again*! We went back to the motel with no worries about performances. He told me about the 'romance' he had had in Ireland when on a solo holiday. The Canadian lady, he heard her in the other room, but had promised Paula not to have any flings while he was away from her on his own.

'So, I didn't. We had a pleasant time together and went to St Mikan's church to see the mummified crusaders.'

Gosh this bloke is something else. He is miles away from his wife, feeling hot as hell and remembers his promises to his wife. Perhaps I began to regard him more fondly at that realisation. There were so many girls and women in his life that never came to anything. He married for sympathy. He had been the underdog yet kept his promises. He was clever, considerate and sensitive. He was making such a fuss of me just because we sing like a well-practised choir in bed. Ah! Well! Perhaps he'd never had it so good.

I endured dinner with Ray, who was a confirmed bachelor and tolerated my presence as if I was imposing on what should have been a great weekend for the blokes. He trotted out very dusty, corny jokes which we all politely laughed at. Clearly, Neil and Doug adored him, so I was tactful enough not to say how I felt.

The rest of the time was just for us. We took a couple of intermissions to go out for a drive, once to the Healesville Sanctuary and once to the Botanical Gardens. Conversation flowed as easily as the sex. We both had a lifetime of stories to tell.

I learned how his young mother, left alone through the war, was impressed by American airmen and fell for the charms of one in particular. Hence, his cousin was actually his half-sister. He and his cousin/sister had recently worked it out for themselves. He had been sent to his grandparents for a prolonged stay at about the time his sister was born and adopted by his aunt. His father's return was not a joyful one. Mrs Scott's infidelity and the sale of his car to make ends meet angered him greatly. Thereafter, his parents were never fully reconciled, but they stayed married and remote from each other.

My life, with its ups and downs was passed on to him. I even told him about the state of play with David.

'Well, his loss will be my gain,' was his comment.

While we were in the Botanical Gardens, he showed me a bench saying, 'Remember I told you how a colleague and I put a stop to TAA and Qantas's price fixing by organising an independent return flight from Melbourne to London?'

'Yes.'

'Well, the organising and coordinating was so complicated and stressful that I was a nervous wreck by the time I greeted the return passengers to Melbourne. I remember sitting on this bench for the best part of a day, completely dazed, unaware of time passing or what I was doing there.'

I was surprised. 'What happened to you? Did you need medical help?'

'No, I just caught the Melbourne Express home and had a few days sleep.'

'Wow, that was some event!'

On that note, we drove back to town to dine. And so to bed.

Our return trip was memorable in that I don't think either of us slept a wink as we lay on the bottom bunk and entertained each other. The window blind was up to permit moonlight to flood our compartment. We got the

Chapter 47   A weekend in Melbourne

giggles as the train came to a halt at Bordertown station and we noticed the stationmaster's boots perfectly aligned with our window.

We arrived in Adelaide utterly exhausted. Neil went to work, put his head on his desk and slept all Monday. I cannot remember how I made it all the way to McLaren Flat, but fortunately I was not scheduled to be at work.

That was the most enjoyable and exhausting weekend of my life; my life as a mistress.

Much later, I found the rough draft of a letter that Neil had written to Ray which shared how he felt about the weekend.

Dear Ray,
How can I thank you for keeping cool on a hot weekend? One way I suppose is to explain how it all happened.

My sex life has been less than completely fulfilling for a long time, so I decided it was about time I found a mistress. This was nothing against Paula as a person and a wife, just at a disparity of libido.

I met Chris Jancarik about a year ago. This was our first weekend away together. Right from our first meeting in October '82 we both recognised that we felt that we were intellectual and emotional equals. Chris has an awareness that I have rarely seen in a woman. Suffice it to say that the weekend was an unqualified smash hit with all the exciting ingredients of a secret romance.

Chris is a high school teacher, 45, and lives on a small farm in the hills. It is a beautifully secluded spot. She has two daughters and an elder son living at home. Her husband, who was a doctor, died of cancer some years ago and she's since lost her younger son in a tragic accident. Chris knows all my circumstances and the importance of the family unit, especially for Joan.

I have come to this position gladly and without remorse. While I have no intentions of hurting Paula, I would not give Chris up if Paula found out and insisted that I should. Rather, I would explain why I need Chris and I _do need_ Chris. After 25 years of being a good and faithful husband, unselfishly trying to maintain Paula's interest at my tempo,

I have grown tired and my patience has worn out. My needs are real and will not be thwarted by restriction to Paula's lower libido. Paula is a loving, sensitive and conscientious person and probably too preoccupied with Joan's health to be aware of what has happened to me, although, God knows, I have given enough warning signs, even to the point where she must know something. What a problem communication can be!

So, there it lies.

I hope you understand my reticence in getting you involved, Ray. But since you are; at least you have a full explanation now. The weekend will go down as the most happy time for both Chris and I, due to your friendship in no small part.

Sincerely,

Neil

CHAPTER 48

DAD GIVES FATE A PUSH

Such a weekend can be exhausting. However, we recovered and life returned to its normal pace of school, farm, children and relaxation with Neil or other boyfriends. Dad became ill with emphysema. He was hospitalised in the Royal Adelaide Hospital and I could not get down to visit him, but I knew that Neil often walked the streets of Adelaide during his lunch hour so that he could smoke and think about whatever problem was bothering him at work. I asked him to visit Dad, knowing that Dad would be delighted at the visit.

When Neil and I met subsequently, he looked grave and said, 'Do you know what your father said to me?'

'No, what did he say?'

'"You know that your wife will find out eventually." He is right, of course.'

'Not necessarily,' I insisted, not necessarily liking my father's interference.

Why has he tried to stir Neil up in this way? I am perfectly happy with the status quo.

'He really wanted to worry me, because obviously, he would like this situation to be resolved in a happy solution for you, his daughter.'

I shrugged it off. 'I am in a happy situation. Being a mistress suits me just fine.'

But Neil wasn't done.

'... so, I am toying with the idea of leaving Paula and coming to you if you will have me.'

I froze for a moment. 'Well, don't let's be too hasty about all this. I'm seriously considering selling up and moving to Queensland. My sister, Jackie, and her husband have a small holding in the Granite Belt and are going through a hard time financially. If I sell up, I can take my financial profit to Queensland, buy a share in their venture, help them over their hump and find a niche for myself and the girls. Jackie and Kathy would be buddies because they both love horses.'

Neil was aghast. 'Oh no! Please don't do that! What would I do without you?'

I liked the man, but this was too much. *Goodness, he's being a bit melodramatic. I had better squash this attitude.*

'You will find another mistress.'

I suppose it sounded callous. This is why I had held back. I did not feel emotionally involved with Neil. I needed to be free and independent. My financial situation was worrying enough for me to seriously consider selling up and throwing in my lot with Jackie and Denis. That way I would still be part of a rural enterprise and not as alone.

We said goodbye that day, knowing that we both had a lot to think about.

Love is reciprocal, or is it? As a child, I felt love from my parents and reciprocated. Falling in love with Xavier was a reciprocated event. We were swept away with first love. Why did it not last?

Loving my children sprung naturally from within and I have never questioned it. How much and when they reciprocated it is different for each child.

I have loved other men and my love was not reciprocated, so I have been shattered and hurt. It was important to me not to be 'sucked in' again. I just needed sex and companionship. However, I know that no one is perfect. We all have our idiosyncrasies, our talents and disadvantages. Could I live with his set of faults? Would it be wise to let him come to live at 'Attention' as a partner? By his own admission, he was not a handyman. Would he soon realise his inadequacies and understand that he really didn't belong on a farm?

He had consulted the bus timetables and discovered that there was an express bus from Mount Barker to the city. He could leave 'Attention' at 8.30 am, drive the old ute to Mount Barker and park it there and be at work at his usual hour, so his working life would go on uninterrupted.

So much for Ann's edict of 'Let the man live alone for six months then decide if you'll take him in.' Yes, I could see that he wanted to jump from his troubled situation to one where he thought he would be better off. Perhaps this was why he protested his love for me; to negate the guilt he would feel at leaving his current family.

I was not deeply, madly in love. I was determined not to be. However, they say 'Better to marry the man who loves you than the man that you are in love with.' I can see that this would lead to a more comfortable life. In all relationships, one partner is more in love than the other, and for life to run smoothly and happily the least in love member has to be kind. I could be kind, and treat him well, as the men in my life had not treated me.

When discussing the situation with me, he pointed out that he had not realised that I was financially stressed. He noted that when he settled with his wife there would be a lump sum available to pay off my mortgage, so that the farm would be ours. I had to admit that it would be a relief for me, but my concerns were now stuck on the thought that I was doing to another woman what Carol had done to me.

But that was a silly thought.

I had been grateful to Carol for taking Xav off my hands.

I eventually said that he could come, but he had to be sure in his heart of hearts that he could live with himself for taking this leap.

A couple of weeks later, on a Saturday morning, our phone rang…

'I have leapt! I am at the Brighton railway station with a suitcase. Will you please come and pick me up?'

View to South from rest stop Barndioota Road, 10 Kilometres North of Hawker

View Southwest from lighthouse, Cape Willoughby

Graduation day, Ted, me, Sue

Peter

'Attention' during renovation

Attention' renovations complete

Jackie and Denis in Manila 1979

Ted and Sue's Golden wedding

Erica, Kathy and Paul with me.
'One word from me and they do exactly as they like.'

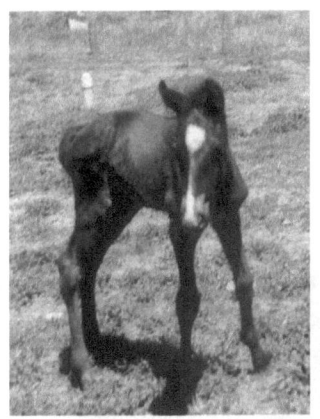

Newborn colt, Zardos

Kathy plays with Zardos

Kathy rides Zardos in a three day event

Doug and Neil, Railway photographers

PART THREE

Maturity

CHAPTER 49

NEIL MOVES INTO 'ATTENTION'

Over the next 30 years, all four of us found a partner. Some of the relationships were successful and others not. What makes some successful and others a failure?

Neil stood in my kitchen.

'I would like to make a cup of tea, would anyone else like one?' He pulled forth a battered lidless bier stein. 'I like a big cup of tea, so I make mine in this,' he said as he put the kettle on to boil.

I was unsure. Did I like this? It seemed like an invasion. Was I really ready to share this space? Well, I had better give it a go!

Later, we sat down to our evening meal together. There were the four of us: Kathy, Erica, Neil and myself. He put a book next to his plate and started reading. I looked at my girls and they looked back.

This was a no-no!

I steeled myself to lay down the rules. 'We do not read while eating together, Neil.'

He seemed surprised. 'Really? I always read while I eat.'

'We do not. It shows a lack of interest in the others at table. This is the time that we share our day and you will learn more about us.'

'Alright then, I will abide by the rules of the house.'

After dinner and dishes, Neil and I would sneak away to the bedroom for 'quality time' together, as it is euphemistically called.

This left the kitchen free for the girls to do their homework. This was not to Kathy's liking. She liked to have me on hand whenever needed and resented Neil taking up so much of my time. Kathy didn't say anything but, because she was as tall as Neil, she would play rough with him. Being a gentleman, he did not retaliate immediately. He had told me that he would not intervene in the upbringing of my children because that was already my area of expertise. Her rough play annoyed him and eventually he had to take a stand.

He was standing with his bier stein full of hot tea when she started elbowing him. He stumbled and 'accidentally' poured hot tea over Kathy. She was not scalded, but she did get a shock and realised that he could play back. The rough play stopped.

Over the next few years, her resentment gradually moved to respect and affection. All my children were moving into their adult lives, helped by us when necessary.

Paul had moved out to live with friends in a shared house while he did his apprenticeship and studied at TAFE. When he inherited his lump sum from his father's estate, I was worried that it would disappear into motorbikes. Neil's expertise with real estate came in very handy, guiding Paul's hand to buy a tidy 3-bedroom home in McLaren Vale. Here, he was independent from us, but not too far away. He let out two of the bedrooms to mates to help pay off the mortgage. Instead of buying motorbikes, he invested in a dog, a large dog, a St Bernard to be precise. He brought home a succession of girlfriends. I always had a friendly chat with them about their employment and how they intended to better their employment prospects. I told them that a woman needed to be financially independent in this day and age.

Both of my girls matriculated and moved on to Adelaide University. They both moved into share houses with other students. Kathy studied for a BSc and Erica a BA. Erica kept her cards close to her chest when it came to boyfriends, so I cannot comment on her progress in that department. Kathy bought home a variety of boyfriends, some we liked more than others. She also brought home a dog called King, because his current owner was not taking good care of him.

Then along came Ralf. He was too good to be true! He was a German lad doing work experience at Balfour's Bakery. He was very well spoken for someone who was working with high school English, extremely well-mannered and obviously adored Kathy. However, it seemed a lost cause as a romance. Ralf's work experience was to fill a gap for him between high school and university. He was due to return to Germany in September to

Chapter 49 *Neil moves into 'Attention'*

start his tertiary education in Economics and IT, while she was in the first year of her university studies and had three years of work ahead to complete a BSc.

He turned 21 on August the 3rd. That was notable because that was Ted's birthday too. A double whammy celebration was called for and Ralf was absorbed into our family and loved by all. And love will find a way, we discovered. Kathy and Ralf spent time together when they had their longest study breaks because Europe and Australia had different academic calendar years.

In her final year, Kathy only had Biochemistry 3 as a subject to study, so she undertook German 1 at uni with no previous experience of the language. She worked hard and passed. Isn't it wonderful what love will do?

She was out of sync with the intake into dietetics, her chosen profession, so she decided to go to Germany and try to get work there while she lived with Ralf who was in the middle of his studies. They lived happily in a very small apartment while he studied and she sought work. Because they spoke German together, she was soon fluent with an Australian accent, which people found fascinating.

When Kathy inherited her lump sum from her father's will, Neil supported her use of much of the money for travel, claiming that travel was an education and mind expander. Indeed, when his girls had been growing up, he had taken his whole family to Britain because he believed in the value of travel and wanted to show them his homeland while they were all together.

However, some of the lump payout she wanted to spend on a diesel ute and a horse float to take Zardos out to equine events. Neil helped her make good purchases and taught her how to manipulate the combination. As a consequence, there was a comfortable feeling lying in bed on a Sunday morning listening to her prepare her own breakfast and lunch, then packing the gear she would need for the day. Her horse and tack had been prepared the day before, then the front door closed and she loaded her ute and horse float. We heard her slowly drive up and out of 'Attention'. She had the day to herself and we had it to ourselves.

When the coast was clear we would have a traditional English breakfast followed by walks through the bush or me weaving while Neil painted, all interspersed with loving. He had an attitude towards bondage as though something in his head had said, 'Women should be kept in chains and always available for sex!' He drew and painted beautiful naked women, but they always had the addition of manacles or handcuffs or were displayed in cages. He possessed a box of manacles and handcuffs and asked most politely if I would like to try his game. He explained the philosophy behind it.

'Women are taught by their parents and society to be demure, restrained and reluctant about sex, but if you had been captured and forced to behave in a wanton way it was not your fault! You could release all your inhibitions and mentally say to yourself that it was his fault. He was forcing this lewd behaviour onto you.'

It worked, and we had an extra thrill added to our love life. It's worth stating that I am not advocating that you all trot down to your nearest adult sex shop for manacles and handcuffs. We all have our own journey in this department. Neil and I trusted each other absolutely, and I understood his attitude and how these toys heightened the experience for him. I insisted that no pain would be involved and so it worked for us.

And where was Erica, our very quiet achiever? She met her birth parents and later told me about both interviews. I was proud that she summed up the situation with such grace, even more so that she was glad that I had raised her. I was always positive and encouraging about her abilities while her birth parents thought little of her achievements. Her Japanese studies progressed well, but her Japanese teacher said that Japanese alone would not make a career and that she would need other skills, perhaps gained by working in an office environment. During school holidays she took herself off to a business school and learned to touch type at a rapid rate, then she was off to university. She moved out of home into a share house in St Peters. It was an exciting time for her, as she was living away from home and independently for the first time. University was a different environment to navigate too.

She worked part-time during the semester breaks, initially at Magic Mountain, until the business shrank to a point there wasn't much work on offer. Later, she worked at The Old London Tavern, in the restaurant as

Chapter 49 *Neil moves into 'Attention'*

a waitress. The work culture in the kitchen was appalling. The chefs used plenty of profanities and quite openly abused junior staff without any repercussions whatsoever from management. She was thankful that she didn't need to consider the job a career move.

As the girls started tripping about, Paul developed itchy feet. Although he was trying to build up a small business, 'Paul's Mobile Mechanic', he toyed with the idea of working on an oil rig. They existed in the north of South Australia where flies, heat and boredom were put up with for the sake of big pay packets. Or he could simply throw a swag into the back of his ute and do a tour of Australia, working as he went.

Neil had a large complement of friends, mainly made up old school chums and transport enthusiasts, who met once a month in each other's homes where they shared photos and videos of transport events that they had filmed. He joined in my life by joining the Agricultural Bureau and meeting the local farmers, and he met all my other friends, including the swingers.

We decided that we would share some activities while keeping some things to ourselves. He had his transport activities and I had spinning and weaving. I was in the habit of filling the weekend with work on the farm and social activities, but in the interest of spending quiet time together my social life was gradually pared back. We still saw all of our friends, just less often than previously.

In many ways, he seemed to me a small boy in a man's body. He loved to feed the windfall quinces to the cows and could make a game of any chore. Packaging a side of beef into meal size packets to place in the freezer was a full morning's work for me, so he took on the most tedious part of the job, that of bagging the mince into 500 gm bags. With small bags at the ready, he would blow one open and place it on the scales. Then his right hand went into the bulk bag and he grabbed a large handful of the cold, wet bloody mince and plonked into the prepared bag, calling out its weight.

'463 gm, not enough!'

Then he had to top it up slightly before screwing the twisty tie around the top. He was challenging himself to get within 5 grams of 500 grams. If he did get a correct weight he would dance around with glee.

I was happy with the situation. He brought more love into my life and a greater financial security. Upon the settlement of his divorce, he paid off my mortgage so the farm was mine. He did not ask that his name be added to the title. His love and trust begat my love and trust. My other lovers slipped away or became good friends of ours. Neil and I never tried to control each other. This relationship was built on mutual care and respect. My first marriage had taught me what I did not want. We truly became a couple and many events that followed we dealt with together. Our relationship became the main warp running through the fabric of life at 'Attention.'

Since I only needed to teach part-time, I was able to take various weaving courses, and from each course I produced a finished article. There was a lovely red rug that Paul admired so much that I gave it to him. There was a tapestry that had Neil's face worked into it that I still possess. It took so long to complete that I vowed never again would I attempt a tapestry.

I bought a large floor loom strong enough to beat out rugs. We installed it in the shed and I produced several lovely rugs, which were given away as gifts over the years.

I must confess that in the first place his protestations of love were much in excess of mine. I had been hurt so many times by falling in love and giving absolutely that I was wary of falling in love again. The slide into love was so gradual and gentle that I never felt 'Oh-oh, here we go again!' But as the years progressed, I cannot say exactly when, I knew I loved him.

He's just my Neil, an ordinary guy. You'd pass him in the street and never notice him.

His manly grace, his charming face, are not the kind that you would find in a statue.

But I can't explain it, it's surely not his brain that makes me thrill,
I love him because he's ... I don't know ...
Because he's just my Neil.

CHAPTER 50

THE GARDEN CONTEST

Neil and I took our first big holiday together, travelling up the east coast of Australia. We were welcomed by the Mitchels—Tom, Mavis and Carolyn—who live in Toowoomba, Queensland.

Carolyn had met Kathy in London when they were both holidaying there and the friendship continues even now. I suppose it was a novelty of meeting a fellow Australian in the foreign city and having a friend with whom you could laugh about the idiosyncrasies of the British.

Our arrival coincided with the Flower Festival. Toowoomba has rich volcanic soil and a semitropical climate which causes their gardens to flourish. Once a year (in September) they have the garden festival and the Council awards prizes for best garden, best street, best shop, and so on. The result is magnificent flowers and blooming shrubs everywhere. Naturally, we had to visit the railway station and it was as blooming lovely as the rest of Toowoomba.

This is marvellous, I thought. We should have a Flower Festival in McLaren Flat and McLaren Vale.

Upon our return, I told the Agricultural bureau what we had seen and what I had thought. They agreed it was a great idea, but how was I to achieve it?

As is usually the case, the person with the bright idea is the one that must organise it if they want it to materialise. So, I laid my plans.

It would have to occur in the springtime when the gardens were looking their best. The main streets of both towns would have to be strongly involved. Gardens in the surrounding countryside should also be encouraged. I would need judges, and prizes to encourage participants.

Judges had to be serious and respected, so I always asked someone who worked for the Onkaparinga Council, someone with botanical or agricultural training, and a previous winner. They were approached well in advance. They were not paid, but they had a pleasant day looking at gardens and given a good lunch. I never had trouble filling these roles.

By visiting garden shops and hardware shops in McLaren Flat and McLaren Vale and telling the owners or managers my plans, I rounded up large collection of donations—usually plants, but sometimes other gardening paraphernalia.

However, people are reluctant to put themselves forward, so I created my own means of coercion.

Everyone living along the main streets would be automatically entered into the contest. Outlying farms could be entered by filling out an entry form giving clear details of how to reach their farm and any special features of their garden. There were things like 'all native plants' or 'no added water.' I explained my procedure in posters and articles in the local newspapers and on a specific morning I escorted the three judges along the two main streets. Each judge gave a mark out of ten to each garden. This way I could arrive at a winning town and three winning town gardens. I then took the judges to 'Attention' and gave them lunch.

In the afternoon, Neil drove the judges to the outlying gardens where they talked to the gardeners and were shown around. They wrote brief reports which enabled me to allot prizes.

A week later, interested residents attended a prize giving at the McLaren Vale Oval. The winning town was announced and prizes given to best main street gardens and to every outlying garden entrant. I did not make that public. Instead, I labelled the prizes best native garden, best hillside garden, best roadside garden, and so on. Thus, every keen gardener went home with a prize in hand and a smile on their face. I told my Beta Sigma Phi friends about the garden contest and the central Council decided to donate a large wooden shield, to which small silver shields could be attached each year announcing which township was the winner. The large shield was displayed for the year in the winning township's country store.

I ran this contest for around five years before it became a burden. When I asked for help and received none, I abandoned it.

CHAPTER 51

THE OBLIGATORY TRIP HOME, AND WHAT FOLLOWED

Neil's father visited us only once, and during his visit he grumpily told Neil that in his day if a man was unhappy at home, he just had to put up with it. Quite soon after the visit he died of a brain tumour, leaving his wife living in their home in Glenelg North. His will left everything to Neil on the condition that he took care of his mother. She was frail and absent-minded. Yes, she did need looking after. So, when we wanted to take The Obligatory Trip Home, we called upon Paul to keep an eye on her by visiting her weekly.

We visited Japan, hoping to catch up with Erica, but she was travelling. Because our trip was already planned when this happened, she contacted the Tanaka family and the Watari family. They both served as excellent hosts.

Of course, the trains had to be experienced. Firstly, the very crowded suburban trains, and then the very fast train from Tokyo to Osaka, the Shinkansen. We visited parks and gardens around monasteries, and we always ate amazing meals, all set out to please the eye as much as the stomach. Even when unaccompanied by our Japanese hosts we found the general population very friendly. They wanted to practice their English on us.

In London, my cousin Dotsy and husband were in the midst of renovating a house. They kindly tidied a bedroom and the kitchen and suspended work for two weeks so that we could have a rent-free place to stay. Neil was in seventh heaven travelling around London on his beloved red buses while I enjoyed the excellent museums, thereby learning some of the history of London, my home patch.

We then spent some time visiting my school friend, Elaine, and her husband Bob. Elaine and Neil fought it out over the scrabble board, and Neil also enjoyed time with a group of railway enthusiasts at Didcot. We also visited the Railway Museum at York. Since Neil needed tips to help him set up the National Railway Museum at Port Adelaide, we were given a VIP tour of the museum and an interview with the manager.

While returning to Australia we both caught the flu, probably from someone on the aeroplane. As I recovered, Neil did not. He seemed to be burning up with fever and just wanted to drink bottles of Coke. One night he was so cold, clammy, and delirious that I decided to take him to hospital.

All was quiet in Emergency. There seemed to be just one living soul, the nurse taking admissions. She gave Neil a jar and told him to go to the toilet and pass a sample of urine into the jar. He was behaving in such a bewildered way that I was worried that he had not understood or had fainted in the toilet. Eventually he staggered out, handed in the sample and collapsed into a chair beside me. All was quiet again. He was sweating profusely, and I was afraid that he would pass out. Suddenly, the whole place came alive. Doctors appeared. A bed appeared. A drip with sugar solution appeared and he was whisked away. The duty nurse explained that there were ketones in his urine. He was a diabetic and would be taken care of. I should go home and return in the morning for a fuller explanation. So, I did as I was told.

After a good night's sleep, I dressed as glamorously as I could in black pencil skirt and soft flowing blouse. *This should cheer him up.*

His eyes lit up as my high heels clicked into the 4-bed ward and the other men peered enviously over their newspapers. That was a moment of joy for us, but the serious stuff was about to start. We were taken aside and given a crash course on type one diabetes. What to eat, when to eat, how to do blood sugar tests and how to respond to them. Neil was kept in hospital for a few days so that he could stabilise, practice his testing and work out how to regulate his sugar flow. He was then released into the care of Dr Tolstoychef.

Dr T amused me, in that he had the same neatness and efficiency as Xavier. His desk was laid out with regimental order, he knew exactly where to find this referral or that prescription. He was a very effective specialist. Within a month, Neil was diagnosed with high thyroid and coeliac disease. His thyroid gland was obliterated with radioactive iodine and replaced with a regular dosage of thyroid pills. I was instructed on how to feed a coeliac. I had to bake his gluten-free bread and avoid thickeners and other gluten-rich products that could make him weak. The bread was only appetising when toasted and there were very few goodies on the market that were gluten-free at the time, but we explored and experimented until he had a healthy diet that answered all his needs. This extra work was a huge chore to start with, but we gradually worked it into our normal routine.

All this meant that our vigorous, spontaneous sex life had to be somewhat modified and timed carefully, because a carbohydrate rich meal had to be eaten prior to energetic activity. However, it was managed because where there is a will there is always a way. 'Bondage' was usually involved.

In my first marriage, I was in psychological bondage. The bonds were only broken when I filed for divorce. In this marriage, the bondage was a game. When the game finished the toys were stowed away in their box and we resumed our normal, well-balanced relationship.

In time, Neil's daughter, Joan, died. Joan had lived into her late teens. No mean feat for a girl born with cystic fibrosis. That was a credit to the great care and devotion from Paula in most part, and Neil, in small part, had given to her. Neil returned to his family for the day of her funeral and was understandably remote for a few days. They had all loved her greatly.

Once Paul was relieved of his grandma-caring duties, he took off to work at Moomba. That was a loss because he was always a great help on the farm.

As soon as Neil's health issues were settled, he returned to work full-time, and I returned to teaching part-time. I fitted in courses leading to an Arts degree in weaving. We managed the farm between us. We managed to raise most of our needed vegies, chicken, beef, and lamb. We even raised geese for Christmas. With an extra pair of willing hands, the organised chaos became more organised.

CHAPTER 52

GOLDEN WEDDING

Sue and Ted had been married for 50 years.

I paused to look back and remember what wonderful parents they had been to me. They had not approved of Xavier, but they had stood aside to let me weather the storms of that marriage without interfering. Then, when I was alone again, they had stepped up to the plate and were supportive to me and my children when we had needed them most.

They had had their own trials and tribulations to contend with at the same time. They had not paid off their house as most people of their age had. Perhaps it was because they had been so generous to Jackie and me, or perhaps it was Ted's gambling addiction. Sue, who was usually the quiet one, had spoken up and insisted that Ted's addiction had to be controlled. He was issued pocket money each week which he could spend as he wished. If he took it to the races and lost it, so be it, but he was not to take any more out of their communal funds.

It was a time to enjoy the now. Phil and Eileen threw a small party for them, and they were congratulated and feted by all their friends. The queen—yes, that queen—even sent them a letter, which they were proud to display.

And there was still time to enjoy a future together.

They had a scheme. They split the year into two halves. In the first half of the year, they worked in the potting shed that Ted had built from nine until four through the week. Ted did hand building and Sue worked on the potter's wheel that Ted had made her. They fired their produce in the kiln that Ted had built. Then in June, when the weather in South Australia was growing cold, they loaded up the Datsun 120Y and headed north. They enjoyed the warmer weather and sold their goods to gift shops and tourist shops along the way. They returned after a couple of months and set to work again. This time, they sold the fruits of their labour to local shops, thereby accruing some extra cash to make Christmas special. They always had a Christmas party because it was their wedding anniversary. At one Christmas party, Dad gave out to each couple a parcel shaped like a large bon-bon. When they opened them, they were amused to find that it contained two toilet rolls. He had a story to tell about them.

'I was out driving last week behind a large delivery truck when a big box fell of the back of it and almost hit my car. I stopped and ran to the box, and called and waved at the truck to stop, but it continued on its way, leaving me with the big box. It was not very heavy, so I stowed it in the back of my car to open when I got home. It was full of toilet rolls, so I decided to share them with you.' Everyone was amused because the term 'fell off the back of a truck' is a term for stolen goods, and as he told the story about 'calling and waving' to the truck, he mimed that this was done very quietly.

Towards the end of the 1980, Ted became ill. He never discussed his illness, but as he wasted away we could see that it must be some form of cancer. Soon, he was only mobile in a wheelchair. As his 77th birthday approached, I was wondering what outing he would enjoy. The answer was obvious, 'a day at the races'. But how could I drive close enough to comfortably wheel him into the stand?

I phoned the South Australian Jockey Club to ask permission to park in the members' car park and walk through the members' stand into the stand where I knew I could make him comfortable. I explained to a dark brown voice that Ted had been a regular racegoer all his adult life and that this would be his last visit to a racecourse.

'How many of you will be accompanying your father?' the voice enquired.

'Just me and Mum,' I replied.

'Give me your address, I will send you a complimentary parking voucher for the members' car park and three free entrance tickets to the members' stand for next Saturday.'

'Thank you very much! Dad will be thrilled at your gift!'

To which he replied, 'Think nothing of it. It's the least we can do for a loyal supporter of the sport of kings.'

Dad was overjoyed at both my thought and the generosity of the SAJC.

The weather smiled on us too. I was able to wheel him through the members' stand into the grandstand, while Mum showed our complimentary tickets at each gate. I parked him in a sheltered sunny spot and acted as his runner. He glowed with satisfaction as I returned with his betting tickets from the bookies ring. We did not try to join the crush of spectators along the rails, we simply relied on the commentators' report for the thrill of the race. Then his ticket was replaced with winnings or consigned to the bin, and the next list of starters was considered. Mum conveyed cups of tea and sandwiches from the refreshment bar and had an occasional flutter with the TAB. Between races, he basked in the atmosphere of his favourite stomping ground. It was a memorable day out for us all.

CHAPTER 53

THE 50TH BIRTHDAY

I was about to have a milestone birthday, the big five zero, and I wanted the whole family there to celebrate!

Paul and Kathy were there. Paul was working at Moomba and, fortunately, was on the Adelaide half of his roster. Kathy was still studying her final year of her BSc at that point and had added German 1 to her workload in readiness to return to Germany to be with Ralf. But Erica was in Japan. Letters from her told us how this all came about. At the end of 1986, she planned to visit Japan for six weeks, with the intention of visiting her host sister, Hiromi, and her family, as she hadn't seen them since 1982. Hiromi came to collect her from Osaka Kansai Airport in her very high-tech car. Much had happened since Erica had visited them in 1982. Hiromi's mother had died, and her father's alcoholism had progressed to a point where he crawled around the house each night drunk. Hiromi had graduated from university and was now working for an airline and looking for a husband, her brother was working as an apprentice chef, and younger sister, Rieko, was finishing high school. As the eldest sibling, Hiromi had an enormous amount of responsibility.

It was an interesting stay, as the father set a curfew for Erica and insisted that she obey it. She did not find his behaviour particularly credible and chose to ignore it regularly. After a month, when she had reached a decision to stay in Japan to teach English for a year while she brushed up on her Japanese, it became clear that she needed find her own place. She found a place in Suzurandai with Simon, and they had a great time that year. No wonder that she was not able to return for my special occasion, even when I told her how very special it was to be.

Friends were invited to my 50th birthday party. The party was planned in Scottish style and guests were requested to dress appropriately and brush up on their Harry Lauder (he was a Scottish singer and comedian). You do not have to be mad to be friends of ours, but it certainly helps! Our friends also knew that we take preparation for fun very seriously, so they begged, borrowed and stole tartan ties, sassy sashes, golf caps, travelling rugs—even long skirts and enough kilts for us to think that the perennial chestnut question about underwear would finally be answered. The local butcher was also aware of the preparations, as he made a great ham and three different haggis. Since not all of our friends knew each other, we gave out name tags on arrival which allowed them to keep their own Christian names, but shuffled them into clans so that they were forced to meet people that were new to them. After allowing them one alcoholic beverage, the clan leaders called their clans unto them for a general briefing of their duties throughout the evening and for practice of their allotted song. Duties involved serving of one food course, washing dishes after a course, and singing to announce a food course.

When we all reformed in the big back room, Pam Taylor announced that Neil and I were to be married here and now! A stunned silence ensued, broken only by Pam making the first declaration of the wedding ceremony. Even when they gained their collective breaths, guests remained attentively silent throughout the proceedings in a psychic feeling of joint disbelief. This gradually dissipated as Pam passed from the reading to the vows. Then I realised Neil was beginning to tremble and sweat, not with emotion but with hypoglycaemia! In all the rush and excitement, he had not eaten at his usual time. Fortunately, civil ceremonies are short and he was fed in time to avoid him slipping into a hypo.

The Scottish 50th birthday then collapsed into a wedding feast. Sue and Ted were in on the secret of the dual celebration and helped with preparation and cooking, but the clans served, cleaned up, washed up and sang to keep the whole event rolling along. The next day we took off on the honeymoon to the eastern states where winter is not so severe.

We took in Queensland, and saw how hard Jackie and Denis were working to establish their winery. There was a write-up in *The Australian* about their Bald Mountain Winery going into production. Then we went on to Brisbane

Chapter 53   *The 50th birthday*

in all its Expo glory courtesy of Greg and Sandy Parsons. We travelled the east coast to Sydney. Cape Byron, the most easterly point in Australia was the most notably breathtaking beauty spot of the coast. It rained so severely upon us in Sydney that we headed home where Kathy had been doing a wonderful farm-sitting job in our absence. She passed German 1, as well as the rest of her BSc. After the honeymoon, life went on as before.

Erica sent us a Japanese student, Yoshi Watari, and later Rieko and Rika, Hiromi's sister and her friend. All these Japanese friends of hers knew that a friendly home would be waiting for them in South Australia at 'Attention', but they were flabbergasted at our isolation.

'Where do you get food?' Yoshi asked. After all, he had not seen a shop, let alone a takeaway for the last 20 km. The little girls returned to the safety of their bedroom and did not venture out between excursions to the kitchen, bathroom or sightseeing trips that we took them on.

Neil's work had changed for the better. Instead of racing around Adelaide's western metropolitan sector, vainly trying to keep up with all planning policy reviews, major development applications, planning appeals, structure planning work and ministerial replies, an overdue department re-organisation had moved most of his work to a new unit and he found himself put out to care for an undeveloped area to concentrate on its development. He cared for about 350 ha of middle suburbia on government land which was intended to lead to new housing for 15,000 people only four to seven miles from the city centre.

I was blissfully happy doing the design and drawing that were part of my weaving course. Later, Neil joined me to study History of Art. We both passed with distinctions.

The veggie garden bloomed, watered by river water, the chickens and geese laid well, fruit trees were bearing, and sheep needed culling. On the downside, the shed was not quite finished. The road was badly in need of repair and then we ran out of rainwater because of the leaky tank.

'Life gets tedious, don't it?'

But to the rescue came Neil. A contractor was commissioned to line and roof the tank so that when the rains came we had a wonderful watertight, light tight, swallow-proof tank to store it in. Neil was determined that the road and the shed be completed before he accepted a three-day week and I resolved to seek a little more relief teaching.

Most of my work was voluntary, but rewarding, nonetheless. We hosted a big Beta Sigma Phi fundraiser. Twenty people dined in the big back room on my homemade Irish stew after a walking tour of Clarendon. I continued to seek help for the restoration of the industrial loom that I had in the shed.

Paul tried a new business, Flat Transport, using a large tray truck to deliver heavy hardware, like wheelbarrows, from manufacturer to retailer. Unfortunately, he lost his driving license for six months due to driving while too merry. His response to the punishment was, 'They can't do this to me! Don't they realise driving is my livelihood!' He survived on odd jobs and help from his friends, and was eventually back behind the wheel of his truck a sadder but wiser man, working twice as hard to make up for lost earnings and managing to keep his business afloat in those hard times for small businesses.

Simon went travelling the world, but Erica stayed on in Japan. Hiromi's father had died during 1988, so Hiromi offered her a place in their family home again. During 1989, Erica studied Japanese, taught English, and lived with Hiromi. It was a year in which she got to know Kiji, Hiromi's aunt, much better. I'd rather have seen her degree finished, but she was 21 and had grown very independent while fending for herself. I had to accept that it was her life and let her live it.

We missed Kathy, but her letters were bright. She was obviously happy with Ralf. They lived together in a very small apartment while he studied and she sought work. She was so fluent in German that she soon found work and was off and running.

CHAPTER 54

LOBETHAL AND THE TAPESTRY

A few of the members of SACSOS (South Australian Coloured Sheep Society) were finding old spinning and weaving machinery and restoring them because commercial spinning and weaving mills were being moved offshore for cheaper production in China. In 1986, I came across a collection of such equipment in the home of a farmer who really did not want to keep it. Sue, Ted and Neil were with me. I was particularly interested in a small industrial loom and said to Neil, 'Could we make them an offer for that loom?'

'We could offer to take it off their hands. Even then, there would be expenses. We would need to extend the shed and to have the loom transported,' he said. I thought he was being particularly mean, but they took us up on the offer and soon it was installed in our shed.

It didn't work. Indeed, it needed a lot of work and I had yet to know how to get it started. I reached out to people being put out of work by the closing of local mills and several visited, but they could not give me the time to restore my loom. A few years passed.

Then I met Fritz Bruch. He had been a loom tuner and manager in the Onkaparinga Woollen Mills in Lobethal. These mills were part of the Onkaparinga Woollen Mills business and when it became evident that it was cheaper to weave in China, they gradually closed down their operations in Australia. He was told, as a manager, that everything was going to go on as normal. People would not be put off work and this message was passed on to his fellow workers. But they did close down, and they did put people out of work. Lobethal had a huge population of workers who were simply discarded. He felt betrayed and so did the workers that he had influenced. He trained as a TV antenna installer. So, at least he had an income.

When he looked at my loom, he noted that it had a warp on it already. It only needed a pirn winder so that we could wind pirns, put them into the shuttles and start weaving. He had control of some of the left-over machinery, including pirn winders and he lent me one. I was therefore able to prepare pirns, that is, bobbins. He visited us on a Sunday and tuned my loom and we wove the existing warp. Then he said, 'You need to prepare another warp of your own design, prepare some pirns and when you are ready I will come back to help you with the weaving.'

I did this for a trial and then set to work on something more ambitious. Neil had bought a lovely, woolen tie while we were in England and suggested that I copy it. I analysed its weave and set about making a warp and pirns ready to weave. Fritz came over and we wove a few yards of the tie fabric. I took the fabric to a tie-maker, and he made me about 100 ties at five dollars each. Unfortunately, ties were just slipping out of fashion, so I was left with 100 unsellable ties. Over the years, I just gave them away as presents.

When we stopped for lunch, Fritz would bemoan the fact that the machinery left behind at the Lobethal mill site was neglected and just shoved into back corners of various sheds. He said he was part of a group of people forming the Lobethal Heritage Association who wanted to restore the machines and create a museum. Neil had played a large part in setting up the National Railway Museum at Port Adelaide and we decided to visit a meeting of the Lobethal Heritage Association to see if we could help in any way. We found a group of people who had worked at the mill, sitting around a table and complaining that the council was doing nothing to help them. Neil asked, 'Are you an official group? Do you have a constitution?'

'What's a constitution?' they asked.

He explained that you were not an official body unless you had a constitution and you had some money in the bank. He suggested that they all put in a membership fee, so one of them had to become treasurer. To grow the account, they should all put in two dollars every time they attended a meeting. They thought this was a bit steep, but Fritz was their leader and convinced them that Neil knew the way forward. Neil wrote them a constitution. They became a proper committee with a President, Fritz, their natural leader, a treasurer, a secretary and minutes, all the usual paraphernalia. They were then ready to approach the council for funds and for a request that all the machines from all over the abandoned site be put together in one shed so that they could be worked upon. The council eventually put aside the worst shed they could find, and, using a forklift, dumped all the machines in this shed. Its roof leaked, its walls let in dust, and it was a very bad site from which to start a museum.

Although Lobethal was an hour's drive from our home, Neil and I attended their monthly meetings and helped with appeals to the council for a few years, but several members of the council seemed be absolutely opposed to the LHA.

I was still a regular attendee to the Hand-spinners and Weavers Guild in Adelaide, and one Saturday morning I got a bright idea. *Lobethal should have a community tapestry!* I didn't know how to go about doing this, so I consulted people who had been involved in community tapestries, namely Ellie Webb and Katerina Urban. They explained how to go about it and said that they would help if I wanted to organise a community tapestry for Lobethal. They were willing to be the hands on if I took on the role of organiser. The first step was to gather input from the people of Lobethal.

We put a public notice into the local newspaper, fixing a time and place for members of organisations past and present to come and tell us about their activities and bring along logos or any images that they would like to see worked into their town tapestry. A large number of people arrived to tell us about the history of their town. Of course, I already knew about the history of the mills and asked Fritz to bring photographs of looms and people working in the mills. Ellie volunteered to be the designer but requested a fee. This is where my work began. I had to apply for grants to pay her, to pay for materials, to pay for worksites and to pay something towards the travel expenses of Katerina Urban and Wilma Badjka.

The next step was to gather a team of volunteer tapestry weavers. Another public notice was placed in the local paper offering a free eight-week course on tapestry weaving to people interested in joining the team. Again, we had a wonderful response from the people of Lobethal. While Ellie designed,

Katerina and Wilma gave the eight-week course. Early in 1998, we had a design and a group willing to weave.

I spent the whole of that year and the next seeking out and applying for grants for community arts projects. I was successful in a few applications. I also appealed to the clubs that were to be included in the design and local businesses for their sponsorship, with limited success. However, we ploughed on and finding a site to set up the large loom was another of my tasks.

There was a vibrant market in one of the large sheds left vacant when Onkaparinga pulled out and I appealed to its organiser. He was happy to have the loom set up in his market, but he wanted me to pay a fee for the space it would occupy. Our finances could not cover it, but the LHA did have a small display of weaving machinery and Fritz came to the rescue. If they moved their machinery back from the walkway, there would be room to erect a large tapestry loom. Katerina and Joe, her husband, spent a weekend setting up the loom, warping it up and hanging Ellie's cartoon of the design behind the warp. Then a roster of helpers was drawn up and work commenced. Locals became regular attendees to the market, just to watch work progress, and slowly but surely the tapestry in all its glory took shape.

Neil's artistic abilities were put to work, creating a pamphlet about the tapestry and the significance of the pictures that were incorporated. We gave these out to interested viewers and I wrote a few updates for the local paper. I envisaged this tapestry hanging in the entrance hall to the museum that Fritz and his friends dreamed about. However, I failed to convey this to the LHA, so that when the tapestry was finished, there was no home for it. I had to raise funds for the proper mounting and protection for this wonderful piece of art and eventually found that the Lobethal Community Association was happy to accept it into their care.

Finally, the saga of the Lobethal Tapestry was due to finish. From then on the tapestry would belong to the Lobethal Community Association (LCA).

The council did eventually supply the LHA with a better shed at the back of its complex. However, it was nowhere near large enough for a museum. The LHA crew shifted the precious machinery and other artefacts into this larger, weatherproof shed. It was still there when I visited in 2018 and the tapestry was housed in the senior citizens hall. So, there is still hope that with local interest the tapestry could hang in the entrance foyer of a Lobethal Heritage Museum.

CHAPTER 55

SPINOFFS FROM THE LOBETHAL TAPESTRY

While we were preoccupied with Lobethal and the weaving of the tapestry, life went on. There was a devastating pilot's strike in Australia, which cost millions of dollars to the air and tourism industries. Kathy and Ralf were living in Germany, Erica and Simon in Japan, but Erica eventually realised that it was time to come home to complete the final year of her BA. It was very hard leaving behind her family and friends in Japan. The culture shock of coming to Australia from Japan was hard, as she felt the two worlds were incompatible. She worked hard at Chinese, Japanese and Asian economic history. Before the results were out she said, 'I went okay'. Erica always sets such high standards for herself that we knew it was in the bag.

Simon came to visit her in Adelaide at Christmas in 1988, and they went to NZ for six weeks together. They stayed at his parents' home and she felt his mother did not approve of the relationship. He had the feeling of being pressured by his family to find a job in NZ and was uncertain about what he wanted to do. So, Erica came home to start the third year of her degree and they did not see each other again. She moved into a share house in Brighton in 1989 and felt lonely and lost for the first part of the year. Later she met Brian and they found a place together in Brighton. Paul was with Ros at that point, still in Adelaide, and were frequent visitors to 'Attention'.

My knees were very painful with arthritis and the doctor suggested that I have arthroscopes on both knees. I was hospitalised for a few days and it took me a few weeks before I was walking again. There was some improvement but nothing miraculous. However, I could walk with less pain, but the farm and garden suffered because I could not be active enough.

One hot, sunny Sunday morning when I was parking in Lobethal to visit

Chapter 55 *Spinoffs from the Lobethal tapestry*

the women at work on the tapestry, I saw a young couple eating their breakfast outside a small campervan. They were young German backpackers who had been working nearby, but the farmer had dismissed them with no wages and they were wondering what to do next.

I could see that they were young and fit and I knew that we could use two such helpers. I told them that I might be able to find work for them and took their names and numbers. They were Ann and Fabian. When I arrived home that afternoon, I told Neil about the couple and he thought that we might be able to help them and take care of a few farm problems. We phoned them and guided them to 'Attention', negotiated a price for the gardening and other work that needed to be done.

The weather was so hot that living in their little campervan was uncomfortable, so we invited them to live in our back bedroom for which they were most grateful. They worked well and tirelessly until we could no longer afford them. When we told them they were most disappointed.

'In a few weeks we are due to fly to Sydney to meet up with Fabian's parents. Could we please just stay with you until then? We will work for no pay to pay for our accommodation.'

We agreed to this, as they were such open, friendly, hard-working youngsters.

They told us about their dismissal from the Lobethal farm. Neil told them that they had definitely been wrongly dismissed and cheated by the farmer. He gave them the confidence to return and confront him. They came back with happy smiles and cash in their pockets. The farmer had still been grumpy and reticent, refusing to pay them but, when he stormed out of the house, his wife had paid them what they were owed.

During their stay, we became great friends, taking them to see some of Adelaide's sights and playing cards in the evening. We were sorry to see them go and exchanged addresses, promising to catch up again sometime.

Another exciting episode which started during this period was the 'Bingle'.

On my way home from Lobethal, I stopped to do some shopping, as you do. When pulling out of my car park, I rubbed against a Volkswagen that was pulling out in the opposite direction. We both sustained scratches.

So, we stopped and exchanged names addresses and phone numbers. The scratches were so slight that we did not bother to take any steps towards repairing them. However, later in the following year we were sent an account from the father of the girl who had been driving the Volkswagen. It was a huge account, much bigger than the repair for a few scratches. We replied saying that we thought the bill was excessive and Mr Schwartz took us to the small claims court. Here, he produced a sheet of paper from a garage's quote book. It was a quote for repairs to Miss S's Volkswagen. I was adamant that something was not quite right here and asked for a second hearing. I was allowed to take a copy of the quote. When I took a closer look I saw there was no date on the quote. *Fishy!* I visited the garage that had given the quote and explained the situation to the manager. He showed me the quote book. The pages were numbered so it was easy to find when the Schwartz's quote had been written. The quotes before and after were dated. For some reason, the date had been omitted on Mr Schwartz's quote. I said this aloud to the manager and he nodded in agreement. He made no comment about the character of Mr S, who was a local businessman, but he said that I could borrow his entire quote book until after the next court hearing.

In court, I pointed out the lack of date and what the date must have been by looking at its place in the quote book. It was much later than the time of our bingle. The judge agreed that because of the date-fixing there was nothing to connect me with the probably false quote.

The judge dismissed the Schwartz case, saying that there was no evidence to support their claim.

I was waiting for Neil to pick me up when the Schwartzs came through the waiting room and Mr S was heard to remark, 'So much for nice little old ladies!'

Neil looked into our rights in this situation and wrote to Mr Schwartz asking for $742.06 to cover our expenses and costs brought about by their false claim. Mr Schwartz duly paid us!

The lesson here is to never underestimate nice little old ladies!

CHAPTER 56

GOODBYE TED

One Saturday afternoon in January, Sue, Ted, Neil, me and Kathy were all together.

Kathy said, 'The plans are laid. Ralf and I will be married in July this year. It has to be in Germany because I am free to travel while he is still in the middle of his studies and my visa has expired. We can only continue to be together if we are married. Will you and Neil be able to come?'

I was sad. 'Well, Teddy is very ill. Your wedding will be a joyous occasion whether we are there or not, and we will be with you in spirit. Teddy is very weak, I don't think we can leave him.'

'Chrissie is staying here to say goodbye to me,' he said with a look of gratitude in his sad eyes.

Just before leaving for Germany, Kathy visited Sue and Ted to say 'goodbye'. She left by the front door, walked past their lounge window on her way to the front gate. She turned to exchange a final farewell wave. Then she stopped, leaned towards the window and planted a kiss on the window.

'We won't clean that piece of window ever again, will we, hun?' said Teddy. We lost him soon after.

Dear Jackie,

It was good that you and Denis managed to come to South Australia for Dad's funeral. Denis wrote and delivered a great eulogy. *Abou Ben Adhem* was the poem I read because it summarised Dad and his faith in and love of people.

Do you remember his funny thumbs? Remember the way that they grew in a curve sideways from his hands? Remember the one that had been sawn off in an accident and sewn on without the middle joint?

Remember how he could press it up against his nose so that it looked as though he had an entire thumb poked up his nose? We would go into squeals of laughter when he did that. We were easy to amuse, weren't we?

They did so much for us. They taught us to walk, to talk, to clean our teeth and other bits, to swim, to ride a bicycle, to drive a car, how to keep on trying, to have faith in other people and not to be afraid of asking a stranger for help. Then, in his last big help to me, he restored this rundown cottage into a lovely home. His aim was that I would sell 'Attention' at a tidy profit and buy a nice little house in the suburbs. But Kathy wanted her horses, and the rest of us became accustomed to country life.

When he was in the hospice, he repeatedly asked me to find some way to let him take his own life. I asked those that I knew in the medical profession and did gain a few extra sleeping pills but was told 'These will not be enough to do the job themselves. He will have to get more sleeping pills to add to these.' However, by the time I returned to Ted's bedside I could see that the staff were maintaining such a high level of morphine in his system that he was in no position to save up extra pills. Even though he was very heavily sedated, he got out of bed each morning, showered and shaved himself, before returning to bed. He did that same routine on the day he died. He was that kind of man, wasn't he?

Do you remember that if we were feeling a bit off-colour as children and didn't want to go to school he would say 'Get up, get dressed and have your breakfast, then let's see how you are feeling.' Most times, by the time we had dragged ourselves through those processes, we felt well enough to catch the bus to school. His 'buck yourself up' mentality had worked again. Was that the spirit that pulled Londoners through the war? Was that the spirit that enabled him to lift himself out of the extreme poverty that he was born into? How did he find/earn the money that it took to do the things he did for us? The new bicycles and proper school uniform for me to go to the grammar school, the dance lessons for me, the riding lessons for you. We took these things as lovely gifts at the time without thinking of the sacrifices Sue and Ted made for us. It is now, as an adult, that I realise how hard they worked for us. What a large proportion of their income was spent on us. Why did they come to Australia? It offered a more promising future for us. My goodness, we were lucky in our choice of parents!

Did you know that when Dad reached retirement age, they still had a mortgage on their house, so he felt that he could not retire? He would probably die before Sue, and should at least leave her with a roof over her head. His solution was typical Ted. He applied for a job as a janitor at Moomba and said that he was four years younger than he really was. Four more years of work meant that their little unit was paid off when he did retire.

When I want to do things for my children or grandchildren Neil is amazed. 'Why do you feel you must do things for them?'

'Because my parents did so many things for me' is my reply.

'My parents never did anything like that for us or our children.'

'Well, there you go. Mine did!'

Enough of that, let's get back to Ted in the hospice. Jackie Searle visited him the day before he died. He was heavily sedated and could not open his eyes. Sue said to him, 'It's Jackie, dear.' He held her hand, but did not open his eyes.

She said to me later, 'He may have thought that I was his daughter, Jackie, but it doesn't matter does it? It's even better, really.'

I would go down to visit each evening after school, leaving Neil to deal with the farm jobs. One afternoon, like any other, Mum, who spent most of her time at his bedside, noticed that his very shallow breathing seemed to have stopped. We called for a nurse who confirmed 'yes, he was dead'. We sat there for a little while in silence, then Sue turned to me and said, 'That's it then. He's gone. We might as well go home.'

It all sounded very cold.

Days later, through tears, she said, 'He's not coming back, Chris, is he?'

Well, I believe he lives on through us, especially when I look at my arthritis gnarled hands with these thumbs that arch out sideways.

Finally, as requested,
This is the poem that I read at his funeral ...
Abou Ben Adhem (may his tribe increase!)
Awoke one night from a deep dream of peace,
And saw, within the moonlight in his room,
Making it rich, and like a lily in bloom,
An angel writing in a book of gold:-
Exceeding peace made Ben Adhem bold,
And to the presence in the room he said,
'What writest thou?'—the vision raised its head,
And with a look all made of sweet accord,
Answered, 'The names of those who love the Lord.'
'And is mine one?' said Abou. 'Nay not so,'
Replied the angel. Abou spoke more low,
But cheery still; and said, 'I pray thee, then,
Write me as one that loves his fellow men.'
The angel wrote and vanished. The next night
It came again with great awakening light
And showed the names whom love of God had blest,
And lo, Ben Adhem's name led all the rest.

Love to all.
Have a quiet weep with me,
Chris

Sue lost all her 'umph' when she lost Ted. Without her companion, she lost her enthusiasm for pottery and enjoying life in general. She expected me to fill many of the gaps that Ted had left and she refused to move with the times. She refused to use credit cards and ATMs. It had to be cash and I had to bring $100 every Friday to her so that she could pay for her daily needs. I could not get her interested in another hobby and was afraid that she would just fade away from life through lack of interest. Sadly, those fears were realised in time, but not before some good years.

CHAPTER 57

THE DEPRESSION WE HAD TO HAVE

The 1990 year opened at a family level with my niece Susan's wedding in fashionable Toorak in Melbourne on January 30. She was marrying a young man somehow related to the British aristocracy and his relatives and friends were dressed accordingly. I am a republican and could not see what all the fuss was about, but Sue, my mum, was highly impressed and had to buy a completely new outfit. I was determined not to be caught up in all the hype. I wove them a lovely large rug with an Australian theme, grey and pink galahs flying against a peerless blue sky. I refused to buy a new dress. My grey cotton one was all I would need because it would be hot. The large reception must have cost Jackie and Denis a small fortune. It was in a very swanky city restaurant, and they supplied all the wine from their Bald Mountain Winery. Doubtless, they were proud of their lovely daughter and her well-connected catch.

I was also proud of my offspring who were struggling with what we were having at a national level, the worst recession since the Great Depression. Paul Keating, our treasurer at the time, called it 'the recession we had to have'. That was all very well for him to pontificate about it as he made the necessary adjustments to make his budget look good, but my children needed work.

When Erica's final year at university had come to an end, she was at a loss to find work in Adelaide. She ended up doing odd jobs in a sandwich shop. Luckily, she was awarded a scholarship to study in Japan for a year which she gratefully accepted. At that point, Brian, her current boyfriend, decided he also wanted to escape to the UK where he hoped to find work to progress his architectural career beyond what Adelaide had to offer. When the scholarship year finished, she managed to get a job as a translator at Koyo Seiko in Tokyo. Brian lived there with her for most of the time, teaching English and working part-time as an architect. They came back to Australia for visits once or twice each year. Fortunately, Koyo Seiko covered her travel costs and her pay was good enough that she was able to buy a unit in Dulwich.

We always welcomed Kathy's letters about her life in Germany and how she was coping with the cold. When she complained to a dentist that her teeth ached when she rode her bicycle, he remarked 'you must learn to keep your mouth closed!' We knew that Ralf was still a student and after working hard to land a job in nutrition, Kathy had been sacked out of the blue. It was tough out there in the real world. But she kept going and found more work, this time cooking for a kindergarten. Meanwhile, they lived in a very small apartment and were so happy just to be together that they did not realise how miserable they were, to quote Topol.

For Paul, the recession meant that work for him and his truck slowed down. He began to think about his future and how I had continually harped on about him being capable of more than truck driving or fixing motors. He asked me what I thought he might be capable of. I turned to Neil's friend Keith and he brought us descriptions of courses in both mechanical and mining engineering that were duly passed on to Paul. In less than a week he returned with his answer.

'Sorry, Mum, I'm not the sort of person who can sit at a desk and study. I'm a "seat of the pants" sort of guy. I think I could be a pilot.'

We were stunned. This was an ambitious goal. We suggested that he investigate what that would involve. It turned out, a lot of theory study at TAFE, which meant sitting at a desk and studying, and practical work in learning to fly, first a single engine, then twin, then navigation, and so on. It looked like a huge mountain for him to climb and an expensive course of action. But he was keen and willing to make sacrifices.

Kathy came home to study a 2-year nutrition course, but she took off for Pfungstadt as soon as that was finished to live with her darling husband, Ralf, until his study was completed. She tried to work in nutrition again, but she had to take whatever came.

One winter we did an around the world trip in the northern hemisphere where it was summer. We visited East and West Germany, Czechoslovakia,

Chapter 57   *The depression we had to have*

Belgium, England, Wales, Canada (Toronto and Vancouver) and West Coast USA, revisiting old friends and meeting with our new German relatives.

Time flew by. It was another 'trailer' holiday. There were so many places we missed, so many things we would have liked to do but didn't. In Germany and Czechoslovakia, our way was eased by Kathy and Ralf, Mariana and Pieter in Berlin, not forgetting Christel from Adelaide who was visiting her mother in Berlin at the time. The Berlin Wall came down while we were there, so we were able to visit both East and West Berlin. We saw the contrast between East and West Europe, the West having clean, well-organised cities, historic castles and palaces viewed from the Rhine cruise or preserved in lovely rural settings. The East was a time warp of rundown cities bullet-pocked walls and peeling paint, smoky 2-stroke cars and trolley buses pitching over subsiding streets. In Prague, we saw palaces and city squares preserved for the tourist, but around the corner, awesome decay where the clock had stopped in the 1940s. For British hospitality, we again had to thank the Bennett girls and Les, the Tailor family, Lindy Leak and the Wiltshires and their friends with whom Neil spent a truly memorable day at Didcot riding trains and exchanging railway memories. While for me, apart from seeing family and friends again, the highlights were living on a farm in the Welsh Brecon Hills and meeting Neil Warburton, owner of a diverse collection of historic looms near Rawtenstall. He creates old-fashioned fabrics for stately homes that are being restored.

In Canada and America, we covered too much ground in too little time, so were left with merely an impression of great highways and life organised around the automobile (cheap car hire and petrol). Life for the ordinary Americans that we visited, Sig and Darlene, and Beta Sigma Phi friends, seemed pleasantly relaxed and like the Aussie lifestyle.

Since Mrs Scott senior was still Neil's responsibility, when we wanted to take the overseas jaunt we had to enlist Paul as her keeper yet again. Fortunately, both survived. Paul continued to study both at TAFE and at flying school. All of this was costly and time-consuming. His girlfriend at the time, Julia, wanted to settle down and have babies, but he felt that the time was not right and tried to end the relationship. Nothing he said would put her off and she continued to live in his house as a tenant. Eventually, he brought the problem to me.

'She just will not go, Mum! I've told her our affair is over, but she stays.'

I tried to think why she was staying put, and I suddenly found a parallel in my own life that was my crush on David.

'Are you still having sex with her?'

'Well, yes,' he admitted.

'That's it! You must stop that!'

'She gets into my bed at night. What's a man to do?'

'You must tell her to get out and go to her own bed!'

'Why? I don't see the point.'

'As long as you keep having sex with her, she will think that you are in love with her.'

'But that's silly.'

'You may think so, but believe me, she is suffering from the "sex equals love" belief. Believe me, I've been there myself. It is a common belief among romantic women. You may not put the two in one basket at present. If you are lucky, you may find them both with the same partner. But obviously that is not the case with you and Julia.'

The romance died and he promised himself not to get involved again until his study was all through. More assets were liquidated, but it was all in a good cause. In addition to his flying lessons, he helped my mum to move into a 'village' and fix things that she needed in her new home. He also removed a huge bough (we counted 93 rings in it) which fell on our shed and the construction of a 50 m² tailor-made addition to the section that had been damaged.

At each step of his course, Paul had to clock up a certain number of flying hours. At one stage, he approached Neil with a proposition. We could charter a Piper Archer four-seater and fly together to Darwin with his new lady friend Heidi, thereby splitting the cost four ways. This appealed to Neil because as he put it, 'Australia has so much space between its interesting features that we have not explored the north.'

The trip took us to Coober Pedy, Alice Springs, Tennant Creek, and

Chapter 57 *The depression we had to have*

Mataranka, a tropical resort with hot springs and canoeing on a croc-infested river where we landed and parked our plane at the rear of our cabin. At Maud Creek, Paul could not read the topography of the remote windsock-less dirt airstrip. We barely landed into the wind but downhill before he realised that we would crash into the range ahead. He had to put on a full throttle to make it over the range at the end of the runway. In Tindal, we were buzzed by F18s who cast their shadows over us while we were waiting permission to take off. Darwin was hot and humid. Paul scouted around to see what work might be available for a pilot of his capabilities. Then we had to return. So, we set off back via Maud Creek again. We were able to arrange for a van to be left at the airstrip so we could actually take a trip up to the Katherine gorge. This time we landed and took off as nature intended, that is, coming in over the range to land uphill, then we went to Ayres Rock for an overnight stay. We flew around the Olgas and the Rock and then on to Adelaide. All this happened in nine exciting days.

The Christmas following the Darwin holiday all the children were home and Paul's present to all the family was a joy flight around the Coorong. It was a surprising and thrilling gift. His expendable assets were running out, so Paul started borrowing from Neil to meet his study costs.

Normal life continued in between all these adventures. Neil was working nine to five in the Department of Planning while I did relief teaching and studied Fiber Arts, and we enjoyed the company of overseas visitors from time to time. However, the Fiber Arts course became more esoteric and I could see the farm and home being neglected. So, I dropped out of school, knowing that I had learnt enough to continue with this hobby whenever our busy life permitted.

CHAPTER 58

NEIL RETIRES

Mother Scott was not coping on her own, so we took her to her GP who reported, 'It's just senile decay. There is nothing I can do for her. Best you let her live with you so that you can take care of her!' So, we brought her to live with us. She really irritated me because she did nothing ... absolutely nothing. She did not read or sew or knit or even talk to us.

One Saturday morning, I was so cheesed off with her unresponsiveness that I sat her at the kitchen table with a bowl of cereal in front of her and said, 'Look, Neil. She is your mother. You must persuade her to eat this cereal and do something! I'm going shopping. You have to deal with her.'

I had a pleasant morning out and when I returned Neil was still at the kitchen table, reading a railway book, while the bowl of cereal was untouched and his mother had returned to bed. I went to see how she was and found her on her bed, curled up in foetal position and feeling ice cold. I cannot repeat the language that I assaulted Neil with on the subject of what it meant to care for an elderly parent. I insisted that we take her to hospital because something was dreadfully wrong with her!

When we arrived, a junior nurse took her temperature, twice, then she called a more senior nurse who repeated the procedure, and then she called an even more senior nurse. None of them had taken a temperature so low! The process was then repeated up through the ranks of doctors available in Emergency until we reached a level of seniority that was capable of action. She was then wrapped in a space blanket and given a room temperature blood transfusion to gently warm her up. She was admitted to hospital for investigation. Investigations showed that she had a very low level of thyroid in her system and that was gradually rectified. The hospital staff recommended that she be placed in a nursing home and 50 phone calls later, I managed to find a nursing home with a free bed,

Chapter 58 *Neil retires*

and we installed her there. She was very happy. All her needs were attended to, and she could do nothing in peace and quiet.

Erica, still in Japan, was distressed by sex discrimination, crowded conditions and pollution. Although her bank account was growing, she decided to come home because she was ill with glandular fever and exhausted. Brian packed up her apartment in Nara for her before returning to Adelaide. They decided to move into her flat in Dulwich together. There was very little work available in Adelaide. They had to survive on an extremely small income. Brian was working for $10 per hour as an architect, and Erica found a variety of work, like temping in offices. Not a rewarding experience for either of them.

Eventually, a few well-paid translating projects came her way, and she was lucky enough to obtain work as an assistant to a professor at Adelaide University. Next, she completed a Grad. Dip. of Education and worked at Pulteney Grammar School, teaching Japanese for a year. She decided that teaching wasn't her vocation and she took up marketing studies at the University of South Australia.

We hadn't seen Kathy and Ralf for two years when they visited us one Christmas. In that time, Ralf had finished his university degree, but he had not found employment while Kathy, after a few false starts, landed a job as nutritionist with an insurance company. She was delighted with the position. They returned to Germany after this holiday to establish their careers.

Paul and Heidi renovated our old caravan in case they needed to take off in it to the Northern Territory. He found flying work at Tumby Bay, so we visited. Neil accompanied him one morning to experience first-hand what the job entailed. Crates of live crayfish were stacked near the Chieftain, so the first task was to get all the crates into the aircraft. It was a three-dimensional jigsaw puzzle. Then it was all aboard for take-off and a flight across St Vincent Gulf to Adelaide while live crayfish scratched at their crates. They then had to unload the cargo at Adelaide and fly back to Tumby Bay for breakfast. This was only a seasonal job, but it enabled Paul to log a few hours of flying a twin engine on his CV.

Paul and Heidi then decided to head for Darwin. They loaded her small car and his large toolbox onto his Flat transport truck and hitched the old caravan behind. They left Bub, their pet Rottweiler, with us and took off for the road trip of a lifetime.

With all the children launched and Suzie settled, we decided on a brief motoring holiday along the east coast. We visited Jackie and Denis at Wallangarra, Queensland, where we witnessed how hard they were still working to establish their winery.

Toowoomba greeted us with its magnificent gardens, warm sun-drenched views and warm reception by the Mitchels. We went on to Brisbane to stay with Greg and Sandy Parsons where I attended a Beta Sigma Phi convention, thoroughly enjoying talking to the 'girls' from all parts of Australia and the US and eating lavishly while Neil explored Brisbane's transport system. For something new, we ventured to the Glasshouse Mountains. The car broke down in Sydney and that meant we 'did' Sydney more thoroughly than ever while the Bluebird underwent repairs, and a fascinating place it is. In Canberra, we found an agent for Neil's bondage paintings, leaving three works with him. By then, Neil just wanted to get home to paint, while I wanted the shed roof fixed so that I could get on with weaving. When Suzie had settled in the village, she met up with a group of women, all living in the village, that met every Wednesday morning and boot-scooted together. Suzie had always been a dancer, so she fitted in immediately. They had matching waistcoats made for their performances in their own and other villages. Her eyes livened up and her cheeks became rosy. It was a marvellous turnaround.

The biggest news was Neil's retirement. He retired with a redundancy package which meant we could buy a few goodies to make retirement fun. A computer was number one. With it, Neil did archival work for the Railway Museum while I was learning to touch type. This newfound talent was for letter writing and keeping chapter lists. My efforts aided the Adelaide membership of Beta Sigma Phi.

Our old TV was replaced with the 'you beaut' model that had a modem connection and took Neil's video eight movies. Most people seem to move on to a new car when retiring, but when I heard that a swimming pool could be purchased for the same price, I decided that we did not need a new car.

Chapter 58 *Neil retires*

Unfortunately, that statement was only partially true. Perhaps we could have afforded the pool, but it dragged other expenses with it, such as replacing over 250 m of water pipe, building a 14 m retaining wall, shifting the meter box and connecting four pumps.

I had joined an organization called LETS (Local Exchange and Trading Society), thereby meeting people who wanted to exchange their talents and produce, using an imaginary point system. We had markets and could also reach each other by phone to access services. Here I met Mike Barton. His wife had died in a car accident right outside their home which left him and their three children traumatised. Because his pension limited how many hours of paid work he could do each week, he took on LETS work two days a week and was very useful to us on the farm. I gave tutorials to help his children with their schoolwork and we all ate together once a week. I really enjoyed the arrangement. It was like having a young family back again.

CHAPTER 59

BOTH MUMS DECLINE

Neil built a retaining wall of sandstone rocks salvaged from a nearby ruined cottage, with a lot of help from Erica and Brian. They visited us on several occasions to help cart the rocks. At the time, she had just left Pulteney Grammar and taken a marketing role at Britax while studying at night for a Grad. Dip. of Marketing at the University of SA. I created a garden above the wall, which meant that while swimming one was surrounded by a spectacular garden.

We had some lovely swinging parties in this beautiful setting.

When Neil's mum died, Neil inherited a house in Glenelg and enough money to buy another house in Blackwood. Now we owned two investment properties, but the real estate market in Adelaide was very flat. He knew that it was a waiting game and that their value would eventually rise, but I was impatient and wanted cash for another overseas holiday. Eventually, I persuaded him to sell one and we took the holiday.

First, we were off to see to friends in England. As we wanted to see different pieces of Britain, we went to Ireland where we were stunned by the greenness and the small stonewall bounded fields. We also visited the Isle of Wight, Scotland, and then back to London. A hovercraft trip took us to France because Paris was a must see. Germany was next and an event shared with Ralf's parents eclipsed everything.

In Pfungstadt, we were housed in what had been Ralf's bedroom in his parents' home. Elke kept a pretty garden and we frequently ate a meal outdoors because it was summertime. One evening we, the four parents, were told to sit over there and wait for a surprise. We sat and waited for quite a few minutes. Then music started to boom from the house ... 'Finally, it happened to me ...' and out into the garden paraded four brightly dressed young people

Chapter 59 Both mums decline

in identical outfits in a conga line. All wore short jackets with frilly sleeves. They had bare, firm bellies and long frilly trousers. They performed a lively dance to the booming song and I gradually identified two of the performers. I recognised Kathy first. Then, a rather tall character with a large curly red wig had a smile like Ralf. Oh my goodness! It was Ralf. I looked over at Elke she was curling up with laughter and pointing at the Ralf-like character. We were overwhelmed with laughter and delight and called for an encore so that we could actually appreciate the performance now that we had identified them. What a blast! I think it was the highlight of our trip.

Another delight had been organised for us. It was a holiday in Schpeck, East Germany. Kathy had booked a cottage for four of us in a rural setting near a large lake and what had been a holiday retreat for the higher echelons of the Communist Party. Yes, the sort of place where those who were more equal than others could come for R and R. We spent a week there, cycling around the countryside and swimming in the lake.

Kathy and Ralf were both working in Germany, but they only wanted to return to Australia if they could find well-paid jobs like they had in Germany. She worked for Alpha Metalcraft Company where she demonstrated to new owners of specially designed cookware how to use them most effectively. Ralf had a job with a very prestigious IT company, SAP. It helped big companies, like Nestle or NAB, by writing programmes to suit the particular company to improve their efficiency. After writing the programme, Ralf had to teach the staff to use the programme. The staff invariably did not want a new system, so his was a thankless job. To me, it seemed that he had an adventurous and romantic lifestyle because he worked in Paris, Budapest or London, until he pointed out that although he was in these different capitals they were all the same to him. He only saw the airport, the hotel and the business office of the company he was working for, and these tended to be very similar no matter what country he was in.

We returned through Darwin where we were able to catch up on Paul's progress. His first job had been with Wimray. Ray, a lovely old rogue, had a charter called RPT (Regular Public Transport). This was a government paid job to fly Aboriginals all over the NT and Tiwi Islands when they needed to attend funerals or health appointments. The pilot was given a list of individuals to be transported from here to there and upon arrival at the airport, he had to check his list and get as many passengers from the list as possible onto the plane at take-off time. He said that it was like herding cats!

Paul was striving to fly bigger and better aeroplanes as he moved onto Northern Air Charter where he flew a Cessna 206 402 X 2310, hoping to become a chief pilot.

Knowing that the children's lives were running smoothly, I visited Sue, hoping for a similar result. However, she had another demand to make of me. A bottle of brandy must be brought along with the $100 each Friday because she needed a nip in warm water at bedtime to help her sleep. She seemed to be losing her lustre, perhaps through lack of sleep. So, that was a reasonable request I thought.

A few weeks later, as I entered on my usual Friday visit, I was pleased to see that a couple of her old friends were visiting. Then I noticed a fresh bottle of brandy was on the table and Sue was fishing in her purse to pay Bob and Freda.

'What's going on, Mum? I've brought you a bottle of brandy and you already have one?'

'Yes, Bob and Freda just bought it for me. Aren't they kind?'

'But one bottle each week is quite enough for a nip each night!'

'Oh, well, if I get lonely it helps to cheer me up.'

'Sorry,' chipped in Bob, 'but we are not the only ones bringing a bottle of brandy. Last week when we visited, Terry and Flo had just delivered a bottle.'

'Oh, Mum, this is no way to carry on. If you are consuming all that brandy every week you are becoming an alcoholic!'

At this point, she went weepy on me and the embarrassed Bob and Freda apologised even more as they sought to escape.

'It's not your fault. I'm not cross with you. You thought that you were being kind to Mum, so please do continue visiting her. I know she needs her friends more than she needs brandy.'

She probably needed more attention from me as well, but I wanted her to get on with her own life and not be so dependent on me. I had the farm to run and Neil to care for and felt that she should do more for herself.

CHAPTER 60

WEDDING IN DARWIN

The aim for pilots in the industry is to work their way up the list of aeroplanes from 6-seaters to 12-seaters. Paul flew Cherokee, Lance, Aztec, Beach Baron and a Piper Chieftain over four years with Wimray. He was then offered the job as chief pilot for Northern Air Charter for one year. He took that opportunity because it would be good for his CV. He then moved on to Pel Air where he was deceived by management. He was employed to do night flights, being led to believe that he would soon be promoted to first officer in command of a jet, but he was passed over when management discovered that some pilots were willing to pay a fee to get that position.

Together, Paul and Heidi were buying a house and repaying Neil for his loan when they decided that they would like to have children and thought that it would be a good idea to get married first. The plans were laid and relatives and friends were invited to a wedding in the Darwin Botanic Gardens. Xavier's brother, Jan, and his wife Anne motored to Darwin. Kathy, Ralf, Erica, Neil and I flew in to attend. The weather was balmy, the setting beautiful, and everyone was happy through the civil ceremony and party.

Kathy and I dressed as the ABBA girls and worked out a couple of routines to mime 'Mama Mia' and 'Waterloo' to everyone's amusement, and some people's bemusement, because I was unrecognisable in a long blonde wig.

Sue would have loved the whole affair, but she was becoming less capable of independent living and had just moved into a single room in the same village where meals were served in a dining room. She was not really happy with the situation. As she expressed it, 'I have to walk all the way down that passage to get to the dining room!'

The newlyweds took themselves off to a hotel, leaving their house at the disposal of family and friends for a few days holiday in the tropics. Paul's debt to Neil had been reduced to $2,000, so we decided to forgive the rest of the debt as our wedding present.

Since we were all together, we were able catch up on all of their careers.

Ralf had finally managed to get a SAP posting in Australia, not in Adelaide as we had hoped—in Melbourne. Kathy had found a job as a dietitian with a company called The Melbourne Dietetic Centre.

Erica was not so lucky. She came to the wedding without Brian because he had taken a contract architectural role in Cairns. Her first few marketing roles in Adelaide were far from satisfactory. Britax, at the time, had a working environment rife with sexism and sexual harassment which she found difficult. She had lasted 12 months. She and Brian were both frustrated from the work standpoint in South Australia. By September 1998, their frustration had reached such a point that they decided to look in Victoria for work. She found Sakata, more on this soon, and Brian eventually found a well-paid architectural role in a reputable firm. However, Erica had decided that her partnership with Brian had run its course. It was mostly just a friendship, so they amicably ended their eight year relationship.

An extra delight for me was a flight out to Bathurst Island, one of the lovely Tiwi Islands where the locals did a lot of artistic pursuits like painting, decorating didgeridoos and boomerangs weaving and sculpture in a casual way for sale through tourist outlets. What interested me most as a fiber artist was a factory for screen printing designs on light fabrics. I could not resist buying a red dress-length printed with an intricate pattern of aboriginal themes in turquoise.

CHAPTER 61

THE HIGHS AND LOWS AS THE CENTURY ENDS

As the century drew to a close, I turned 60 and had a big party, as you do. Paul was all anticipation for the birth of his child. He complained that Heidi had insisted on a new refrigerator and was spring cleaning everything, which he put down to some sort of nesting instinct. Kathy and Ralf managed to become Australians again, and Erica took steps along her career path.

Jessie, a black puppy with soft, labrador ears, was my present from Kathy and Ralf. I fell in love with her immediately. They continued to visit a few times each year. They liked nothing better than planting native trees on the property and building tree guards like fortresses around them. Whenever they visited, Buddy came too. He was a puppy from the same kennel as Jessie. They were great playmates. We helped them move in when they bought a house in Prahran, Melbourne. Ralf continued to work for SAP while Kathy continued with The Melbourne Dietetic Centre and in their spare time, they brought the Prahran house up to modern standards. They did a neurolinguistics programme, which helps you to understand yourself and to make decisions by looking at your life goals. They discovered that their life goals were very similar.

When the owner of TMDC offered to sell them the business they discussed it with us and eventually made the purchase. He was a business manager and she a dietitian. They could make a go of this! But it did not boom as they had expected it to. Here, they made a very wise move. They employed a business coach who analysed the business and told them what was wrong.

They had to work *on* the business more, instead of *in* the business. He pointed out that one-on-one consultations lost money while being a consultant for a nursing home made a good steady income. They listened and took this advice to heart. They sought nursing home clients and worked on servicing them.

John Peter Jancarik was born on the 8th October 1999. We travelled to Darwin for the big event! Both Paul and I were present at the birth. Paul was delighted with his healthy beautiful baby, and I adore John, my very first grandchild.

For Kathy and Ralf, no children came. They had themselves examined for an explanation but kept the answer private. They discussed the multiple solutions and decided to remain childless. They would love and cherish nieces and nephews and other children that may come their way.

Meanwhile, after a few years of being single, Erica finally met her prince—Russell. He was funny, honest, open and attentive. They moved in together in an apartment near the beach and then bought a house together. Neil called it a shoe box, but I pointed out that we all have to start somewhere and they were prepared to work on improvements. They restumped it, pulled down a few walls, gutted the bathroom, revamped the kitchen, painted it inside and out, and installed proper heating and cooling. By the time they had finished it was a pretty cute house, but the one thing they could not change was its location, Seddon.

As noted previously, Erica found a role advertised for a Japanese-speaking personal assistant in Melbourne for a Japanese managing director of a rice snacks factory. She applied and went into the interview in a manner that I found amusing. She questioned the interviewer about the business and what her role was likely to be, as much as he asked her about her qualifications. Hiroshi, the managing director, took a liking to her and she was hired immediately.

They had a fantastic working relationship for more than four years, something she was eternally grateful for. Hiroshi was manager of the Sakata brand which eventually became one of the most successful grocery brand of its kind in Australia. She was delighted to be working with him because he was such a character, married to a beautiful French artist. He liked to break every rule in the book, was a brilliant strategist, mathematician, linguist, and entertainer who loved to cook and who enjoyed nothing more than good company, conversation, great food, and expensive red wine.

On the downside, Sue was frequently having health problems and so she moved from the assisted care section into the nursing home section of the village. She maintained an attitude of 'I am your mother and you must behave yourself' attitude towards me. While in the background, I regulated the amount of brandy she consumed—just a nip in hot water at bedtime.

As I have reached my vintage years, I have realised that I must hand over the reins to the next generation. They are more capable and are *au fait* with modern inventions and accepted way of life than I am. Although saddened by Suzie's decline, I could see that the children were all embarking on good careers. They were readying themselves for the take-over. It is the cycle of life.

Meanwhile, Neil and I were contentedly thriving on the hobby farm. We were financially secure, and secure in our love for one another. I had happily abandoned teaching and replaced it with weaving. Neil loved his painting and writing.

CHAPTER 62

PAUL AND FAMILY IN ADELAIDE

The early noughties saw two devastating events on the world stage. The bombing of the twin towers and the terrorism in Bali frightened the world. I was glad that my brood were all safe in Australia.

When John was just over one year old, the air industry was in turmoil and Paul was feeling disheartened with his career as a pilot. They also heard that Sofia, Heidi's mother, was dying of cancer. Heidi did not want to rush home to spend time with her mother, but Paul persuaded her that if she did not she would regret it after her mother had died. Therefore, they decided to return to Adelaide to regroup, think about their future, and start again. They sold their house. They also sold their best car and most of their other possessions and booked flights on Ansett to return to Adelaide. Between their booking and boarding, Ansett went out of business. Having nowhere to live, their bags packed and still owning one car, they decided to drive to Adelaide. Heidi entertained John while Paul drove with minimal stops. The journey took 36 hours.

Paul, Heidi and John came to live with us for a while. There were two memorable events during their stay. The first was a New Year's Eve celebration. Kathy and Ralf were with us too. Ralf was learning cocktail mixing and we all sampled different cocktails at intervals between our meal and games which made us all very merry.

John invented a game for himself. He ran up and down the passage, stopping to laugh at us sitting in the big back room whenever he reached us. A little later, John had been put to bed and the adults were comfortably seated in our lounge watching the start of a movie. It had a very violent start, something like the sacking of an ancient town. Murder and mayhem was all over the screen. Suddenly, from behind the sofa a young voice announced, 'Those people are not very nice!'

Chapter 62 *Paul and family in Adelaide*

The cheeky little mite was promptly put back to bed.

Stephanie, daughter of Xavier and Carol, had married Grant and they had a daughter, Tierney, born two months after John. That threesome visited us on special holidays like Easter and Christmas so that the cousins could enjoy each other's company. I have endearing photographs of them enjoying Easter egg hunts, cooking together and opening Christmas presents while Kathy and Ralf and all the loving parents looked on.

Erica visited occasionally and told us that after four years at Sakata, the company was growing rapidly and she felt that she wanted to progress beyond being Hiroshi's assistant. She had moved to Henry Jones Foods (IXL) where she had taken a brand management role.

Paul and Heidi both worked at various jobs and bought a house in Marion. John soon went to kindergarten nearby. Since they lived near us, there was an opportunity for me to take John out to the theatre. There were special shows at the Playhouse for youngsters which we both really enjoyed! This created a special bond between us.

While trying to upgrade their house, Paul calculated that it was costing too much. They would be better off simply destroying the existing house, subdividing the block and building two houses; one for themselves and one to sell. Paul carried out most of the demolition himself and asked if we would like any of the materials destined for the rubbish skip. Ralf built me a removable, dividing wall for the shed with the floorboards salvaged by Paul, thereby creating a cosy loom room.

Kathy and Ralf, living in Melbourne, kept us abreast of developments in their business. Eventually, it became so successful that they needed to employ dietitians and other staff. Their staff were mainly young women who preferred part-time work. They were good employers and managed to adjust the needs of the nursing homes to the needs of their dietitians. The girls each had one or two nursing homes near to their own homes to service. The Melbourne Dietetic Centre grew until it had 20 part-time employees and Kathy and Ralf were owner-managers. They worked tirelessly and constantly. Whenever they visited, their computers came with them and our back room became a temporary office. But Ralf also liked hands-on physical work. They continued to plant trees, and at one stage he dismantled our woodshed to rebuild a stronger structure. We called it Ralf's latest erection.

During these years, I had my new kitchen installed. The cabinets were beautifully made and the drawers slid on rollers, but the pieces did not fit together to produce level countertops. Paul said, 'The floor is not level! We have to take up the floor and find out how it is supported to rectify the situation.'

Neil was terrified, thinking that it would never go back together again, but I had faith in Paul. The cupboards were removed, then the floorboards ... where we saw no foundation, just a stump in the centre and cross members radiating out to holes in the walls. Paul adjusted the levels of each cross member, then nailed down a level floor and replaced the kitchen cabinets now level. All done! Neil could breathe again!

Our lives were very busy. My Beta Sigma Phi girls were still an intricate part of my life, and we raised funds for places like women's shelters and enjoyed lunches out together. I made decorative Christmas waistcoats for every member of my chapter and at a local level served Meals on Wheels. Neil helped me with the veggie garden, and he helped his charity (the National Railway Museum) in various ways. On a weekly basis, he picked up Doug and drove down to the Railway Museum at Port Adelaide for the day where they would work on selecting colour photographs for Doug's book. You know, the one that Neil wrote the text for. His latest scheme was selling the now outdated Edmunson tickets. Bags of them visited our big back room and he sorted them into types, making little piles of each type all over the floor until it looked like a miniature city. He then worked out a pricing system. The most abundant were cheapest and rarities expensive. As payment, one of every type went into his own collection.

CHAPTER 63

MADANG, BRIGHTON AND WOODEND

Paul eventually decided that he would return to flying. He put out resumes to various companies and as a result he was called by the chief pilot of Air Link, offering him a job in Madang, Papua New Guinea, flying turbo props. So, off they went. No sooner had they left than Sue left too.

Jackie and Denis visited so that we could jointly settle her affairs. There was no will, but we understood that we were equal in Sue and Ted's eyes. The village had reaped a benefit each time she had moved to a different level of care, but we were not distressed by that. Although Ted had worked to ensure that their house was paid off, so that they would leave something to their children, the fact that the cash coming from the sale of their unit had financed the remainder of Sue's life was satisfactory to us both. 'Attention' absorbed the remaining pieces of furniture while Jackie took Mum's jewellery. The remaining bank balance was halved, so everything was easily settled and a sombre but simple funeral concluded our mother's life.

As is my policy, I also visited Madang where Paul, Heidi and John were living. Because Neil would not venture to such an uncivilised place, I went alone and had an intriguing, fantastic holiday.

I visited John's school and read to the children. They were of many different races but all got along very well. When talking to John about the situation he said, 'I like some of the girls, but I think it is better not to have a coloured girlfriend.' (I wondered where he got that idea?)

I also got to know a few of Paul and Heidi's friends. One couple worked for World Wildlife Fund. The husband was a botanist and we were soon talking plants and how the natives perform agriculture. He offered to show me firsthand and I took up the offer. The walk was very heavy going. The terrain was steep and rough, but I struggled on with him through the jungle. Eventually, we came upon a clearing with a few plants sewn that I recognised like sweetcorn, beans and eggplants, and many that I did not recognise. The garden was planted in clumps rather than rows and very little effort had been made to keep the space in between plants weed free. He explained that they would use this area for a couple of years, which would exhaust the soil of useful nutrients and then they would clear a new area, leaving this garden to return to forest. It was an interesting and exhausting day.

More pleasurable were visits to The Club, situated on an estuary. This offered fine dining and drinking, and to my delight were a couple of pontoons on the deep river that we could swim out to. While we sat talking on the pontoon, dolphins swam past, and when we went snorkelling we saw lionfish.

Paul had also developed a friendship with a man from a nearby village who had a motorboat but could not always afford petrol to run it. So, for a can of petrol, the boat was ours for the afternoon. The village was a group of bamboo huts on stilts. Chickens wandered around at ground level and the bare ground between the huts was kept swept clean. In the boat we visited a nearby sandy island. We all swam and snorkelled together, even five-year-old John.

The water was so pristine that many lovely tropical fish were clearly visible. It was an amazing experience to see first-hand these beautiful creatures in their natural environment.

When Paul was flying, Heidi and I visited a resort, which was only really accessible to club members, but the nationals guarding the gates must have thought all 'whities' looked the same and gave us entry without demure. There was a swimming pool inside, which we occupied alone, giving each other aqua exercises and swimming a few laps. She also showed me the native markets where she had a mission. She was given money by the local CWA to buy fresh fruit and veg to take to the hospital. I went with her to the hospital. It was a series of Nissen huts with timber bunks inside. The hospital gave patients medical treatment and somewhere to rest. Nothing else. Relatives brought food for their sick. We took her purchases to a kitchen at the end of the maternity wing and laid it out for the patients. Those who were able, cooked for and helped the less able.

Chapter 63 Madang, Brighton and Woodend

Work was not running smoothly for Paul, and I witnessed the sour side of Heidi's nature. She instructed Paul on what to say to his boss about pay and conditions and was very indignant and angry when, in the evening, he reported back to her that he had made a compromise with his boss. His result was not what she wanted! Paul tried to explain his boss's attitude, but she reiterated her demands and called him weak and spineless! Again, she insisted what he should say on the morrow. Of course, she was not there to confront the boss and Paul was not able to put across her demands forcibly. The angry performance went on for a few days. Eventually, it was decided that we would just quit Madang and head back to Australia. Their domestic luggage was packed and shipped back to Australia. We slept one night on a friend's boat then flew back to Cairns.

Something was gone from this marriage. Mutual respect and understanding clearly was missing. I was not qualified to delve into the reasons or advise on measures to be taken. Anyway, everything seemed fine again once we escaped the stalemate.

The situation must have festered over the next few years. They came to Melbourne for Erica's wedding in October. It was unseasonably cold and their clothes, especially Paul's suit, were not made for the cold winds that whistled around the rotunda at Brighton where the civil ceremony was held.

Erica looked absolutely stunning in a white satin gown cut on the cross to cling to and emphasise her curvaceous body. She asked me to give her away and later make the speech usually given by the father of the bride.

I have a copy of the speech which amused the guests so I will repeat it here ...

> 'I am going to enjoy this! This is the one point in a person's life when a parent is permitted to tell a child what they think of them and what they remember most about them.
>
> By four years of age, Erica had developed her own peculiar sense of humour. All of you who have watched your children grow up and learn to do things for themselves will be familiar with the sight of a toddler with its boots on the wrong feet standing proudly to announce, 'I did it myself'. Well, one day Erica was sent off to put her boots on. I expected

her to return with boots on wrong feet but said boots could not be found. As usual, I was in a hurry and grew cross as we all searched for the missing boots. Eventually, in my frustration, I yelled at her, 'What have you done with your boots?!'

To which she calmly replied, 'I ate them!' The joke defused the situation and the search continued in much better humour.

By seven, she was forming her own strong opinions about the important things in life and was not afraid to voice them. I told of her damning of the 'Catlick' school and ingesting a pin.

Shortly after, her literary genius began to blossom. She won a prize in a pre-Mother's Day essay competition, 'Why my mother is the best'. Of course, it was not a matter of telling the truth. Indeed, she wrote in the essay what she thought the judges wanted and lied very convincingly. So don't believe everything you read!

At the time I was not the best mother in the world, and they were not the best children! I have a photograph taken at about this time which totally belies our situation. We miraculously all cleaned up and arrived on time at the photographers, all stood where we were told, and smiled on cue ... It made a lovely Christmas present for their grandparents, both Jancarik and Tailor.

I say it belies our situation because at the time I was a carefree divorcee, trying to create a new me and the kids were difficult teenagers trying to define themselves as adults. Life was dishing out problems to us in large amounts and we gave each other a rough time too. I imagined our neighbours at McLaren Flat shaking their heads, prophetically saying, 'They will come to no good that wild bunch out there at 'Attention'. What can you expect? She is a single parent, and they are wilful teenagers!'

In fact, we had a family saying, 'One word from me, and they did exactly as they liked!'

Despite all our disadvantages, we did develop into healthy, autonomous individuals. We did not become drug addicts or have unwanted pregnancies. We must have done something right because eventually Kathy found Ralf, I found Neil, and Paul found Heidi, all perfect mates for us. I think the trick or secret of our good marriages is that you do not need to be like as two peas in a pod. It is better if you are yin and yang, that you complemented each other, that you value the differences, and make each other happy. No two marriages are the same. So, if it works for you, hang on to it! Erica continued her search for the man to make her happy, for she is a 'still waters run deep' person. She takes time to shop around, it takes time to win her confidence and it takes time to form a deep, meaningful relationship. However, I now feel happy that she has found him, she is comfortable with Russell.

And Russell, what does he get out of this deal? Well, I ask you.
I turned toward Erica and continued.

Did you ever see such a beautiful bride? And the wonder of Erica is that it does not end there. Russell is indeed a fortunate man because within the beautiful body lies a heart that knows loyalty and caring love, and behind the beautiful face lies a brain that will keep him on his toes for the rest of his life. So, let me show you where we stand. There is little old me and my gorgeous daughter Erica. Then there are her brother and sister, Paul and Kathy, please come and join us. Then let me introduce those all-important spouses Heidi, Ralf and Neil, please come and join your partner. There is another young Jancarik who grew up without my help. Some may call her lucky, young Stephanie and her doting husband Grant, please come and join us. So, Russell, just as Ralf, Neil, Heidi, Stephanie and Grant have been accepted and absorbed into the fabric of this original, eccentric family, adding their diversity. We want to welcome Russell into our diverse group, that we call a family.

Christmas was spent with Kathy and Ralf in a rented farm at Riddell's Creek. They had lived there for a year. This rental had been selected to give them a taste of rural living while running their business in town, by remote control, only visiting the office on Thursdays. Also, it had easy access to properties for sale in the surrounding area. Kathy had found their next home and they were about to move to Jocks Gully at Woodend.

Kathy and Ralf continued to be good managers. The Melbourne Dietetic Centre went national and then became Leading Nutrition, which thrived.

CHAPTER 64

ZENDER AND MAX ARE BORN

In the summer months, we had the bushfires and heatwaves to contend with. We had to adjust our behaviour, especially in summer. Since the farmhouse was built of stone, it was a matter of opening all the doors and windows to encourage the cool night air in. We woke early to deal with farm jobs in the cool of the morning and then the house was closed down. Doors and windows closed, blinds and curtains were drawn to keep the powerful sun out and we usually maintained a reasonable interior temperature for most of the day.

I wanted us to move off the farm into something smaller, involving less work. So, knowing that 'things take time' I started to clear away STUFF. 'Attention' was a big family home, it had cupboards overflowing. It also had farm sheds containing things that were not used very often. We sold our cows and let most of the open land to the local dairy man for raising calves.

In 2006, the plan was for a family reunion at 'Attention' at Christmas time, but in the middle of the year there was exciting news from Cairns and Seddon which put paid to it. Heidi was pregnant, her baby due on December 4. And Erica was pregnant, her baby due December 14. Both husbands asserted that they would not be travelling to South Australia for Christmas with the olds. What could a grandma and grandpa do? Well, the mountain had to go to Mohammed. Neil was not prepared to visit at that hot time of year, but nothing was going to stop me from welcoming both of my new grandchildren into the world.

I booked flights aimed at getting to both births, despite grumpy forebodings that one could not base plans on anticipated birth dates. As it turned out, both were late which gave me a holiday in Cairns before the birth of the Zender Jancarik on 9 December and a holiday in Melbourne before the birth of Max Mulholland on 22 December.

Chapter 64   *Zender and Max are born*

Paul took Heidi into hospital in the early morning and returned to tell John and me of Zender's arrival and take us into visit. Paul did not seem as joyful as I expected. He was usually a generous softie, but he had no intention of buying flowers. I insisted on a visit to the florist to pick up a blue arrangement to celebrate the birth of a second son. I should have realised that it was a sign of the distance growing between them. Later, I learnt that as soon as she knew that she was pregnant, Heidi had proceeded to freeze Paul out of her life. Zender was cute and very like his over-the-moon-with-joy seven-year-old brother John.

Max was a giant, he weighed in at 9 lbs 12 oz., giving his mother a very difficult labour as you can imagine. She laboured all day with Russell in attendance. Both she and Russell were exhausted before the obstetrician decided that a caesarean section was in order. They took their precious parcel home to their small house in Seddon and proceeded to plan for a bigger home in a better suburb near a good school. They had put a lot of work into converting their 'shoe box' into a cute house. Now it had to be sold and money earned to move them into the better suburb. Russell worked as an office manager for OfficeMax. Erica took a year's leave to care for Max. She then re-joined the workforce for two, then three, then four days a week at Freedom Foods. When Freedom Foods sold its interest in A2Milk she went with it. She continued to rise within the marketing department of A2Milk thereafter.

When we realised that Paul and Heidi were drifting apart, I wrote letters and sent books to try to save the situation, reminding them of reasons why they should stay together. Neil and I thought they were such a well-matched couple, but we did not understand what was going on beneath the surface.

Our swinging friends were maturing with us. I remember an occasion which highlighted our diversity and bonds of friendship. We were all together, naked and sweating in a sauna one evening when the Australian couple mentioned that the war, meaning WWII, had been a difficult because they could not get lollies and their father found tobacco scarce. The rest of us were Europeans, and we looked around at each other and laughed. The English spoke up first. 'Since the British Isles are islands, much of our food was imported so severe rationing was the rule. Everyone was issued ration books containing vouchers for various commodities like meat, milk, eggs. When the housewife went shopping, she paid not only with cash but also with ration coupons. This ensured that the available resources were evenly distributed to the population. Certain things which were deemed important to children, like cod liver oil and orange juice, were only available with coupons from a child's ration book. Mediterranean and tropical fruits were very scare, often non-existent for shoppers.

Then our German member spoke up telling us of the privations suffered by her people, especially after the war. 'When us kids were out playing, we might see a queue outside a shop. That was a sign that there were edibles for sale. So, one of us would immediately join the queue while a brother would run to the front of the line to see what the queue was for, then they would run home to tell Mother what was available. She would issue money and instructions for the child who was moving down the line so they could buy the bread or apples or whatever was available. Harry, the Dutchman, had the last word. He had survived the German occupation. When the troops left there was absolutely nothing left in shops, so communities got together to share whatever could be scrounged. Everything was put into large vats and boiled up into a soup that could be shared. He remembered, as a child, climbing up the side of a large vat that had been used to cook a soup. He would reach in to scrape the inside with his fingers to get anything that was still clinging to the sides.'

What an interesting situation, I thought. We had all survived those hard times and had no prejudice against each other. Indeed, we were shameless sex partners to each other. Our friendship overrode the past.

In June 2008, I turned 70 and planted the Wallemi Pine tree which was a gift from my Beta Sigma Phi chapter. I called the clan together to celebrate. We came together in Cairns. The party was in the new big home that Paul and Heidi had built on an axe handle block. John played 'Happy Birthday' on the trumpet and it made me so proud and happy. Kathy then organised a holiday house in the Daintree for us all to share for a week, with each family having a bedroom. Paul and Heidi were hardly on speaking terms, so it was not a happy time for them.

Chapter 64 *Zender and Max are born*

Soon afterwards, Paul moved out of the family home and rented a room for the two days each week that he was in Cairns. He was working for Air New Guinea on a five on and two off schedule. His boys really enjoyed this time when they would spend time with their dad in his rented quarters, just doing blokey things, whenever he was in Cairns.

All our friends were aging along with us, so sexual activities were waning. As a husband's virility declined, thoughtful wives were less demanding, but our open-hearted friendships remained. One of our swinging friends suggested a dinner party group. The hosts for the evening would cook the main course because that was the most difficult to transport. One couple produced nibbles and sherry, another couple cooked an entrée and brought a suitable wine to accompany it. A desert with a desert wine followed the main, and finally, the fifth couple produced a fruit and cheese board accompanied with port or similar fortified wine. Yes, it was a lavish spread and only occurred about three times a year, but it meant that the same ribald conversations could be enjoyed and a few silly sexy games could be played. We had fun with dress-ups and themed dinners, like cross-dressing or rude food. On one occasion, we all dressed as wives in a harem and hired a professional belly dancer to teach us how to belly dance. On another, Alan the academic and I made up a dance to 'You can keep your hat on!' Before we reached the final chorus, everyone was out of their seats and dancing with gusto.

CHAPTER 65

BLACK CROWE

Neil was always happy to stay home painting or walking, while I had a monthly book club and a twice a month Beta Sigma Phi meeting. To be fair, he did have one outside interest, the National Railway Museum, which took him away from home every other Wednesday.

From time to time, we visited our children. It was the best way to check up on their lives. It was good to escape the winter cold in June by travelling 4000 km north to Yeppoon in Queensland where Neil's two daughters made us welcome, or to Cairns where we saw the Jancarik family. Erica, Russell and Max were simple to visit because they lived in Melbourne, a mere 300 km away. Kathy and Ralf lived slightly closer, so we were able to help each other whenever a big project was happening.

One December we stayed with Erica, Russell and Max for a few days prior to Christmas so that we could be present at Max's third birthday and share a little Christmas cheer with them. The sleeping arrangements were complicated and difficult for Russell. I think that he did not sleep well and in the evening I became the object of his wrath. Erica complained later that more and more this was his mood. He frequently took on more than he could handle and when he was unsuccessful, he lashed out in anger. I assured her that if she found herself unable to sustain her marriage, she was always welcome to return to us. However, they sorted it out between them. Now, this was an example of love and common sense working together. I do not know whether he worked it out for himself or with Erica's help, but I know that together they solved it. He attended a GP and then an anger management classes. Eventually, he became very successful with his job. He gained a new contract for his company and nothing succeeds like success.

Kathy and Ralf were a devoted couple. Devoted to each other and their business, which was one of the things they shared. As a result, their business and their marriage were both very successful. Every winter they took off for a holiday in the southern hemisphere, but they were not joined at the hip. They also gave each other space. She owned horses and was interested in the Pirelli method of horse training. He took the green movement and organic gardening very seriously, and they both put a lot of work into their veggie patch with the result that they were almost self-sufficient.

Remember Anne and Fabien, the couple that I found in Lobethal? Well, their parents wanted to host us for a holiday in Berlin, Ralf's parents were ready to welcome us again, and Joyce Bishop, my Maths teacher/mentor, was inviting us to Barton on Sea. Why not work all three into a trip?

We arrived in Berlin with a day to ourselves. To get an overall view of Berlin, we took the City Circle sight-seeing bus tour. This way we saw Checkpoint Charlie, East Side Gallery, which was 'The Wall' adorned with community art, Tiergarten, Brandenberg Tor, which was close to the huge new Hauptbahnhof. In the evening, we dined at a biergarten in the east. There was a chill wind blowing, but we had to dine *outside* so that the public transport could be viewed. Neil opted for speck while I chose herring. Were we surprised when the meals were presented. Neil's was a smoked leg of pork, big enough to feed a family, and my herring was also large but so tasty that none could be left.

In Fabien's parents' home, the large meals remained the theme. We were taken to see Oranienburg Castle followed by a drive to the canal. We walked along the canal together and saw large barges carrying coal from Poland to Berlin, and manufactured goods back to Poland. After another large meal, we were introduced to Boonekamp/Krauterschnapps (herbal schnapps) which settles the stomach after a big meal, and it did.

We travelled with Fabian, Anne and her brother Leon to San Souci, a huge palace and pleasure garden built for Frederic the Great. It was so big that we all became very tired walking around it. We went into the concentration camp, which was in the same street as their house! It was called Geelenkstatte Sachenhausen (Memorial camp Saxenhouse). It had been used by the Nazi SS during WWII. Upon liberation 1945, the Russians took it over as a prison for political prisoners. In 1989, when the prisoners were released, it was decided to make it a museum because it had so many stories to tell. Many school groups were taken round the camp and the stories told in the hope that 'this will never happen again!'

We had kaffee und kuchen at Anne's mother, Silke's, house. Then, after a walk, a huge dinner, German style, with loads of food on the table. We knew that a diet must start tomorrow! But Clause and Elke were of the same mindset and dieting was postponed until we were out of Germany. The weather was balmy while we were in Pfungstadt, so we ate at lovely outdoor restaurants and in their garden while we congratulated each other on our talented and well-matched children.

I had not seen Joyce Bishop since I had been a student at Sir William Perkin's Grammar School fifty-seven years before. She did not seem any older to me and still inhabited the schoolteacher persona. She insisted that we take sandwiches for our lunch when we went on outings and always rose early to make them. On one occasion, we were going down a ramp to a beach when a young man on a bike was coming the other way. She stopped the young cyclist with a firm voice.

'Young man, this is a pedestrian path! Please dismount and wheel your bicycle!'

I was mentally cowering, expecting a rude response from the lad, but his response was somewhat sheepish. 'Oh, sorry, ma'am,' he said as he dismounted, lowered his head and pushed his bike past us. Some schoolteachers never lose that air of command.

While we enjoyed her company, she told us a little of her life with her mother and older sister. They had lived together in this house. As their mother had aged, Joyce and her sister had cared for her. Then, after their mother's death, Joyce had cared for her aging sister until her death. Now that Joyce had retired, she maintained the house and garden herself. She had many friends and pen-pals, some visited her from time to time. She showed us a precious possession, a one person campervan. In the summer months, she enjoyed driving and camping at beauty spots all around Britain.

Over the winter months, my health became shaky. Neil had to cope. We felt that that was what marriage was about at our age, propping each other up. First, I had a bad back, created by some violent coughing. We solved this by moving out of the waterbed to firmer beds, having loads of painkillers and good physio. Then, a very sneaky chest infection disguised itself as worsening asthma and got itself really entrenched before antibiotics were sent in. As a true Tailor, I was stoical about keeping on with household jobs and activities. However, that amount of activity, plus antibiotics, did not shift the blighter. So, I was re-paraded before the doctor who prescribed a second batch of antibiotics and Neil put his foot down. I was to rest. Well, an evening meal had to be concocted somehow but apart from that I was to rest. Neil was then diagnosed with heart problems and whisked into hospital for a triple bypass. He needed extra care afterwards, but his recovery rate was speedier than average, so we must have done the right thing.

Then, surprise! Surprise!

I always had an interest in acting and so did Neil.

'But,' he said, 'I could never remember the words.'

An opportunity arose that would satisfy us both. Richard Lane told us about auditions for a radio play to be produced by the Black Crowe company.

We went to the auditions and both got parts. The producer had written a radio play based on Dickens' *A Christmas Carol*. Neil got parts as Bob Cratchit and Mr Fezziwig and I got Mrs Cratchit and various other voices because I could do the posh English accent and a Cockney one.

We met the rest of the crew a little later. It was an interesting mix. Most of us had more than one part and we all had to learn to be foley artists; that is, we made the sound effects at a side table when we were not actually speaking into the microphone. After a few weeks rehearsal we were ready to go because we didn't have to learn parts. We kept our scripts with us throughout.

We presented the play at several venues, usually nursing homes, and it was very well received and fun for us too in the lead up to Christmas.

After several productions there was a closing party and we were each presented with a framed memento, which included a solo photograph, a group photograph and a sheet describing our contribution to the play. I have kept Neil's because the photograph of him shows him with such a twinkle in his eye.

CHAPTER 66

EVENTS IN FNQ

Paul, far away in Cairns, was not visited as often as his sisters. We kept in touch by letters and phone calls. I knew that he had moved out of his family home and rented a room while he was in Cairns, seeing his boys whenever he could.

Most of his time was spent flying with Air New Guinea in and out of PNG, mainly to Asian destinations. He had reached the post of Captain on Dash 8s, but he was stuck at that level because he was a white officer flying an airline run by nationals for nationals. He considered flying for different airlines, but he could not find anything that gave him his R and R in Cairns, enabling him to see his boys on a regular basis.

In snatches, I learnt that he had bought a house which was in need renovating.

He sent us pictures of his sons with his pretty girlfriend, Corina. She was a New Guinea national, an air hostess. No surprise there. We prepared ourselves for a New Guinea daughter-in-law, but were soon told, 'No, Mum, her attitude is fully national. We do not see life through the same window. It is hard to describe, but we just have very different attitudes. I suppose you would call it cultural differences.'

Then the administrators of Air New Guinea found themselves in a situation where they had more pilots than planes to keep them all busy. Paul waxed lyrical about the inefficiency of nationals when it came to organisation. The only way out of their dilemma was to give enforced, unscheduled leave to pilots selected at random. Since he was helping personally with his renovations, he would normally have leapt at the chance of additional leave, but unfortunately there were no jobs for him at that time. He was most annoyed when he was told that he had been selected for leave.

Chapter 66 *Events in FNQ*

'Well, Mum, there is nothing for me to do here, I might as well take a holiday. I think I will go to the Philippines for a month.'

'Oh no, Paul! You will come back with a wife! The Philippines' chief export is wives!'

'I don't care if I do, Mum. I am a man who needs a wife.' So off he went and did return with a potential bride. I was horrified. How could they possibly know each other well enough after such a brief encounter?

'Well, she is a lovely girl, and you can meet her when you visit in October, because I have invited her to Cairns to see if she likes it.'

Yes, we met this shy, petite Filipino girl, Rhosa, when we arrived at his almost complete house. He was still away working, so Neil tried to introduce her to timetables and buses so that she could get around Cairns. Her English was very limited, but she made it clear that she preferred to drive and Paul would supply a car when he arrived.

He did just that and then they investigated what procedure must be undergone for her to gain the appropriate visas to live in Australia and to bring out her children and eventually become an Australian citizen. It was quite a long and involved process, but they felt that they could manage it together. Marriage was the first essential step and the sooner the better to set the ball rolling for her applications. They were certain that they were right for each other and so they started with a very simple marriage ceremony on the beach.

Before long, Heidi had the news of the wedding and was conveying it to Kathy and Erica with extensions like, 'I knew that he was having affairs before he left me', and 'He is a lothario like his father was'.

When I tried to say that she knew nothing of the sort, that none of us knew what had gone on inside their marriage, Kathy asked me, 'Why do you always take Paul's side when there is a dispute?' to which I replied, 'Firstly, I know what a softy he is and he is my son!'

'What do you mean?'

'Let me put it this way, Kathy. I can see what a loving couple you and Ralf are, and what a tolerant, loving man he is. But if, for some reason, there should be a rift between you two, guess whose side I would automatically line up on? You are my child!'

She was still willing to swallow Heidi's version whole. A large rift was opening between my children and I could not stop it.

CHAPTER 67

WE ARE GOING ON A JOURNEY

We returned to 'Attention'. My mind was busy with thoughts of how I could bring my family together again. Erica gave me the benefit of her opinion on this topic. 'You have a good relationship with me. You have a good relationship Kathy. You have a good relationship with Paul. Why can't you be content with that?'

'Very sound thoughts, Erica, but I do have an answer. When you no longer have me, I want you to have each other.'

Neil was busy finishing off the text for Doug's book. One morning, while I was tidying the kitchen, he came in with a worried look on his face.

'I cannot get this last paragraph onto the computer!'

I frowned. 'Is there something wrong with the computer?'

'I don't think so. It's complicated. Will you come into the office and see if you can do it?'

'Sure thing. Now, what are you trying to write?'

He told me that he was trying to explain why there are three railway gauges in Port Adelaide. I had listened to this weird story dozens of times before, only half-listening I dare say. But it was a story that he could tell in his sleep.

'So?'

'Well, I cannot seem to be able to write it into the computer.'

'Okay. Give it to me slowly and I will type it in.'

He did, and I did. While I was typing, my thoughts were running wild.

This is very strange. Neil has a vocabulary to beat any that I know, he has made his livelihood by writing reports and explanations and this bit of railway history is of great interest to him. Why can he not write about it?

We discussed that when the job was done and he had no explanation.

Our GP, Daniel Bourne, was the next port of call. He made light of it, saying that Neil would quickly recover, but I insisted that a brain scan was necessary. Just to placate me, Daniel ordered one and an appointment was made for a week later when the result would be in. Both of our favourite doctors were in the room when we were called in. After we were comfortably seated, Daniel looked straight at us and said, 'We are going on a journey. Neil has a glioblastoma, which is a nasty cancer in his brain. We will send you to a very good brain surgeon who will take over the treatment. He will know how serious it is and what is the best course of action. Please remember that we are also here to help and support you whenever you need us.'

We were told that from here on Neil was not permitted to drive. I was to chauffer him wherever necessary.

After looking at the first MRI, Mr McDonald said, 'Neil's tumour on the brain is one of two types. One responds better to chemo than the other, hence on Monday 20th June, shortly after 4 pm, I will operate. I will take a biopsy which will be rushed through laboratory analysis to tell me which of the two tumours Neil is hosting. If it is the one which responds to chemo, I will remove only a small amount, but if it is the one that does not respond well to chemo I will take as much as I can surgically. Neil will be in intensive care until he is ready to return to the ward. He will spend a couple of days in hospital before being released into your care. I would then like you to visit again on 27th July. Somewhere in there, other treatment will commence depending on what type of cancer I find.'

Neil found it hard to believe that it was him we were talking about because he continued to feel very well. He had to undergo radiotherapy, which was given for half an hour every day for two weeks. He was given chemotherapy in the form of pills administered in a defined order by me each morning. He was sent to a speech therapist for help with his articulation. We visited the brain surgeon every three months for a fresh check-up. Good news was that brain tumours do not send out secondaries into other organs. This one just had to be treated aggressively to keep it in check, because it would never be completely defeated.

Since this was all news to us, it took some time for us to come to terms

Chapter 67 *We are going on a journey*

with it, to settle our raw emotions and to work out how we would live our lives from then on. Fortunately, all aspects of his treatment occurred at the same hospital so we became very familiar with it, where we parked and how we spent the day.

There were many people interested in his progress and I dreaded the thought of constant phone calls and having to reiterate our progress endlessly, so I wrote a letter to all interested parties and asked them not to call. I would send out monthly health bulletins to all and ask for only email or snail mail replies.

Neil's daughter, Heather, was on our doorstep within days of my first bulletin. She was a great help as a subsequent report shows.

> Having been forewarned about possible side effects of chemo and radiotherapy, we decided to take advantage of the five-day break in treatment and the presence of Neil's daughter Heather to take a holiday in the mid-north of SA. We visited Clare, Burra, Peterborough, Port Augusta and Quorn. All of these places have great tourist attractions relating to our state's early history and some, of course, to early railway history. We visited and enjoyed them all. We rode the Pitchi Richi Railway from Pt Augusta to Quorn and back behind steam. Heather wangled a ride on the footplate for Neil while our loco was shunting in the Quorn yard. Since Neil is not permitted to drive and I am only fully on the ball during the morning, Heather took over the driving in the afternoon. This enabled us to cover the distances involved in the short time available and enjoy all the attractions.
>
> Heather was replaced by Karen, Neil's other daughter. Karen fortunately drove Neil in for one of his appointments which enabled me to sleep (bliss) and prepare the evening meal. Chemo is administered at home to a strict timetable, which has to be fitted in between meals and radiology visits. Neil is in good spirits and is not suffering any of the dreaded side effects, which is not surprising because most of the pills are designed to counteract the possible side effects. The steroids make him very hungry and food puts his blood sugar up so, anticipating an insulin dose at each meal is proving our biggest challenge at present.

Thank you for your cards, emails and offers of help. Karen will be with us for another week while we settle into the routine and I can work out which visits I must attend. When the routine is established, I will be able to ask for some help in driving Neil to radiotherapy on some mornings while I do other things. That would be a great help.

Many thanks, Chris

CHAPTER 68

LAST CHRISTMAS

And so our lives were taken over by his treatment and decline. We drew what pleasure we could from each other's company and sought out extra pleasures that were within our reach, like the coffee shop that sold gluten-free goodies to eat with our coffee. We always stopped there after a hospital visit. I continued to send out bulletins, like the following...

> Dear friends,
> Here we are again, three months on. We went to Mr McDonald again yesterday for the MRI and a verdict. The tumour has not grown, but it has not shrunk either. Mr Mc therefore suggests that we keep going with chemo. We have an appointment with Dr Cheong, an oncologist, on Monday, so we will go, and if she agrees, we will start another three months of chemo. What else can we do?
>
> Dr Cheong is a charming Chinese lady who talks in a very relaxed way about Neil's progress. Each time, she asks him to write a sentence and to draw a clock-face showing a given time. Each time it becomes more difficult for him to perform these tasks.
>
> Thank you for your continuing letters of support.
> Chris

The rest is not easy for me to recall, even now, but I have a letter that I wrote to Joyce Bishop after Neil's death which covers many events, including the loss of my younger sister, Jackie.

> Dear Joyce,
> He's gone. My lovely Neil died on the 4th of February and I am alone

with my memories. What wonderful memories they are!

We were so glad that we took that last trip to England and Germany.

Soon after our return, Neil was diagnosed with glioblastoma and the doctors told me that he would last months, not years.

Well, we went walking and talking and getting about for two years after that. Admittedly, the talking became difficult because the tumour was on his speech centre. But we understood each other pretty well after almost 30 years together, so we communicated well.

Last winter, I had a foot operation and the kids persuaded us that I could not look after Neil on one leg, so a plan was made for us to spend time at Woodend, with visits to Melbourne as guests of my daughters and their husbands. Then we moved on to Yeppoon, Queensland, as guests of Neil's daughters Karen and Heather, and their husbands. Finally, we visited Cairns, Queensland, where we stayed in the home of Paul and his new wife, Rhosa. There we got to know her two lovely children, Daniel and Rosemarie and were frequently visited by John and Zender, Paul's sons who live with his first wife Heidi. It was great to share the lives of our children and do with them the things that they do on a regular basis. The markets, the footy games, the gardening—just ordinary things that give their lives colour.

The grand tour took about two months, so by the time we returned home I was able to walk and drive and carry on as before.

Then came a big shock. My sister, Jackie, was dying of pancreatic cancer. If I wanted to see her one last time, I must rush to Brisbane. Neil went into a respite care facility while I spent five days with Jackie's family in a palliative care suite while Jackie fought it out with the Grim Reaper.

Neil and I were glad to be reunited, but about two weeks later, he fell and cracked his femur. The doctors at the medical centre were sure they could patch him up and have him walking again in a few days, but he never left his bed again. He went from hospital to an aged care facility. I was able to bring him home for short visits. He came for Christmas Day when his daughters were with us and my daughter Erica brought her husband and son to visit, which made it a real Christmas party. He was delighted.

He came home for his birthday in January, and on a couple of other occasions. Each time he was less aware of his surroundings, but he kept on begging for a repeat visit.

His daughters both took time off work and stayed in Adelaide, wanting to be with him at the end. With his right side paralysed, due to the tumour, and his speech becoming more and more difficult, the doctor eventually put him into a morphine-induced coma and he died five days later.

There, now you have the full story you can grieve with me.

I am gradually finding a spot for him in my psyche because I know that he will always be with me. Then it will be time to move on.

All the best to you, dear friend, Christine.

CHAPTER 69

PICK YOURSELF UP, AND MOVE ON

I had been through bad times before and knew that they had to be endured. This black cloud, like all things, would pass.

This is the annual letter that I wrote to all my friends at Christmas, 2013.

> Thirteen is unlucky for some. At first, I thought of this being a cow of a year for poor little old me. Neil died on the fourth of February, my gallbladder kept giving the painful reminders of its existence, while my lungs were in such bad way that the surgeon was fearful of operating. Putting the property on the market so that I could move closer to my children meant a lot of work to keep the house and grounds clean and tidy for inspections. I cared for Kathy's two dogs, as well as my own, through the winter and tried different lung specialists and antibiotics. Eventually, the surgeon saw enough improvement in my lungs to extract a gallstone the size of the pigeon's egg and I felt so lightheaded that I planned two overseas trips to Vietnam and the Philippines and bought new carpet for the lounge to increase the chance of selling the place. These items almost exhausted my bank account because everything had to be paid in advance. Meanwhile, although we were getting interested viewers, no offers were coming. So, the real estate agent kept coaxing the price down. Jessie, my dear little dog, died in July, then I fell and broke my leg, and finally, I had a troublesome cyst removed from my neck.
>
> I hope you're still with me ... not abandoning me as a moaner. I'm sure you know me as a glass half-full person. The troubles are but a backdrop to the great positives that have shone throughout the year, like black velvet used to display diamonds.
>
> Neil's death was a peaceful end to two horrid years since his

glioblastoma was discovered. His funeral saw the little church at Kangarilla bursting at the seams with old and new friends. Both Scott and Jancarik daughters gave moving eulogies depicting Neil as a fun-loving, caring father and Doug's told of his mateship while I said the following.

'I would like to talk about love, real, generous, giving, sharing love. The timid and the cynical might say, "Why open your heart up to love when it always ends in pain? Often what starts as romantic love does not stand the test of time and ends in painful separation. Or if the love proves to be more enduring it will end with the death of one of the lovers, leaving the other bereft and in pain. So why give yourself over to it in the first place?"

'Here's the answer—because the alternative is to go without the happy times together, the long, deep, meaningful discussions and the companionable silences.

'I do not mind being the one left behind to pay the piper.

Thank you, Neil, for investing in me and letting me invest in you, because as a consequence we have had all the things that make life meaningful and significant, such as getting married, sharing our children, the ecstasy of sex, hope, mutual support, friendship and laughter.'

A scrumptious spread supplied by my friendship group and Auntie Helen eased the mourning into a celebration. All our daughters were with me to plan and carry out the funeral and scatter his ashes in the forest where he loved to walk.

My search for a good lung specialist has borne fruit and I can now walk, swim and laugh without falling into a coughing fit. My showpiece of a gallstone is frequently displayed. The trip to the Philippines was a great eye-opening experience in many ways.

I saw how people living in third world conditions can still make the best of life and are happy with it. The happiest people are not those who possess the most, but those who need the least. Also, I rediscovered my son. He is so happy in love with his Filipino wife that no service to others is too much for him, he is generous and considerate to his wife's family and children, and he made my stay interesting, and comfortable. The warm atmosphere was great for my lungs and this made me re-think where I will settle when the house sells. The broken leg prevented my trip to Vietnam and the travel insurance restored my bank balance. It also roused my children into caring mode. Kathy deserted her husband and business in Victoria to nurse me for a week. Rhosa, Paul's wife, and her two children came to Australia to take over from Kathy. Paul joined us as soon as his work shift released him. All this attention from my children reminded me of the wall hanging that Kathy bought for me when she was a cheeky teenager. It said, LIVE LONG ENOUGH TO BE A BURDEN TO YOUR CHILDREN.

Well, I thought, *I have managed that!*

Through the year, I have been supported, helped and cheered by my girlfriends, Neil's transport mates, and wonderful neighbours. Honestly, how lucky can one girl be?

Finally, after a lot of work and heartache, the property known as 'Attention' sold on the seventh of November. The packing was done with the help of friends and neighbours. The furniture is on its way to Cairns where Paul and Rhosa will store it for me. I intend to spend a couple of weeks enjoying gentle goodbyes and Christmas cheer with South Australian friends. Christmas and January, I will spend in Victoria with my Victorian children. Then, when the wet season is over in Cairns, I will head north, buy a small house in Cairns and take up grandmotherly duties and a new life.

I hope that Christmas finds you as contented with life as I am and that you look forward to an interesting productive and fun-filled 2014.

Love, peace and joy to all.

Christine

CHAPTER 70

THE MEMORIAL

Our dinner group friends will remember Neil because I gave to each couple one of his completed bondage paintings. I have kept just one, which I have to hide from my daughters. The remainder I have had to destroy. Sorry Neil. No one else would house one.

We never talked about it, but I felt sure that Neil did not want a tombstone in a cemetery. He would like to be remembered somewhere significant to him, like the National Railway Museum (NRM).

So, I hatched a plan. At a meeting with the management of the National Railway Museum I told them that I knew that he had bought the first locomotive for the collection and that because he was not a hands-on man, he had worked in many behind the scenes ways to establish and keep the museum running. When the current site for the Port Dock Railway Museum was being sought, Neil was employed by the State Planning Department of SA. He had been able to use his knowledge and cognisance of how things operate within government to ensure that the site landed in the right hands. The most recent contribution Neil had made to NRM was the organising and setting up a pricing system for the sale of Edmondson tickets. All the proceeds of which have gone to NRM.

In addition, I was willing to make a donation to NRM if it could result in a permanent acknowledgement of his services.

He had painted at least three really good railway paintings I would give them to the museum. At his memorial service, friends were asked to make donations to NRM, instead of flowers. I collected $300.00. Then, to boost the fund, I gave Neil's collection of Australian transport books to the NRM bookshop, and a few train and bus models that he had cherished over the years, on the understanding that the proceeds go into the fund.

They suggested that as he was fond of 800, which was currently under restoration, my donation could go to finance 800's restoration and his services could be acknowledged there.

They were good as their word and now alongside the restored 800 at the National Railway Museum, Port Adelaide, there is mounted a plaque acknowledging Neil's part in helping the NRM and the restoration of 800.

CHAPTER 71

THE SOLO JOURNEY

'Well, Kathy-o, I have to get my Rav4 and myself to Cairns, so the best way of doing that is for me to drive there! I have driven Adelaide to Melbourne several times, so I should be able to do it.'

Kathy seemed horrified. 'Mum, it's a very long way to Cairns. Take a look at the atlas!'

I took the atlas to my room. I found Woodend and Cairns and had to admit that it was indeed a very long way. On the other hand, I had friends in some of the towns in between. So, with the aid of emails and phone calls, I planned a trip for my little Rav4 and myself to Cairns, stopping off wherever I had a welcome, and a few stops where I would have a motel stopover. Kathy lent me a couple of audiobooks to listen to. They relieve the boredom without taking your attention off the road when you are doing a long trip. Maybe it was courage, maybe just obstinate rashness, that motivated this 75-year-old widow to embark on a solo journey.

The first stop was Canberra where Solange, my Beta Sigma Phi friend, and Gerry lived. We spent a very pleasant day there with a great visit to the art gallery. She said that the great advantage of living in Canberra was that whenever a world class art or theatre show visited Australia, its first stop was always Canberra.

Dubbo, just 409 km to the north, was a motel stop. A long leg of 636 km to Stanthorpe and my brother-in-law, Denis, was a very wearing day. I organised the day so that I could stop for lunch in a small country township with a good bakery. After a satisfying takeaway and drink, I drove to a quiet backstreet, put my legs onto the passenger seat and a cushion behind my head and snoozed for about an hour. When I woke refreshed, I was ready to move on.

Because he lived on his country property, Denis met me in town so that I could follow him back. He was not surprised that I was taking this solo trip because he had been married to my headstrong, single-minded sister, Jackie, for 52 years. She was famous for courageous long, cross-country horse rides even into her 70s. He constantly referred to her as a wonderful woman and she was clearly still with him in spirit, for he had not cleared away her personal things. Even half-finished teddy bears sat where she had left them. Theirs had been a long and caring marriage. They had worked side by side to build a productive winery. When they retired from the winery, they had bought a slightly smaller, very picturesque acreage so they could stay in the district that they knew so well and she could keep her horses. His life consisted of caring for the property and playing golf, and he introduced me to the 5/2 diet which he swore by and I later took on myself.

A mere hop of 145 km took me to Toowoomba and Mavis Mitchell. I had not known her long, but our daughters were friends and she trusted me with her home because she had to leave town for a family event while I needed another day's rest.

Refreshed by this rest, I took off early on Sunday morning for my trip to Theodore. It was a bit of a swerve inland because I wanted to avoid the coast road that I thought would be very busy. My route was definitely not busy. This was the only section of my trip that actually scared me. As I approached Theodore, I had not seen a township or a service station or another car for hours. I was hot and tired and the fuel gauge was running on empty.

What if I run out of fuel or have any other sort of trouble here in the middle of nowhere?

The hot monotonous road went on and on as my fear mounted. Finally, I was in Theodore, but it was deserted. I could see no resting place or service station. Rather than use my last drops of petrol searching town for petrol, I locked my car and left it while I walked through the deserted town. Eventually, I heard male voices coming from a tin shed up a side street. I approached it with a nervous, 'Cooee'.

The voices stopped and a couple of blokes emerged from the tin shed.

'Where is everyone?' I asked.

'Oh, it's Sunday, so everyone's gone to the pony club.'

Chapter 71 *The solo journey*

'Is there a service station in town? I'm almost out of petrol.'

'Sure, love, just a few hundred yards up the main street.'

I thanked them gratefully. In the servo, there were two more people. I filled up with petrol, revived myself with an ice-cream and asked after a hotel.

'Sure, love, we've got a lovely hotel. Just turn left at the first intersection and there you are!'

There was a receptionist at the hotel, and I thought, so now I have met 5 residents of Theodore.

She showed me to my spartan room and told me that the evening meal was served at seven. I turned on the noisy air-conditioner and slept until seven. The cuisine ran to steak and salad, but I was in no mood to be picky. Food and a cool sleep were all I needed.

Sleep unravelled my tension and I was ready to head for the coast via Rockhampton. I knew a welcome would await me in Yeppoon, at the home of Heather and Greeny. I was not disappointed. Yeppoon is situated on the tropic of Capricorn and has an idyllic climate. I spent two days there enjoying the tropical beachy/hippy village atmosphere and their good company. I even found time for an aqua aerobics class at the swimming pool.

The final three days were spent uneventfully, travelling the Bruce Highway northwards, passing through Mackay and Townsville and finally rolling into the welcoming arms of Paul and his family in Cairns.

CHAPTER 72

SETTLED IN OUR HOME

While I had been travelling, Paul and Rhosa had been house-hunting for a home with room for a family of six and a granny flat. They knew that I would want a large garden and no home in the tropics is complete without a swimming pool. To find all this in good condition would have a price tag too great for us, but they had found a compromise. It was a Queenslander with enough room for the family upstairs and a large party room and garage downstairs. Paul could already envisage the charming granny studio apartment with its own bathroom and kitchen that he could create from the party room, and Rhosa could envisage the improved bathroom and kitchen that she wished could grace the upstairs house. I had money in the bank and Paul had all the knowhow to get these jobs done if I would pay for materials. An agreement was soon struck, the house bought and we were living in the mess of renovations for about six months.

To the rear of the house, a long sloping lawn ran down to the back fence. That had to be converted into a garden that I could get around. Paul soon had plans in his head for a garden of connecting terraces, with lawn paths down each terrace and strip garden beds on each side of each path. The whole thing called for retaining walls and a lot of earthmoving. He built the retaining walls of pine and timed the whole project so that the earth moving equipment could be conveniently hired when needed.

Meanwhile, I had been attending the local permaculture and seed savers club meetings. These helped me to work out a planting scheme. A banana circle was a must and just before the earthmoving equipment left us for the last time, I asked the driver to dig me a banana circle in the lowest corner of the garden. Bananas are planted around the circle and the hole in the middle becomes a compost heap. All garden and kitchen refuse goes into the hole to feed the bananas.

'Well, madam, I can try but due to the shape of my bucket, it will have to be a 'banana square,' he said.

I was happy with that and in no time we were producing our own bananas, pineapples, paw paws and many vegetables. The strangest thing that I had to learn was that winter was the best time for gardening if you wished to produce European type veggies because the summer was just too hot.

The refurbished bathroom was installed upstairs and Rhosa was planning the new, improved kitchen, but my cash was not infinite and the existing kitchen, although shabby, was still functional, so we never quite saw eye-to-eye on that.

I was still writing to Joyce Bishop. Here is what I wrote in May 2015:

Dear Joyce,
You are still there! Hooray!

Every morning I wake up and say, 'I'm still here! Hooray!'

I fell as I left the permaculture meeting two weeks ago. It left me with a very bruised right hand side and a cracked pubic bone. This will take two months to heal in a person of my age. That means two months of doing very little.

Last week, I went to the buy-back shop at the Cairns dump and bought for myself a white plastic chair to put in my shower recess so that I can sit to scrub my feet. It was not cracked, but it was grotty. It served my purpose very well. However, the day before Mother's Day Paul brought in a brand new plastic chair for my shower and took the dirty one outside saying, 'That's better. Happy Mother's Day, Mum.'

A card from Erica, including a gift voucher for a nearby day spa experience, arrived on Friday. Early Sunday morning, a phone call came from Kathy. She was bright and happy. She was on her way to a horse event and checking up on me to wish me a happy day.

On Friday, the children had brought home their gifts for Rhosa and hidden them with much secret glee in my wardrobe. Through

Saturday, they were checked on several times. On Sunday, they were duly presented with love and laughter. Well, that's Mother's Day done and dusted I thought, but not so. Paul and Rhosa appeared with a prettily wrapped box and card. The box contained a solar lamp in the form of a frog emerging from a manhole, holding a telescope to his eye which was the lamp. At the back was the powerhouse, a tiny solar panel. I was delighted. On top of that I cannot contain my joy at the wording of the too elaborate card obviously selected by Rhosa, but written by Paul

'WITH ENDURING LOVE AND ENCOURAGEMENT, SUPPORT AND TRUST, THANKS, CHRISSIE. WE LOVE YOU, MUMMY'

Thank you for the delightful British calendar that you sent. When I told my grandsons that this calendar came from a lady who is thirteen years older than me, they looked at me with utter disbelief.

'No way, Grandma. How old is she then?'

'Well, you do the math. You know that I am seventy-eight. If she is thirteen years older, how old is she?'

'Gosh! Ninety-one! No one is that old!'

'Well, perhaps you will believe it in thirteen years time when you come to my ninety-first birthday party!'

It was all too huge for them to contemplate.

Life in Cairns is just wonderful for me. My asthma disappeared in the first month. I had a knee replacement late last year and it has taken me most of this year to get back to walking normally.

I was instructed to spend most of my life resting with leg elevated, so I have nearly finished writing my autobiography. Well, I have nearly finished the first draft. I will do a second draft by changing the names to protect the innocent and not so innocent and fixing up the obvious faults. Then I might try to publish. I have had a marvellous life. I might even say 'three marvellous lives' and now I'm having a fourth.

It is good to be useful in helping my grandchildren with their homework and giving little bits of extra tuition where needed. My oldest grandson, John, is so clever and hard working at school that he has achieved B+ for all his subjects. He is consequently in a dilemma. What does he want to study at university?

I have friends in a book club that I formed on arrival and friends in a theatre company that I joined to exploit my acting ability. So far I have been Antonio in *As you like it* and a witch in *Macbeth*. This year the company is producing *The Taming of the Shrew*, but I am not acting because I am putting all my effort into the autobiography.

I do hope that you're keeping well and active. What does a ninety-one year old do for fun? Do you still drive? How are your eyes holding out? I still enjoy driving and reading and maintaining my beautiful garden, so it is sight that I find most precious. I am a little deaf and my grandchildren mumble—except when they want something.

I am so lucky to have an optimistic, positive personality. Life is marvellous for me. I do hope it is for you too. We must have a happy ending because if it isn't happy, it isn't the end. This has been such a happy day that it seems a great note to end on.

Much love, Christine

Ralf

Ralf and Kathy on their wedding day 1987

We write our annual letter.

One of Neil's superb photographs of the Onkaparinga River.

Our wedding.

I learn basket weaving in the NT

Proud father, Paul with happy son, John

Neil painting

Tierney and John cooking in my new kitchen

Lobethal tapestry takes shape. Katherina helps Wilma and volunteer weaver.

Spring at 'Attention'

Zender with guitar

Zender and John with icecream

Neil the radio star

*At home in Earlville. Back; Rosemary, John.
Front; Zender, Paul, Me, Daniel.*

ADDENDUM

I was seventy-eight in 2016 and now we are in 2022, so you do the maths. I'm not ninety-one yet, but I am so active that I may just get there. It has taken a few years to reach this point in my story with all the details filled in. I still feel that we are a part of all that we have met. We are like pebbles in a stream. We rub against each other as we are washed along the rapids of life knocking and rubbing against each other to form our ultimate shape.

I have had a few more trips, encounters and adventures in those six years and now find myself resident in the delightful Victorian country town of Kyneton. I am connected by rail to my daughters and their families. In the winter, I hasten to Cairns to take up residence with Paul and his family. I am always welcomed into my children's homes and that is a blessing because I love them all dearly.

Because I am a regular visitor, I have a bird's eye view of all three marriages and I think that I may be able to answer the question I asked at the start of Chapter 48. I am not privy to the bedroom scenes, but I know from my own experience that passion fades with time to be replaced with friendship, respect and balance. Respect gives you the ability to discuss your differences of opinion without the discussion descending into a squabble or argument. Balance is the most difficult to describe, and the balance point is not necessarily exactly in the middle, but it works for the couple concerned.

Much water flows under a bridge in six years. Kathy and Ralf have sold their business at a good price and are very active young retirees.

Erica is now the head of marketing for a dairy company in Australia and New Zealand. Her son, Max, performs very well at school, especially in Japanese, which is no surprise.

Hiromi, in Japan, is married with two sons, and is current deputy head at a high school.

My grandson, John, will be 23 this year. He has just finished a Bachelor of

Aviation and is finishing off his flying tests that will make him a commercial pilot.

Paul is a training captain for Hevilift in PNG and is planning his retirement. He still supports and loves his school-age sons who are thriving and performing well under his guidance.

Although David lives on in his ivory tower, several of my friends have died. I think they do this to prepare one for the inevitability of one's own demise. I am becoming relaxed about that idea because I have finished the book. I know that I leave three well-balanced, caring children in this uncertain world.

However, I do not think that I have learnt it all, because life always has another lesson in store.

ACKNOWLEDGMENTS

I want to thank all the characters I have encountered through my life and have influenced/educated me, thereby finding their way into my story. I thank my children, who helped and encouraged me, even though they disapproved of some of the content. I'd also like to thank the librarians at the Kyneton Library who helped me over many computer hurdles, Will Plumridge and Denis Parsons for photographs, Paul Staska for advice on matters Czechoslovakian and finally, friends like Bill, Marcia, Lynda, Sue and Ken for critical readings of the manuscript before it reached the professionals. Lastly, I'd like to thank my editor, Rebecca Wylie, and designer, Luke Harris, who converted my ramblings into a real book.

www.ingramcontent.com/pod-product-compliance
Lightning Source LLC
Chambersburg PA
CBHW031231290426
44109CB00012B/251